Travels With My Daughter:

An Experience of Motherhood

by Laura Fraser

Dedication

To all those for whom shards of glass have lodged inside your hearts.

May we learn and then relearn, every single day, how to dislodge what seems so permanent. Because only then can we learn to hold what has seemed so wounding in our open palms, as our feet carry us in a direction most mysterious. A place where we discover a campfire roaring, around which others have been gathering since time immemorial, and are already dancing... And where, close by, the animals' hooves and paws have smoothed down what was once rough, so that now it is smooth.

It's a fire around which women of all ages and backgrounds are standing, the heat of which is so strong that it can be felt by those not yet ready, or able, to make the walk. Like a memory calling them, from not so far away after all...

Here, on this earth, is where we place these shards of glass.

Hans Christian Anderson wrote of Gerda and Kai and the pixies up high who relished destroying all that they couldn't understand. The thing that the pixies didn't realise was that the power that beat in Gerda's heart was more powerful than any mischief they could create.

Similarily, whatever disharmony, distress and disruption that may have played out in your life, please know this: a time will come when life will grant each of us in struggle the chance to discover that what has felt so binding is actually only our own version of these shards of glass, and all we need to do is simply acknowledge that they are there, reach in, remove them kindly, and with much tenderness, and then place them down beside those of others. Because when we do this, we get to see that those jagged edges that we once feared so much, and contorted our entire being around, fit effortlessly into these other shards, so that what's slowly forming is a new mirror. One that we are learning to peer into to discover: we're never as alone as we feel we are.

To all those who are learning to peer into the mirror: this book is for you.

"The Path isn't a straight line; it's a spiral. You continually come back to the things you thought you understood and see deeper truths."

Jaylene Moreau

travel redefined

Sometimes, we don't get far. At other times, our front door doesn't even open. The back door does, though, out of which we go into our garden; home to a re-wilding project that's ravaging in earnest. Out here, amidst our unmown lawn, roses and wild orchids are emerging from nowhere, along with plumes of ragwort, tufts of ferns, dandelions and the white fluffy plant that you blow at to set the fairies free. At the far end of the garden stands our threshold to the rest of the world: nettles about five feet high that are currently acting as a fortress to a thick wad of blackberry bushes. The flies have got to the juiciest first. We don't complain too loudly.

It's out here that most days, my daughter Evie and I come, along with our dog Bongo, who's come to live with us now that we've more to offer him then a graveyard in Kilburn. come. Although sometimes, the neurotic mother in me hurls herself fretfully into focus.

"We must go somewhere!" she'll screech. "We must do something!" she'll shrill. And so, dog and daughter are herded into the car, and off we go to the Land of Something. Other times, though, another part of me whispers back: *But what's wrong with here? Everyone's content with where they are...*

Occasionally, this truth sinks in, causing the breathless pulse of paranoia to subside, if only for an afternoon. Which leaves the three of us free to walk off in search of adventures. Like out here in our garden, under the wide-open blue, or rather, grey wind-swept sky. Of course, life isn't a constant, so I don't always feel at ease in our home environment. Sometimes, the tiredness from another night struggling to sleep blows me so off centre that all I want is to be utterly alone: a mother bear in her cave.

Grrrr.

Generally, however, I like hanging out with my daughter. The last five years most of my days have been spent with her. For the most part, this has involved us doing something that to the uninitiated might look like nothing, but to us is something. Possibly this has been a mistake. Who knows, maybe when I'm eighty years old, I'll look back, sigh and speak of the regret I have of all the time Evie and I spent with one another.

But I don't think so. And I can only hope that when my daughter turns her gaze back to look at the shape of her life, she doesn't say, *Oh, I wish Mama had hung out with me less*. But rather, *we had a good innings, Mum and I.*

And even though, more often than not, our travels involve a climate that's soul-crushingly British, these days, I look at my passport with its blank pages, and less and less do I feel a mourning for that. Or at least, I mourn them less. Because something else is blooming that has the potential to be even more enticing than the extraordinary joy that comes with foreign travel. Something that I don't need to stand in any passport queue to access. Journeying to it requires very little, in fact.

I just need to remember.

And because these first five years of motherhood have been about settling and making peace – maybe most of all, with myself – it's become an irony of my life that I'm growing up, travelling not the contours of this globe, but the inner terrain of my heart.

Devi

Motherhood almost didn't happen, were it not for Devi.

We met on a main road, in the hills of northern Spain, where I was on a friend's week-long raw food retreat. After a cucumber and celery juice that only the most fanatical of us would call breakfast, we headed out for our morning hike. As we crossed the main road, I saw a large white dog who looked as if she was trying to catch a ride with one of the passing cars. But as we came near, she ran off. The following morning, we headed out to the hills for a hike, and there she was, beside the road again, doing her best to fling herself at passing cars in an apparent bid to be taken anywhere other than where she was.

My mother's side of the family sees trips away as, yes, a chance to meet people and to warm our skin in the golden sun, but also, invariably, to rescue dogs. It's happened on too many trips that we've made an animal friend not to suspect that the real reason we go away is simply to make another. This is the stock that I come from: see a dog in trouble, do what you can to help. So as the others walked on, I retreated and walked towards this lupine creature; a befriending mission in mind.

After realizing I was missing, our trainer, Yuri, who was leading the hike, asked his assistant to take over, and raced back to join me. The dog clearly needed a vet: she had a large, deep welt above her left eye that, although it had narrowly missed her eyeball, was oozing a deep yellow pus. She was also emaciated, wore no collar, and her teeth were brown with decay.

It took about twenty minutes for the dog to trust us enough before she'd allow herself to be beckoned away from the road. And another ten to get her to follow us back to the hotel, where, a couple of hours later, she lay under general anaesthetic in the gardens, whilst her eye was cleaned and stitched up by a local vet. All of which was witnessed by a very understanding hotel manager keeping guard.

When Devi woke after her mini-operation, she lumbered about in such a way that I was worried that the anaesthetic had been too strong, and would kill her.

But the dog had spirit, and despite being weak, survived.

⁂

canine, not cannibal

That night, unable to find any local charities who had room for another stray, my room-mate, Samantha, agreed to let Devi share our room.

"I hope she doesn't eat us," she said, getting into bed with a sideways look at Devi who was spread out on the floor. A mother of two, hers was an understandable concern, and though I assured her, "Oh no, she'll be fine," inwardly I was making fervent prayers to the Lord that this canine was as peaceful as I sensed she was.

The following morning, after saying a quiet thank you on discovering that we remained gloriously uneaten, I stood to open the sliding doors that led out to the garden, so that Devi could pee. After struggling with the handle, I finally managed to heave the heavy glass door open, turning around to watch as Devi climbed awkwardly on to my small single bed, before lying down in the identical position to the one I'd slept in, with her head resting on the pillow where mine had been. And just like the Grinch, my heart bloomed two sizes right there. Later, Devi and I bonded, chasing each other around the garden, simultaneously taking turns to chase and be chased. I felt like a child who'd discovered the best playmate ever; albeit slightly stronger, larger and faster. For Devi was such a huge dog that where I sprinted, she merely lolloped.

After our play sessions, I called, emailed and Facebooked whoever I could think of who might be able to help find Devi a home. As is not unusual for Spain, all the local stray dog centres were full, and since I was leaving in a couple of days, I was running out of time to find her a home. (I was advised against bringing her back to the UK, due to the stress that quarantine causes an animal; advice that I would come to regret following).

On my last morning we went for our hike and, just as she had with the others, Devi came with us, walking beside me, no need for a lead. I felt with this dog a kinship that I've only ever felt with one other: Bongo, with one key difference. Devi was female, and perhaps because of this, I felt in some way that she was a direct expression, albeit a canine one, of some deep part inside of me that I too often pushed away. Such was the strength of our connection that, in place of any doubt dominating our relationship, I felt a deep sense of trust in this lupine creature whose spirit was opening up something inside me.
⬚

a mother roars

It wasn't just trust that I felt towards Devi, but a deep-seated sense of protectiveness, which was gifted a moment to express itself on that walk we took with the others that morning before I left for the airport. Along the way, our group passed by the bottom of a drive where three dogs of varying sizes pummelled down the gravel and out of the gates, hurtling towards Devi, all ferocious barks and bolting bodies. Devi's nature, so friendly and open, made her turn towards them, confusing them for friends. As she trotted towards them, seemingly oblivious to their intent to attack, I was filled not with fear at what these dogs might do, but a very clear sense that my role was to protect this animal. A moment later, I found myself sprinting towards those dogs, bending down as I ran to grab whatever rocks and pebbles I could to hurl at them.

Some people say that animals are *just* animals, but when we bond with them, and care for them, we're given extraordinary opportunities to practice love, compassion and anything else that we look for in meditation or other spiritual practices. That dog seemed a drop of the divine; hence her name. She felt sacred to me. And in that moment, she gave the maternal instinct that was beginning to stir inside of me, space to roar. Such was the strength of this feeling that I would do whatever I needed to do to protect her, as I ran towards those dogs to stop them hurting her, that I remember it as clearly as if it had happened this morning.

It was with something like heartbreak, then, when at the end of that walk, rather than coming back into the hotel with me as she had after every other walk, Devi carried on down the gravel path that led back to the main road. On her way, she stopped twice to turn and look back at me, before once again crossing the road and disappearing into the woods on the other side. Sensing something different was happening, I ran after her, calling her name. On seeing me once again deserting the group, Yuri came to join me for one more rescue mission.

It was he who found her, about a ten-minute walk away from the hotel, in a clearing in the woods, being tied up by her owner. A man who kept her chained all day and night, in an area where she was kept alone as a guard dog for a dilapidated building that didn't look like it needed guarding at all.

Devi's owner told us that her brother, who'd guarded the area with her, had died. Of what, we were not told. Around her lay shards of broken glass, a large aluminium dog bowl with some dry dog biscuits, and a murky bowl of water.

I felt utterly powerless to do anything about the situation. It was clear that the man didn't know what to do with her, and yet, for whatever reason, he wouldn't let go of her. Not knowing what else to do, I said goodbye before walking back to the hotel with Yuri in silence, tears blurring my eyes.

magic whispers

Thankfully, my mother is made of a more resilient nature when it comes to animal rescue. Two weeks later, she was doing the same course, and discovered that Devi's owner was more than happy to part with her – for a small fee. Yuri's parents, who lived in the hills a couple of hours away, offered Devi a home. There she made friends with their other dog, who was equally mammoth in size, and became a mother to a stray kitten.

After a month or so, I went out to visit Devi to see how she was settling in her new home - as I said, my family takes our animal rescue seriously. However, although the purpose of the trip was to check on a dog I'd only known for a few days, once there, I was to have a conversation that would change the course of my life.

Over breakfast, where we feasted on home-made rye bread and jam, Yuri's mother Ines shared with me stories of birthing all four of her children at home. One detail in particular struck me: for the birth of each of her children, only Ines and her husband were present. Such was their shared sense of trust in their ability to bring their children safely into the world, that they didn't have so much as a doula to support them.

They clearly did a good job, because Ines's sense of peace was such that two of her children were born with their amniotic sac still intact. And as I chatted with Ines about her experiences, I felt something move inside me that had, up to that point, been something I'd sworn never to do: to have a baby. Ines was an anomaly to me. I'd never met a woman who not only spoke so positively about labour and pregnancy, but whose face still glowed with the memories of it. Her wholehearted and gutsy approach to both bringing her children into the world and the manner in which she and her husband raised them, inspired me. Such was the power of this afflatus that motherhood could lead to an experience not so much where one is lost, but perhaps found, that whatever pathways had become fixed in my brain dissolved right there. Causing a rather swift recalibration to occur that went something along the lines of: *motherhood, maybe it's not so bad after all.*

Two days later, I went home. And although I left without Devi, I returned to England with something else: a pulse of longing for a child. And a certainty that when that time came, she would be a daughter.

As for Devi, she was only to live one year more, after a farmer shot her when seeing her in his field of sheep. Ines's other dog, whom Devi had befriended when she joined the family, died shortly afterwards.

Cause unknown. Suspected: a broken heart.

the scent of motherhood

I sniff the air; something's changed. My nose is drawn to the forest floor where it presses itself against the wet mulch of leaves, as if trying to understand the dialect of the wood that for whatever reason seems suddenly a little more conversational.

I can only fathom that somehow, being pregnant – as this baby and I oscillate between worlds, not yet born, not yet a mother, with the emphasis on waiting, growing, evolving – something's happening. SO that whilst my ears may still need hearing aids to hear correctly, and my eyes contact lenses to see, right now, here in the woods, with Bongo and Piglet, my mother's Jack Russell by my side, I'm finally discovering what it means to use my sense of smell.

The forest smells good. Interesting, and also mildly frustrating; nature being a class that I've not paid enough attention to. So just as I know only a few names for the cacophony of wild flowers growing alongside country lanes in the summer, and can only identify the pigeon cooing, the crow's squawk, the blackbird's song and the buzzard's soulful call, I've lost the ability to identify these smells wafting up to my nostrils, and instead lump them all into one generic smell: the forest.

As I carry on walking, I inhale a torrent of smells. Like refugees pouring through a gate that's suddenly opened, my basic humanity restored. Because who knows? Maybe that's the path parenthood takes us down: restoring what's lost in us, while reminding us of what's most magical.

retreating

In the final months of my pregnancy, realising that this was going to be the last time that I would have the freedom to go on retreat for a while – which turned out to be the only premonition about parenthood that I've got right - I booked myself onto a self-led retreat, in a Buddhist centre in east Essex. While there, I oscillated between yoga, walking in the woods, and meditating. Which in reality meant feeling the physicality and aliveness of my unborn daughter's movements in a way that I hadn't been able to before, whilst contemplating what a deeply spiritual song *Doh-Re-Mi* was.

Apart from two others who left on my first day, I was alone all week, as lunch and supper were solo experiences left outside my door. My first morning, then, was the last time that I saw another person for the next six days. As I sat on a chair eating breakfast in the small courtyard behind my bedroom, I sensed something familiar about one of the two other people there, and glanced over at him.

"Anthony!" It was my wandering-monk-traveller friend, who I'd last seen in a retreat centre in the northeast of India, about two hours from Dharamasala.

He walked over. We chatted. The specifics of which I can't really remember but I do remember the tone of our conversation, and more specifically its impact. Any anxiety I had about being alone and pregnant - would I go into labour when there, and oh bugger, why hadn't I found out where the nearest hospital was? – calmed, if only a little.

Some people we don't need to see often. Such is the strength of whatever quality it is that they embody, that even the thought of them can calm us, as if they were seated next to us holding our hand. Others hold memories for us, a place in time that we can relive at the mere thought, or sight, of them.

To think of Anthony is to recall three extraordinarily special months spent at the centre of my Buddhist teacher in northern India. Three months spent sharing all our meals together, over which – along with another student, Alex – we talked endlessly about dharma and practice and everything in between.

The randomness of seeing Anthony in a tiny little retreat centre in East Sussex felt like a blessing. And then he went, and so did the other woman there, and it was just me, the babe inside me and the thoughts that always whirl.

Before you give birth, it's a lovely thing to be surrounded by those you love, and who care for you, so that you can spend those final days before the gargantuan effort of labour nesting and resting.

When I think about this retreat I wonder, if I were given the choice would I do it again? With any other retreat experience I've had, the answer would be an emphatic Yes. With this one, however, so close to the birth of my daughter, it's a No, I think most definitely not. It was too isolated. The sense of feeling unsafe which had lain dormant for long enough to suggest that the insomnia that'd started at the age of sixteen had been successfully remedied, was sparked once more.

In fact, as it was to turn out, those month spells of sleeplessness that had speckled my life in my late teens and early twenties were only a dress rehearsal. As I edged closer to motherhood the nights of waking and worrying began once more, as my brain started an incredibly convincing campaign to retrain its ability to fall asleep: *Nights aren't for sleeping, dear lady. Oh no. You need to stay AWAKE.*

Five years later, I'm still struggling to convince it otherwise.

here we go
part i: the beginning

I'm in child's pose and my waters have just broken. Three underwear changes later, I plump up some cushions to sit and meditate. After five minutes or so, my partner Ben walks into the room, and lies down on the mat, places his head in my lap and stays there for ten minutes with his eyes closed. Neither of us says a word; he doesn't know that the labour has started. The due date is a week away, and we're geographically misplaced, as we're meant to be having a home birth in London, not here at my mother's in Sussex - something that she'll be enthusiastically reminding us about in three hours time.

After he leaves the room, convinced that this is the orgasmic birth I'd planned for, I head out to the garden, Bongo and my mother's dog Piglet by my side, feeling myself slip into a haze of blissfulness as I drift about the garden, taking in the colours and shapes of the plants, flowers and general herbaceous features until the thought comes: what happens now?

Not having attended any birthing workshops - *"We'll be fiiine. Women have been doing this forever..."* - I was all trust and no knowledge. The only thing I'd seen was a DVD called Orgasmic Birth, where women with sparkling eyes and joyous groans, birthed bumptiously large babies in the ocean's water, whilst dolphins cavorted in the background.

Sensing that there was something that needed to happen, but having no idea exactly what that was, I retreated to the silence of my bedroom, and made a phone call. In retrospect, I wonder, *oh dear lord, why oh why did I make that call?*

⏾

part ii:
how long till we get there?

"Hi, I think I've just gone into labour: my waters have just broken."
"Right, what's your NHS number?" the lady on the phone asks.
"Um, my paper work's back at home in London. My due date's not for another week... I'm uh, actually registered with the Royal Free in Hampstead."
"Right," she says. "You need to come in straight away because if your waters have broken, there's risk of infection to your baby if it's not born over the next twenty-four hours."

And so Ben and I, along with my brother Charlie, troop over to the local hospital in Chichester, where they check me. But although my waters have broken, my cervix is clamped shut, and so I'm sent home. Later that afternoon, with labour apparently stalled, I go for an acupuncturist appointment, to see if it'll help the labour along.

Thinking me in more advanced stages of labour then I was, the acupuncturist Gabriella comments, "You're very calm with the pain."

So brave think I. Labour, I can totally do this.

And then I go back to the hospital again. My cervix is still shut, so we return to my mother's once more and I take a walk in the woods with Charlie, returning after not too long because the contractions are heating up, and there's a hill I need to negotiate that's starting to look a little bit foreboding.

Later that evening, two friends come for supper. Halfway through, I make my excuses and head upstairs to my room. My friend follows me.
"Are you okay, Lau?"
"I've no idea what's coming next," I say, lying in my bed.
"It'll be okay," she says, rubbing my head, neither of us entirely sure.

And then it is night, and I lie on my side awake with contractions. The following morning I eat a bowl of porridge for breakfast. I'm glad I do; it's to be the last thing I eat for the next thirty hours.

part iii
geography: essential, really

They say that the hormone you want present during labour is the one that helped create your baby in the first place: oxytocin. The ones you don't want, or at least only in minimal amounts, and only towards the end when the baby needs some extra *oomph* to make its final transition, are cortisol and adrenalin.

Unfortunately, in this moment, I have *a lot* of the latter pumping around my system, and an absence of the former. As a result, my cervix is still refusing to open and my sphincter muscles have shrivelled up into a tight ball of unresponsiveness. Meanwhile on one side of the house, my mother is bellowing to Ben that whatever happens, what is *definitely not* going to happen is her grandchild being birthed in her home. Thankfully my German stepfather is on holiday in America with his daughters and ex-wife. Needless to say throughout the pregnancy there had been a campaign of sorts to persuade Ben and me that a home birth was a most irresponsible choice. Unfortunately, the more that people clamoured that we were making a wrong decision, the more I trusted that for us, it was the right one.

But my mother remains unconvinced.

So that whilst I'm on the phone with my Peruvian housekeeper, Camella, arranging with her to go to our house in Kilburn to pick up my pregnancy notes, and bring them down on the train, Ben and Mum are locked in a battle of increasing intensity. Watching from the sidelines is one of my mother's oldest friends, Alan, unsure that this is the kind of fun he had been looking for on a weekend away from London. My brother, previously incredibly supportive, has started looking slightly wan. So rather than be in the bosom of love, surrounded by chilled out people who are saying reassuring things like *oh yes, carry on, dear*, the atmosphere around me is ever so slightly volatile. It's not so much a question of will anyone blow, but who's going to go first.

After four hours, which may only have been ten minutes of managing train times, coordinating with Camella and responding to my contractions, I pass the phone to Ben, who's in mid-negotiations with my mother.

"Here, you guys deal with this," I say, and stagger up the stairs to spend the next two hours vomiting into the loo.

☒

part iv
Hollywood, not Buddha; London, not Sussex

Which is where I am now; doing my labour breathing, curled around the base of the loo. There's a knock on the bathroom door. It's a midwife from the local hospital who looks at me, aghast.
"Love, what kind of breathing is that?" she asks, watching me, all huff and dramatic puff.
"It's the breathing you're meant to do," I reply.
"Says who?" she asks, approaching me.
"Well, the movies," I say, my tone quietening. Because although I'd been convinced that my long-established yoga and meditation practice would see me through labour just fine, such is the white hot inferno that is the *reality* of labour, that in the end, it's Hollywood, not Buddha who appears to have the most influence on my mind. As a result, I'm not copying the quiet Zen of the Dalai Lama, but the exaggerated huffing and puffing actresses do in films when 'doing labour.' The kindly nurse takes pity on me and demonstrates the deep, calm breathing that might be more effective.

It helps.

As it does when she says, "Okay, poor pet, I see what you need," and begins rubbing my lower back with a gentle, warm maternal motion that instantly brings about a sense of calm, and acts as an immediate and effective pain reliever. And yet my cervix needs a little more persuading because it's unconvinced by the surrounding theatrics and is still refusing to open, so after a little while my friend with the reassuring touch leaves.

"Call me if anything changes," she says, walking out of my bedroom. I watch her go whilst lying on my bed and then head back into the bathroom, because at least in here I can manage the pain. It's only when someone comes to check on me, with ashen face, unblinking eyes, and a look that says, *oh Jesus, are we all going to survive this?* that the pain gazumps up, and I'm in agony.

And then around 11 p.m., Ben and I retreat to the hospital. Nothing's progressing, so, defeated, I get into the car, my mother waving a hearty "Goodbye!"

When we arrive, parking our car as intimately close to the revolving doors as possible, a harassed-looking nurse ushers us into a side room.

"It's a busy night," she rasps, before quickly walking away. And there we remain, with me hobbling between the bed and the loo to throw up.
"Where's the nurse?" I croak at Ben.
"She's coming," he replies, lying on the sofa in the room. One thing is clear: she isn't coming any time soon. Two hours later, I stagger out into the hall, throwing myself through the door of the nurses' waiting room like a drunk in search of some whisky. Two nurses look up at me.
"Please, someone has to come and help," I beg.
"Someone will be with you soon," replies one of them.
"No, lady, someone has been on their way to see me 'soon' for the past two hours. I need someone now!"

By the time I make my way back to the room and onto the bed, a nurse is there. She gives me an injection for the vomiting, and then tells me that she's going to give me the pain reliever.
"But I've planned for a natural birth," I say.
"If you don't take it, you need to leave," she replies.

"But we've waited two hours to see you," I counter. She shrugs her shoulders in response. The communication's clear: my labour's taking too long, take the injection or leave. I'm about to admit defeat, and then he's there.

"Wait Lau, wait. Let's call Liliana, and see what she says." Ben calls our doula.

"Don't do it," she says. "Because if you do, they'll then have to induce you, and that birth you've planned for, and wanted, will go." I've no words left, I'm used up, gone, emptied.

Ben replies for me. "I'm taking you back to London."

So we hobble away from the hospital room and into his car. He drives us the ninety minutes back to London at 2 a.m., with the back seats down and me on all fours in my t-shirt and underwear, groaning and moaning the whole way, with contractions every four minutes or so and a car tail-lighting me a part of the way, it's full light beam unwavering on my raised pantied buttocks.

At one point, we stop at a petrol station, because the pain's got so intense that every jolt is like being stabbed. I need fresh air. Actually, hell to fresh air, I just need a pause.

"What's going on?" a concerned man on the night shift asks, running out towards us as I lean over the bonnet of the car, groaning.

"She's in labour," Ben responds.

"Oh *no no no*. Please, not here. Please don't have your baby here," he begs, the whites of his eyes enlarging with horror. No room at the inn indeed, so I get back into the boot of the car, and on we go. "I'll be at your home at 12 p.m.," says Liliana on the phone a few minutes later.

"No way," I reply, as Ben relays this to me. "You tell Lilianna to be there as soon as possible. I'm having this baby *now*." An hour or so later, we get home. It's 4.30 a.m. I stagger upstairs to the first floor and into the shower. As soon as that first drop of water touches my head, I finally get the first desire to push. I'm home: the place I'm meant to be, and so the mammal in me relaxes, and finally the process of birthing my baby can continue as it had begun.

Or almost. I end up pushing for four hours.

part v
hello

When Liliana arrives half an hour later, I've moved to our bath with a mental state about eighty-seven solar systems away from sanity and, seeing this, instead of speaking, she sinks to the floor and prays. Or almost. She meditates instead, holding a space so that her presence fills the room and calms me as I oscillate from lying in foetal position to crouching on all fours and pushing with everything I have (another basic error, as I learn *after* the birth. Apparently only novices push; the trick is to wait until your body begins the pushing of its own accord. Until then, you just need to breathe your child out...).

Half an hour later, two NHS midwives arrive who I'm later told were going to delay as well until Ben, in his best motivational language possible, emphasised the need for them to come *immediately*. They arrived shortly afterwards.

"Okay, lovey, I see what's needed," one says, seeing me curled in a pathetic heap in my bath, having not eaten since that bowl of porridge. With all the vomiting, my strength is somewhat weakened and my will greatly reduced. I don't know if she really does this or if I've imagined it, but I remember this marvellous woman from a bygone era rolling up her sleeves as she starts to tell me when to push and when to pause.

"Love, you're going to have to move," says the other midwife slowly and kindly about ninety minutes later, because our bath is as big as a loo and I'm having problems opening my legs wide enough so I can actually birth my baby. We move to the next-door room, our yoga room, so that a cycle is coming close to being completed, because just maybe now this birth can finish as it started.

Because it's here where I can finally let rip, bellowing like a water buffalo, roaring like an elephant and, unfortunately for one of the midwives, biting with the ferocity of a labouring tiger as an unfortunate hand travels *a little too close to my jaw* just as I am bearing down. Luckily, she is made of golden stuff, and rather then admonish me, simply cheers me on.

"Wonderful, Laura! Wonderful!" she sings, as if I'd blown her a kiss. Encouraged, I roar, grunt and moan to my heart's delight. And after the chaotic confinement of the previous two days, it is delightful. To be surrounded by three incredibly supportive and experienced women, who all have the same message: *don't hold back, trust your body, and GO.*

And then I'm done.

"Look, can we stop this, and come back tomorrow?" I ask.
Everyone looks at me wide-eyed . "No love, you're nearly there, come on, *you can do this.*"
"Um, actually, no, I don't think I can. I'm done," I say, quite convinced that I am, and in the merit of pausing for, if not the day, at least a rest and lunch.
"You can do this Laura, come on." And the look in their eyes is convincing and I'm kind of easily influenced so I push some more, and the ring of fire thing happens which, at the time, I think is me being ripped wide open.
"What are you doing to me?" I bellow at the midwives who're crouching down by my legs and pressing something against my vagina. "I'm ripping!"
"No, Laura, we're stopping you from tearing. It's all okay. You're fine. It's all okay."

16

Unbeknownst to me, as I'd taken out my hearing aids so could barely hear what was being said around me, my doula was asking the midwives to "Cut her! Cut her!" because I'd been pushing for four hours, and I think there was concern about my ability to finish the job.

But the midwives didn't cut me, and miraculously, there was no tearing. They tell me maybe I need to chill out a bit on the roars and focus instead on deep, slow breathing. My vocal exclamations make room for silence, and peace fills the room as my breath deepens and slows. And then there it is: the orgasmic birth experience I'd been inspired about, and whose tremors are building up through my entire body, if only for a moment. So that although the general experience has been hell, traces of heaven linger, no matter how short their apparition may be.

⁇

part vi
Krishna comes to Kilburn

"Do you want to know what sex your baby is?" asks one of the midwives, bringing the baby towards me as I lie on my back in the middle of the yoga room.

"No, not yet," I say, just wanting to hold onto this incredible mystery of not knowing for certain what sex my child is, only knowing in that silent way that we doubt too often.

So, the void expands and there we lie, my purple-skinned, dark-haired baby and me. And then I lift my child off my belly, and she's a girl, and down she comes again. Ben walks into the room and comes to lie beside us, and the nurses place her on my chest instead of my tummy so that Evie can make her way to my breasts on her own, but they've placed her in between my cleavage, so she's wiggling up to my chin, and I have to keep pushing her down again. Then she finds my breast and starts suckling, this bright purple bloom of a baby.

And there she is: Eve, Evie, my daughter, as a life slips away and a new one dawns.

⬚

part vii
windows: the new phone

Later, Camella comes to clean the room and the towels (an act that she may still be in recovery from, "The blood, Laurita! The blood!"), and Ben and I go to bed to sleep with our daughter. When we wake a couple of hours later, we walk downstairs to the kitchen, with me holding Evie, and notice two cards lying on the doormat. We look at each other with surprise: from whom? We hadn't even told our parents yet that she'd arrived.

They're from our neighbours, congratulating us on the birth of our child. "We hear congratulations are in order…," one begins. I blush with embarrassment; it's a Saturday morning in mid-August, and it seems families across Kilburn have awoken confused: are they in north London, or have somehow been transported to an African savannah, where not too far away a hippo is giving birth?

And yet, besides this residue of embarrassment, there it is: an experience of labour, which included brief interludes of a freedom I'd love to invoke again.

Without the middle bit, perhaps.

unmasked

Mum is holding Evie in her arms for the first time, her little head resting in the nook of her left arm. I peer at my mother's face, at the expression it holds; one I've never seen before. Or since.

And then my brother, Charlie, holds Evie, and there it is again: bewilderment and devotion entwined as his entire body relaxes; simultaneously strong and gentle.

Sometimes babies come into the world and a halcyon period emerges where old feuds are temporarily forgotten, masks and roles dissolve, and a relating occurs amongst family members that can seem so natural and easy, it's only a wonder that normally this kind of relating can seem a frustrating mirage.

But for now, my mother, brother and I are hanging out, not a whisper of tension in the air. No therapist needed.

magic intervenes

A few days later, Ben and I decamp back to *Little Halnaker*. When we arrive, we need to take Evie to the local hospital for her newborn check. We enter the room, the doctor runs through the checks, then looks at her notes – a file which had been started when I had come in whilst in labour – and looks up with the kind of expression no parent ever wants to see on their child's doctor. "I'll be back in a minute," he says.

About ten minutes later, he returns with a colleague, a serious-looking woman who manages to channel a sense that something grave has happened but at the same time, that there is nothing to worry about at all.

"I'm very sorry to say," the doctor says, "but we need to put your daughter in intensive care for a couple of days. She needs to go on an antibiotic drip *immediately*." Ben and I look up from cooing at Evie, our eyes unblinking, mouths agape.

"When you were in labour, you came into St. Richards. On one of those visits, a nurse took a swab. We have the results from that test which show that you had Strep B. This is serious. We need to put your daughter on a drip."
"What is Strep B?" I ask.
"Group B Streptococcus is a bacteria that can be found in the vagina. Women can have it at anytime, but if it's present during labour, and if you haven't taken antibiotics, then it can be fatal to a baby. Because you had a natural birth, there's a chance that your daughter may have it, and it's very serious. We need to take her and put her on a drip. It'll only be two days."
"But why are we only being told about this now?" I ask, holding Evie close. "Why has no one called us to tell us before?"

The doctor shuffles his feet, clears his throat and says things that I think he intends to pass as an explanation for the fact that no one followed through, but just sounds like bullshitting.

Ben gets out his phone. "We're calling Liliana." Luckily, we get through straight away.
"I think this is nonsense," she says. "Don't let them take her. I'll call Michel, and call you back." Unbeknownst to me when we chose Liliana, we chose the most experienced doula in the country. Liliana has worked closely with the natural birthing pioneer Michel Odent, who's been advocating for natural births since the 1970's. It's safe to say he has probably been present at a few thousand more births than either of the doctors in the room with us right now.

Five minutes later Liliana calls us back.

"Michel says there is absolutely no need for Evie to be taken away. Call him." I dial Michel's number, and this wonderful French accent comes booming over the phone.

"This is completely *ridikuluss!* If your child is still alive, then there is 98% chance that she will remain alive." Which is kind of reassuring, but that 2% leap from 98 to 100% seems an awfully large one when you're a first-time parent. Even so, when I get off the phone, we tell the doctor that we'll be taking our daughter home. That she needs to be close to her mother, and to nurse as often as she needs to, and to lie in the nook of our arms as we snuggle around her, skin to skin, lying in our bed. When we tell him who we were speaking to, he blanches and becomes incredibly apologetic.

"We are so sorry if we upset you at this wonderful time. We didn't mean to alarm you."

"How was the check, by the way?" we ask him.

"Oh, absolutely fine. Everything's fine. She's a healthy baby. It would have just been a precaution."

Taking a five-day old child away from her mother to plonk her in a cubicle alone, with tubes all over, and feeding her antibiotics to mess up her immune system is an awfully big precaution, I want to say, but don't. Instead we walk out.

The UK doula website that I'd been encouraged to go through when looking for a doula has hundreds of doulas. When I'd scrolled through in my first trimester, I chose two women. One on account of her kind face, although when I called her she already had a birth around the time of my due date, so wasn't available. And then Liliana, because I liked the fact that she was older than everyone else and, therefore, I assumed, more experienced. When Ben and I met her, we went on gut, which is to say we liked her unconventional approach. (She's famous amongst the NHS midwives in north London for not calling them until the very last minute when the baby is practically born). But her confidence in womens' ability to birth with minimal interference reminded me of Ines, and so the decision was made, perhaps before we had even realised we had one to make.

Often, at the crucial moments in my life, it seems an intelligence is at play that brings people, animals, information and situations into my life that completely shifts the status quo in a way I most likely would have missed had I continued clutching the wheel and screeching, "That way! We have to go that way!" And even though I still don't have the unshakeable confidence in what, intellectually, I have absolute conviction is true, if someone were to ask me what my life philosophy is, I would reply "less Buddhist, more magic." Because it was magic then that we had the right doula with the right friends, so that in a time of need Liliana was able to come through for us in a way that we never could have fathomed when we chose her.

⏹

a return

And now here I lie, awake in the dark, Evie asleep by my side. Some nights it seems as if a brilliant orb of wakefulness illuminates the room around me. Others, there is just a desolate sense of isolation. As I lay here next to my daughter, my breasts full of milk, ready to feed and unable to sleep, my thoughts lumber and stumble over one another inside my increasingly bleary head: *again and again and again.* The later it becomes, the more appear, followed by armies of others: a new one, an old one that is neither old nor grey.

Some nights I lie here thinking of other mothers, not just those in London, but all those in the nooks and crevices where humanity has pushed them, lying awake in their beds. I connect to these mothers, if only through the bounds of my own imagination. It's the potential of it that matters, so that even though I lie here unable to sleep, I feel buoyed, supported and not totally, utterly alone. In the day, people jest about the broken nights, "Keeping you awake, is she?" And I smile and nod, when inside I'm thinking, *but it's not her.*

If we're each gifted an internal compass, then perhaps our job as parents is to nurture our children in such a way that they grow up learning to trust theirs, no matter if they find themselves amongst others who don't know such a thing exists. Because if they've witnessed just one person (and what more powerful person could there be than your parent?) trust their own compass, even in the face of great adversity, then the gift we impart and share with them is that they must develop an unshakeable confidence – above and beyond the convictions of others – to know when their compass is leading them in a direction they need to go. And if they are able to discern what is will and what is genuine insight and intelligence, then the direction their lives will take can be assured by one thing: it will be touched by magic.

perils of perfholicism

This is it. The ultimate parenting book, the one that'll answer all my questions and quell all my fears.

"It's meant to be a great book, read it," a friend says, handing me *The Continuum Concept*, which a mutual friend had suggested to him. And though neither of these friends are parents, nonetheless I have projected such wisdom onto them both that I take them at their word in the worst kind of way: unquestioningly. And though I find out later that the author never had children herself, it didn't matter, because inside this book was the Promised Land. So here I am, a *bona fide Continuum* devotee.

The book's message can be distilled down to one salient point: *carrying baby good; putting   baby down bad.* And even though the woman who wrote the book was commenting on a South American tribe in which there were countless members of the tribe to carry the babies, but r here in Kilburn there's only me, an occasional visitor and the post-natal doula I've hired, who's currently lying asleep on the sofa with Evie in her arms whilst I do the housework, I'll be darned if my daughter's going to be placed on anything remotely stationary. Which means Evie spends her nights lying down and her days being carried. Everywhere.

The book also says something about not looking at babies too much; that this infatuation we have with our children is overwhelming, and incubates spoilt rotten scoundrels. Children learn to see the world from the gaze their parents hold, the author Jean Liedloff argues. If that gaze is always locked on them, then that's a sure way to overwhelm a child because children don't want to be the centre of their parent's universe. Instead they want to discover the universe through the gaze their parents hold. My eyes think this is absurd. They want to look at my daughter, so when she sleeps, I peek glances at her, reminding myself to look away as soon as her little eyes open, worried I'll overwhelm her otherwise.

There's an *Aesop Fable* about a father and a son who walk through their village with their donkey, doing their best to follow every piece of advice thrown their way from well-intentioned neighbours. If someone says the father should be carried on the donkey, this is what they do. If another says the son should be carried, then this is what they try. Eventually they end up carrying the donkey on their shoulders, but as they walk over a bridge, they trip and drop the donkey, who falls into the river below and drowns.

Which is to say that eventually the awkwardness and strain involved in not looking at my daughter allows me to realise how close to me that river runs. The next day I drop off the book at a charity shop and then throw the NHS red book - where you're meant to document the weight and length of your child, which leads to competitive conversations amongst parents about what percentile of growth their child is in – into the bin. Bugger it all. I can see my daughter's feeding well and that she's growing. I trust her. And I'm going to trust myself.

And so, Evie and I learn to look at each other once more. It takes a couple of months, perhaps, before the eye aversion ceases to be. Although sometimes, there goes the legacy once more causing me to pause and refocus as I look into my daughter's eyes, softening my own gaze as I peer into her own, so brown, beautiful and searching.

love & presence: not much difference?

In 2009, I got to meditate, unexpectedly, with some nuns whilst working in Cambodia. As I sat behind these women, I had my first inkling that their loving and my loving were quite different. Their loving was a state of awareness; something I had a tangible sense of as I sat meditating behind them. It was a force field that emanated out from them, and could be felt as keenly as a ray of sun on my naked arm.

However, unlike my haphazard claims to love, their love, was an ode to something quieter, and more mountain like. *Their love*, was the love that we connect to in those impossible moments of presence. Or, when we're outside, walking in nature, where our awareness is expanded, and we realise, to this there is no boundary. Or the very tender open-hearted love that we feel for our children, or close friends, or dogs, or mountain ranges, or maybe even gurus. It wasn't focused and narrowed, but expansive and broad. It wasn't exclusive, but indescribably *inclusive*. Nor soft and sweet, or cuddly and reassuring. Nor addictive and fleeting, and I don't think it was particularly personal either.

Now, when I look at Evie, I see what feels to be that place that is the source of us all: a place that's heart-poundingly raw and compelling, drawing me in, in such an incomparable way that I'm left pulsing with awe at the infiniteness of the whole thing and of this sense of seeing a human oscillating into being, as a part of them continues to surf the cosmos. But as the days bloom to months, and my daughter spirals out into the world, it seems to me that she has to learn this thing called love, or at least, grow into what we associate as love. To do this, she has to first leave this place from where she's come. And thus another human follows this bizarre formula that our species has come up with, whereby the young grow up thinking of love as an external entity that is either given to them, or denied to them; depending on how they behave, and who they become. As opposed to relating to it as an internal source, to which they can always reconnect, and from which they can discover their own bespoke compass, which if they spend the time learning to trust and understand will direct them towards events and relationships that will bring meaningful, extraordinary and magical things into their lives. And that this compass is never further from their reach then the thump of their own hearts. So that rather than I love you because you are like this, or I love you because you make me feel like this, the wish would be that they grow up simply loved, because that's the source of us all.

But because I can only turn to my daughter with more of a hopeful heart, than one completely identified in anything like the indestructible nature that it really is, so that I might more truthfully reflect back to Evie her innate wholeness and goodness, I take her outside into nature as often as I can. Out to nurse under the trees, to walk through the woods, and with increasing frequency, to spend as much time as I possibly can getting lost in London's Hampstead Heath, where I lean against the trees to stare at the open sky and listen to the birds singing their chortled songs, all of which stir in me a reminder of that wholeness that I must have identified with more certainty not so long ago.

Because whereas I forget, and stumble, offering poor caricatures in lieu of simply embodying to Evie a truth of who she *really is*, not so much a personality becoming, but a portal into an experience of infinity, nature just intrinsically gets it. And so out we go, again and again, so that Evie can refamiliarise herself with that state she first started in and that of knowing truly what love really is, not a thing that so much owns and possesses, but gives and creates.

Which is to say that outside amongst nature, I discover a place where instead of demands made, acceptance is unconditionally given, and in that graciousness it's easier to accept the too easily diminished truth that Buddha spoke of: who we are is okay, and actually more than that, who we are is basically good. Because I forget this, my hope is that the more time we spend out here amongst the trees, with the dogs and whatever horses we come across, the more often Evie will see heaven mirrored back to her, whilst her mother continues to stumble on.

Love and presence: maybe there's not much that separates them after all.

brief but beautiful

My uncle has come to visit. He lives in Amsterdam, and is staying at Halnaker for the weekend. He likes to tell stories and is telling one right now about his partner Julia, and of the contentment he saw in her when she became a mother to their daughter India.

"Do you feel it?" he asks me as we sit in the kitchen drinking tea, with Evie sitting in my lap.
"Yes," I reply. "I do."

Because I do. So that for an interlude in my life, this most elusive of emotions is actually settling into the kernel of my cells as if it feels safe to actually hang out. Whereas before my focus was always *out out out*, for a brief interim it's now *here, here, here,* as the rest of the world slips away, and here I am, in this soft oscillation of life looking after my child.

In moments like the first night of Evie's life, where cursed by the witching hours and unable to sleep, I took her downstairs to the sitting room, where I danced with her lying cradled in the nook of my arms, the light of the moon sprinkling on our shoulders. The contentment appears too as I sit nursing Evie under the tree in the field at the bottom of *Little Halnaker*, hidden under the soft swath of branches above us. And as I walk across Hampstead Heath, carrying her swaddled in front of my chest, her belly meeting my chest as if there she lived once more. And though mini tornadoes are beginning to thunder around me, in my own heart, somewhere in a place where no tornado can access is this soft and incredibly resilient place of utter contentment.

So here we are, mother and daughter, perhaps the both of us spiralling into being, leading not so much to huge transformative changes, but smaller, more significant internal ones, the like of which sustain my life in a richer and more complete, yet perhaps wholly unambiguous way.

⏾

holding on

Evie's lying on the floor in the sitting room, her arms lying beside her, her gaze focused on the wooden things dangling from her play gym above her. She's been staring at them for a while, whilst I'm sitting on the sofa about three feet away. Attempts for her hand and the dangling things to come together have been misaligned, and for a moment or too, she's simply been lying there, deep in ponderment.

And then she does it, she lifts her left arm from the floor and raises her hand towards the wooden circle, and the tiny red bell hanging about twenty centimetres above her, in a slow, specific gesture. She stretches out her arm, and then clasps her fingers very deliberately and, with the full weight of every single second counting, around the circle and bell, her fingers dipping through the circle, so that they wrap around it.

And she's done it: the first time that Evie's learnt how to hold onto something. Except now she needs to learn to let go, which, judging by her intense focus, isn't so easy. Because she's holding on and she's watching the fact that she's holding on, and she's looking at her fingers in a mixture of wonderment that they've done this and utter puzzlement: because *how oh how are you meant to let go?* And then I watch her figure it out. It doesn't come easily, nor naturally, but a bit awkwardly. She looks intensely at her hand which she tries to dislodge but it doesn't work; still her fingers wrap around the dangling circle and bell.

The more she stares at it, the more difficult it becomes. Until finally, after an exorbitant amount of focus, her fingers unfurl, her grip releases, and her hand plops back down to the floor. So that just as when she'll come to start speaking in about six-months-time, before she learns to say yes, Evie will first learn to say no. Likewise, before asking for less, first comes "more." It seems, before we humans can learn to let go - with grace, at least - first we need to learn how to hold on, and with as tight a grip as our intention, skill and ability will allow us.

confidence pending

Evie's hungry.

We're on an overland train heading to my secret garden: Kew Gardens, a large and magical area of green located to the west of London where, between Hampstead Heath and here, we're spending an increasing amount of time. It's us two, and about five men on the train. I can feel my breasts being pumped with milk, as my body responds to my daughter's hunger. She's getting increasingly fidgety. But *Christ*, I just don't know if I can do it. To take out a breast and feed my daughter - the only woman in a compartment. I wish I was one of those women who can breastfeed in public, my child is hungry and clearly that's the priority so to hell with any awkwardness, *la di da* let's unbutton, and hey, here's my splendid breast, *go feed* my darling child.

But I'm not.

I'm me. Fine to be nude on a nudist beach. Fine to be topless by a pool, in the changing room, but I just can't get comfortable exposing my breasts to feed Evie when others are around. I watch with fascination as friends feed their babies with no hint of awkwardness in crowded cafés. Then I try and replicate it, but at the first exposure of nipple, I'm heading to the bathroom to feed there instead.

I'm fine outside, somehow the great wide expanse of sky and trees seems to soften my lack of confidence about feeding her in a place densely populated and with a reduced circumference of space. It's the enclosed places where people are packed together where the sense that I'm doing something incredibly socially wrong becomes so intense. There's also the not insignificant detail that, whereas some women can feed their child without exposing any breast, my mammary glands are fairly curvaceous creatures. With a lot of breast tissue, as well as a lot of nipple, it's kind of impossible to feed in a way that doesn't feel totally inappropriate. Which is bullshit really, it's just a matter of confidence. But confidence pending, please don't ask me to feed all insouciance in a café whilst conducting conversation with a friend across the table. I'd probably only spray them with milk anyway. Which means that in the absence of anywhere to go that's private and with about fifteen minutes left till we arrive at Kew station, I walk Evie around trying to distract her. When we finally arrive, I bolt for the nearest café, the back of which is totally empty. I place myself at the furthest table, unbutton and finally feed my daughter.

Breastfeeding: a joy to do, unless you're out in public.

⟨⟩

parenting skills from a lion

The teeth have arrived. Evie's bitten me. It's not an understatement to say it hurts. Luckily for my nipple, I'm prepared, having recently watched a video on YouTube of a lion mothering her young.

Without thinking about it, I roar. Not a terrifying mama going to clear the jungle kind of roar, more a *hey, honey, you've got to stop.* Post roar, my five-month-old daughter looks at me, her eyes open at this new and unexpected sound. Then she goes back to suckling, and never again during that feed, or after, does she, or will she, ever bite me again.

relief

It's a large room, with one small desk, and some toys scattered around the floor, and a doctor sitting in one corner with Evie in her lap.

"She's fine," she says eventually, after running through various tests and passing her back to me. "Her hearing is absolutely normal."

For maybe the first time since walking into the room, all the muscles in my body relax, and I exhale for the first time. I can't remember too specifically, because you push these things away, but I think I can't help but think *oh my god, thank god: Evie's going to be able to hear.*

some benefits & challenges of being deaf

At night, storms may rage, people will shout and I won't hear a whisper of it. And I know this is the opposite of what I should do, but it's what I do do, because sometimes when I meditate, I take out my hearing aids and those outer distractions, such as the radiator making obscure sounds, or people talking, are removed, and all I'm left with are those inner distractions (which are, unfortunately, slightly harder to contend with).

My father died when I was seven years old. Shortly afterwards my lungs started to struggle to breathe, and my ears to hear. Although the family joke was, "Say the word shopping and she'll respond," there was one family member who felt that something a little more significant was happening: my grandmother. Trusting this, my grandmother took me to the local village doctor for a hearing check, who declared that I was "simply slow to respond." And that was that.

At least for four more years, until I started boarding at Woldingham, in Surrey. During my first year there, we had various routine checks, one of which was a hearing test. Again, the doctor made a similar conclusion, yes I wasn't responding to sound normally, but no, there was nothing to worry about. It was only a matter of me paying more attention.

A year later however, I was still struggling to hear properly. This time it was suggested that my lack of hearing was due to too much wax. However, after the wax was duly expunged by my GP in London, I returned to school with no noticeable improvement. But apart from a friend who had also had great bowls of wax removed from her ears and who enthusiastically declared what a huge difference it had made to her hearing, no one asked if the removal of the wax had made a difference, and so I didn't tell anyone that it hadn't.

I learnt to stretch my ears in those subjects I enjoyed (English and Drama) and to get through the lessons I didn't (everything else). When GCSEs loomed, I simply revised old exam papers, working out what questions were due asking. A strategy that worked more or less okay through my A Levels, and even whilst reading history at Trinity College, Dublin and then later transferring to Goldsmiths College in London. And other than the fact that I had to listen to the television on the highest volume, sitting with my nose pressing against the screen if I wanted to hear what was being said, I convinced myself that my ears and I were fine. And although my friends knew differently (they just got used to speaking really loudly when talking with me), life bumbled along.

It wasn't until I worked as an intern for the late, great, life-changing Dr. Barbara Harrell-Bond in Cairo, Egypt over the summer of 2005 that my lack of hearing prowess was called into question.

One of my roles during my internship was to act as the secretariat for the weekly meetings between the local refugee organisations. Faced with a myriad of different accents, I floundered. When I passed on the minutes to Barbara, she commented that they "were the greatest piece of fiction ever written," on account that absolutely none of them had any relationship to what had actually been said at all.

Half-way through that trip, Barbara, who was generally economical with her words, (emails were distilled to one liners on the subject line, we didn't do greetings each morning, just simply got on with what was needed), looked at me and shared with me a story of a refugee whom she'd worked with who was deaf, and how it had affected his life. The message, and compassion, were clear. When you go home, Laura, it might be worth going to get your hearing properly checked. And because she's a woman who I came to admire deeply, I booked that hearing test with a specialist on Harley Street as soon as I returned to England.

"It's kind of interesting that you can talk as you do," said the hearing specialist, "being this deaf." And I went back a week later to collect my new hearing aids and she placed them in, leaned back in her chair and asked, "How does that sound?"
"This is super person hearing right?" I replied, convinced that she'd turned the hearing aids in my ears up to a higher than normal frequency, and was simply testing that they worked.
"No, Laura, this is normal hearing."
"Well, if this is normal hearing, then this is something I have no recollection of ever having."

Afterwards, I walked outside, able to hear the swish of my hair, and the jumble and jangle of things moving around in the bottom of my handbag. When I got into my car, I turned on the tape player, and was overjoyed to be able to listen to all of the words of my favourite Rod Stewart songs. Maybe hearing wasn't so bad after all. Something confirmed to me later in the week, when I discovered while waiting for a friend in a café the joys of something previously denied to me: the art of eavesdropping.

There're not only losses that come with being deaf, there're benefits too. Benefits because there can be so much conversational baloney taking place that inwardly I sometimes thank god I'm deaf. Because if you're deaf you can kind of get away with shrugging your shoulders, pointing to your ears and saying "I'm so sorry, I just can't hear very well."

End of conversation.

But then, I don't really mean that, or at least it's not the whole story, because the world has so much to say. And now my daughter's here, and she's speaking to me, and sometimes I miss too much.

snores of a silent world

They say that the voice is a small facet of how we communicate with one another. Compared to the words we speak, our eyes, our faces, and the way we hold our bodies say so much more. This is the world, then, that those of us with hearing loss start to familiarise ourselves with – which in itself can lead to disconnections with others, because such is our focus on what a person's face is doing that we've zoned out on what they're actually saying. Something that when it comes to giving the right response puts the deaf person in an awkward conundrum. Do you admit you didn't hear what was said and ask the person talking to repeat themselves, or do you try and bullshit your way through it and offer a smile of understanding or a frown of comradeship? More often, it's the latter chosen, because the thing is, people don't generally like being asked: "Can you say that again?" Not all people, just some people. So I try and avoid it whenever, if ever, I can.

Herein, the gift of getting older, for now, whereas before I put my hopes in the power of a smile getting me through a conversation in which I was struggling to hear, now at the ripe old age of thirty-five, I tap my ears, smile and say "I wear hearing aids, please can you repeat that?" And maybe it's just that my tone's got more confident, but the mumblers seem to have gone away.

However, confidence in our right to hear something is a great part of the deaf person's journey. But learning to feel that we matter and not only need to hear this, but want to, so that we feel okay to ask people to repeat themselves, is only half the battle. The other is that the person speaking responds without condescension. Because it doesn't mean that we're stupid, or slow or not paying attention (quite the opposite) if we ask you to repeat yourself, it means we care. Too often in our world we're too rushed, too in our own world to hear the plea behind the deaf person's communication: slow down, speak louder, I want to participate too.

Evie's been incredibly patient with my hearing. Because although there're days when I seem to say with increasing frequency, "Say that again love," she'll always repeat herself. Never with irritation. But with patience. And a kindness that touches my heart.

And if it's something important she wants to say, she'll come towards me, lift up my hair and, peering into my ears, ask, "Have you got your hearing aids in, Mama?"

Although if this question comes when we're in the bath, what normally follows is a wave of water being *swooshed* into my face. So maybe concern isn't needed; instead, just appreciation, because it could just be that motherhood is reinvigorating my relationship to the world of sound so that although it may have been the death of someone I loved that shut down my hearing, it may be the birth of someone I love that's awakening it once more.

⧉

home

I once lived in an apartment on London's Ladbroke Grove. There were three rooms, four, if you counted the small loo by the front door, the seat of which was permanently broken. It was cosy, it was warm, it was a good home. I slept some of my deepest sleeps there, meditated with friends there, danced alone in the sitting room, and set up a company that lasted a year there. It was also the place that *Monday Meditations* were born.

Knowing that I needed some support if I was going to establish a regular meditation practice, I started sending out an email to anyone I knew, who either already meditated, had definitely mentioned an *interest* in it, or was, I thought, potentially thinking about it, and invited them to come and meditate with me.

There were regulars and irregulars. People who came once, and people who I never saw again. Friends brought friends, who became friends. It became my go to, and sometimes even my dance card when I met people.

Sometimes there'd be just me, sometimes me and one other. Other times a bit more, so that we'd spill from the sitting room into the hall, which was just space enough for one bottom, and then on we'd flow, moving into my bedroom, circling the foot of my bed.

This home was also the place where I taught my first yoga client: the estate agent who'd sold me the apartment. Our classes would happen in my kitchen, beside the fridge. Later, I taught another client there. An absurdly good-looking blond man, whose looks prompted me to pour extraordinary effort into pretending that his handsomeness had absolutely no effect on me whatsoever. Subsequently, I delivered a sermon of a class, speaking in a voice devoid of any intonation in my best attempt to appear professional. He lasted two classes.

This home was also the home of a morning routine at which the mother that I am now looks back at and weeps. I'd wake at 5 a.m., having participated in a mammalian phenomenon that remains, almost five years into motherhood, woefully elusive: deep sleep. I'd then meditate for an hour, before making my way to the fridge, out of which I'd pull a plate of home-made raw chocolate cake, of which I'd cut a slice, then head to my sofa, which I'd lie across while enjoying that cake *very, very slowly*. After the slice was finished, I'd turn on a CD and do my yoga practice, after which I'd shower, have a second breakfast, and then be at my desk by 9 a.m.

This was the home I lived and loved in. It was accessible by friends, being close enough to tubes and centrally located enough to be an easy destination. So that even though I lived alone, for the most part, I rarely felt alone. Instead I felt safe. Well, mostly. Apart from the day I came back during the Notting Hill Carnival and someone got shot outside my front door and I went up to my first-floor apartment and the music boomed, and voices called, and I felt scared and hid under my duvet.

That home was a whole ecosystem to me. I almost never needed to leave it. It provided so much: nourishment for my soul, a place to sleep, wash, somewhere to entertain friends, a place to meet new friends, a place to work, to explore, to learn, to come back to.

Which brings me to love, or at least learning to love. Because in that home I got awfully confused about what is this thing love? Falling, tumbling and hurtling into love that somewhere along the way I found myself reflecting: *hmmm, maybe this is anything but love.* And yet and yet and wonderful yet, that home was where my daughter was conceived.

Now some years later, for various reasons, Evie and I have moved five times in the last three and a half years. By the time she turns six, we will have moved six times. A house for each year of her life. Not having a place to settle has been discombobulating for both of us. In many ways, Evie's first years mirror my own childhood. Immediately after my father's death, we lost our homes in London and Sussex to the banks, to pay for what remained owing. Afterwards, we moved to live with Nicky, my mother's eldest brother and then onto my grandmother's home in London (a wonderful period where I never had to do any of my own homework), before settling in Battersea. However, in all that disarray and turmoil, my family found something that will stay with us forever, however often we may forget it. And yet, even though all the parenting books, websites and magazines are forever highlighting the importance of consistency, I think there's something they're missing: we can live in the same home throughout our whole lives and never find our way to our hearts. Of what use then is a home?

So that it's not so much that our homes, however glorious or impressive the bricks and mortar may be, are where "the heart is," our homes *are* our hearts. The homes we live in, then, are the cherries on the cake. And if they're anything like the one I lived in on Ladbroke Grove, then what a damn good cherry that is.

⏹

a longing answered

When I sold the apartment on Ladbroke Grove, it had made a good enough profit that I was able to buy a four-bedroom home in Kilburn. When Evie was around four months old and we started spending less time at my mother's in the country and more time in London "(Darling, you have a home in London, why don't you use it?")", most of my days were spent wandering about trying to befriend local mothers; the hardest friends of all to make.

Or at least a segment of mothers are so very hard to connect with, and they're the mothers that look most like me: white, middle-class British. We're not the most inclusive of characters; in fact, most of us act almost protective of one another, excluding anyone else who comes our way. Whereas some, like the Somali and Iraqi mothers who lived close by, were so incredibly friendly and welcoming that I soon stopped trooping over to the larger playground in Queens Park, where groups of largely white women mingle in their twos and threes, and instead started heading to a much smaller, grottier playground only a few minutes away from our front door, to meet the locals who lived nearby. Because although some mornings I'd see things that you just hoped weren't what they looked like (syringes/broken vodka bottles), such was the strength of companionship around that tiny playground that it felt a much warmer place to be, if a little less aesthetic.

So it is to this patch of earth that Evie and I would make our daily pilgrimage.

"'ello Tony," Evie waves every time we pass Tony whose dry cleaning shop sat at the top of our street. Tony always waves back. Sometimes we walk in and chat for a few minutes. He works hard; business is tough. And on top of that, it's isolated work because, apart from the people who rush in and drop off their clothes, most don't seem too keen on stopping for a chat, so for most of the day Tony's going about his work alone.

"What to do?" He asks, during one visit, shrugging his shoulders. I inwardly shrug right back.

Next stop is *Crystal DIY*, the shop of a Polish family, and husband and wife team Nick and Elma. As with Tony, these two have become an important part of our day; to walk past and not say hello doesn't just feel unfriendly, it feels inappropriate.

It's here where I buy candles and batteries, and the occasional doorbell. Nick's also taken on the role of handy-man, which has seen him address everything from leaking washing machines and roof work (although our neighbours were less keen on his exuberance in tackling issues on their roof too), to putting up and then taking down wooden huts in our garden, to anything, anything, and always at a good price.

After *Crystal*, there's the local graveyard where we go for picnics, to climb trees after storms have ripped them from the ground, play hide and seek and occasionally re-home a burgeoning family of slugs and snails that have been colonising our garden. Then there's *The Olive Tree*, a family business run by another husband and wife team, Greek Costas and his French wife Virginie. Evie and I come here for a warm lunch of rice and dhal, and sometimes to buy food, with Evie pillaging their carrots and trying her damndest to eat a Medjool date without me noticing, and which, if pilfered, is always given free of charge.

Costas plays welcoming host behind the till, sharing his views on all aspects of life with such emphatic sensibility that most of his customers will, if not join in, at least stand and listen. It's been here that I've met some fellow neighbours. As our visits increase, and Evie gets older, Virginie starts to come out from behind the till, to sit on the ground at the back of the shop where she and Evie play card games together. And when I'm running low on cash, they let me run a tab, which is community spirit in action, as it sure as hell doesn't do their cash flow any favours.

Afterwards we head over to the playground across the street. Most of the time I sit and 'write' on my phone whilst Evie runs around, singing and playing and making friends with the local kids. And even when I intend to write a story whilst Evie plays, most of the time I sit there on the bench watching and enjoying and feeling my whole system infused with the warmth that love and joy bring to us. Watching Evie holding hands with her new friends, whose parents are maybe Iranian and own the café next to *The Olive Tree* and whose kids are friendly and inclusive to Evie. They teach her nursery rhymes with words like "stinky winky" that make them all laugh and giggle like old men holding onto their bellies as they chortle over a shared sense of humour before running off to push her on the swing. Occasionally I get up to help on more precarious parts of the playground, such as the raised pathway that she loves to totter across.

Some days, the girls aren't at the playground, so Evie and I will walk across the road to the café and ask if they want to come and play. Sometimes their friends will come too, and the mother will stay back, but the father will occasionally walk over. And when we walk them back, the mother will open her arms wide, gesturing towards the drinks and say: "Please, please take something, what would you like?"

"Thank you, that's so kind, but that's okay," I reply, embarrassed because they don't have much, but she insists, and so I take a bottle of water.

Elma, too, from *Crystal* will give Evie little gifts: an old plastic doll, a small football. And they're all given with the sweetest, kindest gift of all: a hopeful heart. A heart that says I thought of you and I got this, hoping it'd be something you like. So here I am, a beam in my heart blooming. Because this is it, a longing in my heart made good: community, unfolding in unexpected ways.

something else

I've locked myself out of the house; something that I've been doing with increasing frequency. Which along with occasional misplacements of my debit card and mobile phone forms a triad of losing some of the more essential aspects of my life. An SOS for help perhaps: I've lost my way, someone please come find me. Or at the very least, a reminder of a familiar refrain in my life: *hey lady, you gotta slow down; things are getting a little out of hand here.*

This time, because it's cold and late, rather than wait on our doorstep, I've walked over to Elma's shop.

"Please can I stay here whilst I wait for Ben?" I ask.

"Of course," Elma replies, saying yes with her whole heart, because whilst many might say this, not many would really mean it. After ushering us in from the wet November night, six-months-old Evie and I hang out with Elma and her mother, who doesn't speak a word of English, around their electric fire by the till. When Evie gets hungry, I head to the loo to feed her. As accommodating as they may be, breast-feeding isn't for everyone, and some folks might be a bit surprised to come in for a light-bulb and find a lady feeding her babe by the till.

dropping anchor

So keen to protect my daughter from any suffering I worry has come too soon for her young life, and guilt-ridden by the absences of all that I wish was there for her, and paralysed to move forward in the direction I know is inevitable, here I am again, another night, totally awake, wondering when sleep will come. At some point, it dawns on me what I need to do. But of course, I resist. At least for a few more hours. Eventually though, the prospect that sleep may come when I do this thing propels me on. Kissing the top of my daughter's head, I close my eyes and turn around, so that for the first time since Evie was born eight months ago, my back is turned on my daughter.

The act feels symbolic and pulses with a significance only an eight-month sleep deprived mind can assign it. And yet, what is meaning other than the significance we assign to the otherwise everyday occurrences that make up our lives? In becoming parents we seek utter availability to our children, so that they might grow up knowing they matter. It is only when we realise how far we have drifted from our own sense of wellbeing that we seek to retrieve ourselves, as we look out to sea and wonder: can I throw anchor here? Are the waves calm enough, is there no risk of a storm coming close? Only then, after our eyes and senses have surveyed the horizon, do we slowly start doing what we've needed to do for longer than we even know to admit. We turn our backs and fall asleep.

I'm ready. Finally, I'm ready. I've loved this part of mothering so very much but in the last month have noticed resentment replacing contentment. In other words, I'm ready to take my body back as belonging fully to me. The journey of breastfeeding between Evie and me is coming to a stop.

Aiming for a smooth transition, I've been preparing for a couple of weeks.

"My body's stopping making milk, but it still makes love," I whisper to my suckling daughter as she feeds. "My body's stopping making milk, but it still makes love." I sing softly as she nurses in the crook of my arms.

As the time comes closer, I'm reminded of my mother's dog, Piglet. After returning from a three month trip to India in 2007, I came to visit my mother and was greeted by two newborns and an exhausted Piglet with rings under her eyes, who clearly hadn't read any of the eastern wisdom about taking care of what you eat in the first forty days, as her ribs were showing, and she could barely shuffle her little body across the room to collapse onto one of the dog beds; beds that she had previously ignored in preference of her little hut cave.

Her puppies fed all the time, and judging by the faded look in her eyes, throughout the night as well. Her nipples, previously so neat and pretty, were now swollen and hanging heavily from her body. If anyone who she loved and trusted came near to pick up the puppies, she would look at us with gratitude. This devoted mother, who was giving everything to her puppies. One of which wasn't feeding well, and who we weren't sure was going to make it because he was getting weaker while the more boisterous one was thriving. But Piggy was so tender, encouraging and loving to the weaker one, letting both of them suckle whenever and for as long as they liked, that slowly the weaker one began to thrive too.

And then one day I was hanging with Piggy in the dog room, and one of the puppies went to feed, and she stopped him. He tried again, and again and she turned away, only this time she continued turning, slipped through the door and headed off to the kitchen. Just like that, with a glaring absence of guilt, or internal recriminations, Piglet stopped feeding her puppies. Her message was clear: my job's done, darling boys, you can look after yourself now. And though she continued to clean and play with them, the feeding from her body bit was over.

Fast forward seven or so years, and here I am, lying in bed with Evie having just woken, and before she has a chance to feed, Ben picks her up and takes her downstairs for breakfast. And I lie here, waiting and wondering: will she resist? Will she cry?

She does neither.

Nor does she the following morning, or the third, or fourth, and then we're there, four days before Evie turns twenty-one months old, our breast-feeding journey is finished. In the days that follow, my lopsided breasts return to roughly the same size. There's no pain, nor, more significantly, any internal niggles of doubt. In fact, this is one of the few experiences in my life, and certainly in motherhood, where I've managed to set a goal, achieve it and then move confidently on; no doubt lingering. And notably it wasn't the advice of others I listened to, but simply a sense inside that said this is alright, go with it, and stop when it feels ready and right.

We sell ourselves short when we only confine our teachers to individual forms and species. As a mother, some of my most influential teachers about how to mother have been not from a fellow member of my species, but from animals. Often we can see, in worlds not normally associated with our own, symbols or motifs for experiences that we're moving through that reveal to us a way not previously conceived of.

To these teachers then, may even more appear!

crossed wires

"Hmmm, this isn't good," says Richard, the *Feng Shui* man who mum has sent around as a gift to the house. "Lots of cross wires of information. This will have and has had a very disturbing energy on a relationship."

"Funny you say that," I say to him. "Because I just found out that the couple I bought the house from are getting a divorce."

"Hmmm, yes," he says, furrowing his brow. And then he heads out to the garden and sticks some pins into the soil, as he does to the tree outside our window on the street, which stands beside an electrical birds nest of wires where all the cables and wires of the street concertinaed into a *Feng Shui* nightmare. Or rather a very real one that's erupting in the centre of my very own home.

⍰

kindness of wasps

There's a knock at the door. It's our neighbour's nanny who's noticed that there's a wasp's nest under the guttering above our kitchen. She comes in, and Evie and I, along with her and the two kids she looks after, march through the kitchen, out into the garden and look up to watch the wasps swarming in and out of their hiding place.

"You must get rid of them," she says. "Yes," I say. And then I go onto Google, curious to see if there's a way of working with the wasps because life's expensive, and besides, nature's been around an awful lot longer, and we humans have become so logical as to be totally incredibly 100% illogical, so maybe there's something to learn.

Online, I read Shamanic articles that write of wasps as positive things, and that rather than condemn them for being nuisances, praise them for their organisational abilities. They can help bring order to the chaos in our world, the article says; in other words, I might just have found my muse, albeit in insect form. Afterwards I get to work: drawer by drawer, day by day, leaving the big cupboard underneath the stairs for last. As I clear the detritus of my life, I feel my mind and body responding. With challenges in my relationship draining my energy reserves, I don't have the juice to practice yoga, but this last week, I've practiced nearly every day, and I haven't done that since giving birth nearly two years ago.

After a week of cleaning, hovering, binning, bagging, filing and dusting, as the drawers and cupboards of my home become ordered and spacious, I move onto my to do list, and start ticking off more items than I can replace, all the while having more time to write, and hang out with Evie.

Meanwhile, a friend has posted a reply to my status update asking about how to get rid of wasps. *Ask them*, she suggests, *why have they come to your home?* And yes, it's summer, which is a pretty good reason, a logical one, a rational one even, and yet, maybe it's not the whole reason. So I think about it and the metaphor, 'a wasp's nest' comes to mind and I think of our home, and what it's become lately. But before I can ask the question, I find one in Evie's room and then call pest control, and whilst waiting for the man to arrive, I look out at the nest with all the wasps buzzing in and out, and I ask: please tell me, what is it that I need to learn from you?

And the answer that comes back? *Be kind.* I think of the ebbing away of kindness between Ben and me. Not all the time, but a lot of the time, and I wonder where it went. Later, after the pest control guy has come, and the wasps nest is no more, I stand in Evie's room looking out at the guttering. I feel the absence of the wasps, maybe even their sacrifice. Their message, "be kind," is so simple that it's so easy to waft it away, *yeah yeah, but I want the deep stuff.*
It's my loss that I do not more readily realise quite how deep kindness is.

let it go

Our lives have *Frozen*.

Whereas other films have come and gone, Frozen has appeared, and remained - with a surprisingly resilient shelf life. Whether in the form of a DVD, the songs, or one of those Elsa dolls that everyone seems intent on giving to Evie at-any-possible-opportunity. Or the snowman in large plastic form which still to this day haunts the toy cupboard, refusing to be lost or even destroyed by willing canine teeth.

And then there's the song.

"Let it gooooo!" Evie sings, her arms out wide as she runs around in the park. "Let it go!" she sings as she runs up to me where I sit at my computer stressing out. "Let it go!" she sings as she sits in her pram, as we toddle along the streets.

When not singing, or watching the film, Evie has been developing her skills as a highly committed graffiti artist. Her canvas? Every orifice of our home, including the sandpit, dirt patches in the park, and if we're lucky, the occasional piece of paper.

Desperate for some variety, I try one night to show Evie *The Little Mermaid*. My plan is quickly vetoed. "Let it go, Mum," she says. Reluctantly I do, and on goes Princess Elsa.

another chance

My grandfather's gone into hospital. Mum, Evie and I are flying out to Norway on the first flight available. We arrive early evening on Monday, after two plane rides, one of which is delayed followed by more delays of anything remotely delayable, and a long taxi ride, after which we stagger, bleary-eyed, into the hotel lobby where my eyes swim to a stack of magazines sitting on the reception desk that have the word 'Arundal' splashed across the top.

The next morning I check with the receptionist to make sure that we're actually in the place where the film Frozen is based. "Yes," she says, "although their pronunciation is way off."

I walk over to where Evie and her beloved Dodo are having breakfast, the magazine in my hand. "Bubba, guess where we are?" Her eyes open with curiosity. "We're in Arundal," I say in a desperate bid to raise the tempo of the visit, and to turn this trip into a jolly little adventure for my daughter whilst trying to communicate telepathically with my mother, who's contemplating the potential death of her father, the parent she adores and loves with all her heart.

I point to the magazine with a picture of the landscape on it, "It's the home of Princess Elsa, bubba," a beam of a smile soars across her face: to be in the place of ones' heroine! And though she remains silent, I can see the impact that this is having on her system: her body softens. Mum winces a smile and gets up to make her way back to the hospital where she had stayed throughout the night, and will remain for the next two days, sitting vigil by her father.

"The hill's very steep, Lau. Get a taxi."

"We'll be fine, mum. We'll walk."

We follow shortly afterwards; Evie sitting in her pram which I'm pushing with extended arms and a puce face. "The hill's steep" was not an understatement. On the way up, we pass a shop where four big-nosed trolls sit in a shop's window display. I stop and unclip Evie, who climbs out of her buggy, pressing herself close to the window, entranced by the sight of them.

When we arrive at the hospital, I call my mother, who comes out to look after Evie so that I can see grandpa. Later we speak to his doctor who says it can go either way, and it's in this not knowing space that I'm reminded how hard it can be to say to those we love: I f*****g love you because maybe in a moment like this that's too much, because to admit the depth of how much I do care about my grandfather is to let him know that time is running out.

A decade or so earlier, my grandmother Dean was taken to hospital after having being found lying on her sitting room floor. After checks, it was determined that she needed an operation. Before she was taken into theatre, the whole family came to wish her luck. Just before I went to say goodbye, my grandfather walked in. Seeing him, Dean pulled out her hairbrush from her handbag, and immediately started brushing her hair.

Grandpa walked around the foot of the bed and came to stand beside her, where he reached out and patted the bed and said something like, "Come on, old girl, spirit of the war and all." And whilst he offered words of encouragement, my grandmother sat there, propped up by the pillows, listening and perhaps wishing for something a little less general and a little more personal to them. "I love you, you were an amazing mother to our children," and quite possibly, "I'm so sorry I hurt you." But the moment was lost, and with my grandmother's hair now fully brushed and coiffed, my grandfather walked out behind the curtains that made up the small cubicle in which she rested. I stayed behind a little longer, struggling to articulate quite how much this woman meant to me. A woman who'd been like a second mother to me, having stepped in to help my mother raise my brother and me when my father died, whose cupboards were filled with endlessly glorious items to dress up in, and whose drawer beneath her mirror I loved to peruse, simply for the joy of discovering more about this woman in my life who felt so good to be around. A woman who introduced me to the world of opera, to Shakespeare, who adored books as much as I, and who always encouraged me to "Write darling, write about it."

But because denial feels more comfortable than reality, I didn't thank her for those wonderfully supportive and loving letters she'd sent to me during my time at boarding school, always written in that reassuring turquoise ink, or the bottle full of chocolate milk that she'd always left for me in her top drawer at home in London, so that all I had to do was pull open the drawer, lie back on her bed, drink and be soothed. Or tell her how the way she loved animals, particularly of the canine variety, had been inherited by all members of the family (and endured by our partners), or how much I appreciated her generosity of spirit, which meant I was allowed to play with her precious small china animal figurines that lived along the mantle that ran over her bed, which lesser mortals may have worried that a child of my age would have broken. Or for all the ways that various rituals of hers became sources of reassurance for me, from the exquisitely deliberate and elegant way she'd paint her finger nails, the same colour every single time, to the way she kept her hair aloft with plumes of hair spray, the lathering of her eyelashes with Vaseline each night, "to make them grow, darling," and even the way she commandeered that place on that sofa that only those who didn't know better would sit in. Although such was the sense of divine ownership that she had infused that spot with that were another human to sit in her place, such was the *froideur* that could almost instantly be detected, as if the sofa were telepathically whispering to the unsuspecting bottom that perhaps there might be other seats in the sitting room that it may like to explore, that few ever made the mistake of confusing it as anything other than the matriarchal throne.

But whilst I was all too ready to accept my denials conviction that all was well, my mother wasn't so convinced. "She's not well, Lau," my mother said to me when we got home later that afternoon. The doctor called whilst we were having supper. He asked for us to return to the hospital, he needed to tell us something. Still I clung to my façade. "The operation went well! She'll be fine!" My mother's silence indicated that she knew otherwise. When we arrived, the doctor was waiting for us in the hall. Without saying anything, he gestured to a little room to his left.

"Great," I told myself, "he just wants to take us somewhere private to say how well it all went." On seeing him gesture to the door of the room, my mother sagged. I placed my arms around her, as we turned towards the room.

"No no, Mama! You've got it wrong, it's all fine." Except it wasn't. When the doctors operated, they discovered that my grandmother had been right: she wasn't well. It was the hospital who'd been wrong. Instead of being sent home the first time she came in, she should have been trusted as someone who knew her own body, not dismissed as an old woman wasting time. During the time it took for them to decide to operate on her, a blood clot to the brain meant that her organs weren't receiving oxygen; as a result, my grandmother died in the operation.

Now here I am with grandpa, simultaneously frozen with caution at the worry that I might overwhelm him if I say goodbye and terrified of losing the chance to tell him how much he means to me if I don't.

"When do you think I'm going to get over this?" he asks me later, as I sit next to him propped up in a chair in his hospital room. He's struggling to breathe, as well as being exhausted by not having slept for two nights.
"I'm not sure, grandpa," I reply.

Afterwards, mum and I chat because no one is telling him what the doctor told us earlier: Grandpa isn't going to get over this. It's only a matter of days.

A year previous, my grandfather had made a speech at Evie's first birthday party, "From the oldest member of the family, to the youngest," he said, raising a glass to toast his great-granddaughter. For some moments, we only realise their preciousness in retrospect, whilst others we manage to show up for as they're happening. For me, that moment with Evie's great-grandfather honouring her was one of the rare moments in my life of showing up, and saying THANK YOU as the moment was actually happening.

just say it

That afternoon, I spend as much time as I can by my grandfather's bed. His lungs and heart are weak. For various medical reasons, he's been unable to sleep for days. He's not only dying in discomfort then, but in disorientation and exhaustion. It's decided that the kindest way to let him die is by starvation. I stay by his bed as long as I can whilst family members take it in turn to hang out with Evie outside.

I stand by his partially raised bed, which is raised so that it might be easier for him to breathe whilst he attempts to sleep. He wakes with a start from his sleep apnea, which causes him to stop breathing for a moment. He's anxious, scared, and bolts up into a sitting position.

"It's okay grandpa. You were just sleeping. When you're sleeping, your breathing stops just for a moment. I have this too, sometimes. It's a bit scary, but you're okay. Lie back. Go to sleep, you need to rest." He lies back, his mouth open as he falls asleep before he has time to exhale.

Eight seconds later, the cycle repeats itself, and so on. I don't know how long I stay with him like that, other than knowing that just as I would comfort Evie, to reassure her, that this is what he needs: the knowledge that someone is standing close by and there is a voice speaking calmly to soothe him back to peace. Eventually the cycle ceases, as he's able to rest for longer periods.

At one point, I'm joined by his Norwegian wife Berit, and one of her sons Marius. Then mum comes in, asking me to take Evie, who needs to go back to the hotel for her supper and bed. Grandpa's sleeping. I walk over to kiss him on his head, nothing in me wanting to leave.

"I love you grandpa," I say, reaching over to touch his hand. Immediately as I touch the back of his hand he sits straight up, grabs my hand and looks directly into my eyes, saying, "Thank you, darling," and then falls back into a sleep.

I'm so touched by this privilege of being with my grandfather and having this moment to truly say goodbye to him that as I walk out of the room, I cannot stop the tears from pouring out of my eyes. Finally, a death was happening to someone I loved and cared about where I was both able to be actively with them and to also acknowledge how much they meant to me. Subsequently, it's not an understatement to say that those moments with Grandpa are a few of the strands of my life that I'm most grateful for. Death happens suddenly, or with a warning. To get a warning may seem brutal, it may seem unfair. No matter, it's still a warning, a chance, an opportunity to say all that you would be denied saying were the death to be a sudden one. Our lives so easily fill with regrets, largely because typically we play the game that we believe we have forever and tomorrow, or the day after, or the year after, or the decade after, when we can make amends. And yes, Ms. O'Hara may have been right, tomorrow is another day, but it's today that counts.

☐

reconnecting

The next morning, Evie and I come down to breakfast to find my mother and brother already there. They had spent all night beside Grandpa, reading him Buddhist prayers and playing him music. He died as night slipped into dawn.

After breakfast, we travel with Berit and her three sons; Peter, with his daughter Julia; Harald and his wife Warsan and their son Isaac; and Marius. Along with Evie, my mother, my brother Charlie, and my uncle Maneeshi, we go to Berit's home in Tungen – where Grandpa had his heart attack.

The house sits on the edge of the water, leading out to the sea. The water's warm enough to swim in, and so we do. However, this being a trip that no one's brought their swimming gear for, I'm in my underwear. Something my mother offers her visual opinion on, with a glance that lets me know she'd probably be happier if I wasn't exposing everyone to this particular pair of flesh coloured maternity pants that I'm wearing. She looks, and I turn away, pretending I haven't noticed.

Evie scampers around the rocks, enjoying the chance to be naked and outside, as she and Julia play. It's rare for my family to come together, which is a loss, given the fact that it's a family that includes people from Rwanda, Norway, Germany, China and even bonny Scotland: the potential! However, often characters are at war with each other, or at the very least, at woe. So, whereas the dramas of life can separate, here, the finality of death connects. As we sit together, overlooking the water, later preparing food together or chatting near the children, my heart roars yes, and of course the time comes when we say we should do this more often, and everyone agrees. However, nearly three years after this has happened, that once more has yet to happen.

Later, when the kids have gone to bed, we sit in the barn that my grandfather designed and built, and I hear stories about who he was to them; his other family. After dinner, when everyone's said goodnight and gone to bed, I go outside under the stars, crouch down and start singing. I think Evie's the only person who doesn't question the ethics of my singing; whereas other family members and close friends might not be so polite about my vocal abilities, Evie simply joins in.

But tonight, I need not worry about offending anyone; it's the stars and I, and of course the water, and I don't think either are too bothered about my tone-deaf attempts at lyrical combustion. Sitting down I start to sing, imagining myself out there in the countryside of the deep south, in a place where sorrow can always find a melody. The resonance of the words causing my body to feel a connection to the pulse around me, and also quite possibly to my grandfather; his energy still perceptible amidst the air around me as I say goodbye, not only to him but to a dream whose reality, it seems, is not to be.

The following day, Mum, Charlie, Evie and I head back to London. It's a somber day, not least because grandpa's died, but also because it's the day that Ben and I were meant to be getting married.

However, ten days after returning home, Ben and I decide to separate. Two weeks later, he moves out.

🞐

expression

It's a rainy night. I've my phone in my hand as I follow Google Maps to where I want to go. When I get there, I walk into a cavernous hall, with about sixty people taking off their shoes, drinking water, stretching and chatting.

The dancing soon starts, moving from flow to lyrical, then staccato where we stagger step by erratic step, closer to chaos. As I move around the room, something stirs inside, and though I'm on no stage, have no training, and certainly no audience, no matter: I've my imagination. So that in the movement I am more than me; a dancer dancing on stage who is transforming the grief and loss that've nestled around her solar plexus, and is instead giving them life. As I leap about the room, finally able to be as physically expressive with these emotions as I'm somatically able to be, tears start to flow. Because everyone's so focused on dancing, I don't need to wipe them away, and so they slide down my face, liberated in a way their peers so rarely feel. In return, I'm able to feel a cleansing that, if I had habitually quashed them back down, would have been denied.

The dance floor is one of the few places where those secret hurts and longings that we have no way of acknowledging, not only to others, but even to ourselves, can be liberated. Instead of pushing them away, or wading through long elaborate explanations of why and what and when, here on the dance floor they're released by virtue of being allowed not interpretation, but an expression contained within conscious movement. Here on the dance floor I can dance my own private homage to whatever's dark and sore inside. Here in the absence of words, connections are made that speak of worlds far larger than the one I call my own, and through which I so frequently drift. And as my world and the world of my daughter moves towards a reality that I've wanted so much to avoid, the only thing I can do is dance, so that what may otherwise have remained trapped, is freed.

the sadness dance

"How are you?" people ask. A question to which the politically correct thing to do is just smile, shrug your shoulders and say "Oh fiiine." But one evening, at a friend's house where the journalist Rachel Kelly's talking about her book *Black Rainbow,* which goes in-depth about her experience with depression, tired of social niceties, I reply that "I feel as if my skin's been ripped off and I'm a rippling mass of nerve endings walking around with nothing to cover them."

Luckily for my friends, Rachel begins her talk, and our conversation comes to an end. But the sadness doesn't. In fact, wherever I go, there she is, Miss Sadness forever keeping me company. What to do?

Buddhists say watch what arises, *let it pass.* But nothing about this sadness feels transient. It's a lumpen thing setting up home in my heart. At least until I come across *The Language of Emotions* written by Karla Maclaren. It's in here that I finally find the inspiration for communicating with the sadness. So that suddenly this lumpen heavy state that sits like cement in my chest has started to oscillate just slightly. In other words, sadness has found its flow.

Sadness is an emotion like water, writes Karla, *it wants to flow. If we block it, it crystalizes.* To get it flowing again, she suggests a technique where you breathe deeply, then move your arms in gently flowing movements, releasing the sadness whenever you feel it.

I start incorporating this fluid movement into my life – in the bath, the shower, whenever I remember - until the sadness technique becomes the sadness dance; finally something that I can share with my daughter. Because Evie needs a skill to support her, too. So that dancing becomes a release for the both of us – and at the same time, a tool that we can use that isn't too heavy for a two-year-old, but still provides an outlet for whatever confusing feelings she may be dealing with as well. Because although Evie's too young to be able to cognitively understand what's happened, she's the perfect age to feel what's happening; namely that her home life has shifted from one of tension to one of sadness.

"Mummy's sad," Evie sometimes says, "Lets dance!" Sometimes I am, and so we dance, and sometimes I'm alright. "No, bubba, I'm okay." "Evie's sad," she'll say.

"Then let's dance." The beauty of the sadness dance is that it's kind of impossible to dance with your child and for a smile not to appear. Because dancing in its nature is expressional and also, in a way, maybe just a tiny bit devotional. We're giving ourselves over to the spirit of something larger than this eclipsed version of ourselves that we so protectively live our lives clinging to so very tightly.

So the sadness dance became a part of our everyday lives; in fact, we dance so much I'm wondering if we'll ever stop. Eventually, though, the dance grows bored of the four walls it's being confined to, and we find ourselves dancing outside. At that playground near our home one afternoon, the younger sibling of one the girls whose family owned the local cafe falls over. Immediate tears tumble down her cheeks. Evie and I help her up and place her down beside her sister and friend on the bench.

"Do you know the sadness dance?" I ask her. All three shake their heads, looking at me with serious expressions. I look at Evie and she looks at me with that big smile of hers, and we start moving our arms, jingling our heads, stomping our feet and swirling about as we show them the sadness dance, except not looking quite so sad. The girls watch, open mouthed, then the dance pulls them in and there we are, four girls, one woman, dancing under a tree by a bench on the side of Kilburn Lane, temporary pain forgotten, or at least flowing into something else.

a glitch

In the days that follow the decision to separate, all I want is to get away from the bleak darkness settling in my home, but I feel at a loss as to how, so that sometimes the containment of the whole thing becomes too much and one morning I find myself storming down the stairs. And I don't know why or what preceded it, only that I feel obliteratingly angry. A powerful emotion that storms into view as my ego's attempt to provide an anecdote for the utter powerlessness sweeping through my heart. And then I hear her, my daughter, not yet two, making her way carefully down the stairs behind me.

"Mama, I miss you!" she calls out to me, tears pouring down her face. I stop immediately, and run upstairs to her, open my arms and hug her as tenderly as I can. Not yet able to traverse that fine line of being engulfed by the tsunami of emotions that hit you when everything you didn't want to happen is happening and the feeling of powerlessness to do anything about it.

As parents sourced from imperfect lives, we can want so much to cup the world in our hands - if only for a moment - so that we can go to our children and say *hey, this is what you're a part of.*

When life changes in ways that we'd hope it wouldn't, sometimes we find ourselves with hearts hanging limply and eyes averting contact with others, simply because a voice inside taunts us with images of how far we've drifted from the parent of our ideals. And yet, amidst those ever-beating wings of change, little portals emerge in unexpected moments, in places that previously I hadn't even thought to look, and that have contributed to whatever healing is taking place for us.

So that healing is happening, and continues to happen, not when externalities steady, but when my heart relates to the changes, not with regret at what I've interpreted them to represent – i.e. a departure from what the early years should be like - but with something else that I'm not even sure I have a word for yet. Maybe because it's the thing that cannot be named, but only expressed or felt. And that no matter how many shards of glass may lodge in our hearts, or in the hearts of those around us, it cannot and will not fade.

⸺

powerlessness

And so a life I've been clinging to, in the hope of avoiding something that in the end ends up being unavoidable (Evie, having to move between homes, having only just turned two) begins.

The first weekend, Ben comes early. After I've put Evie in the car, I stand in the street watching them drive away. Evie sitting in her car seat, all the toys she wanted to take with her loaded in her arms. "I love you!" I call out. Furious waves, a little face staring out the window. *It's all okay!* A puppet's smile on my face. When the car turns right at the bottom of the street, tears pour out of my eyes. As waves of hopelessness smash into splintered foam on that eternal rock of hopefulness; the human heart.

I walk back into my empty house. The usual flotsam and jetsum hadn't had their time to accumulate on the floor, and the tidiness creates an eerie-not-comforting feeling. Something, or rather someone, is missing. I stand for a minute by the stairs: what to do? And because there's nothing else to do, I dance...

rushing

"Bubs I've lost my phone, do you know where it is?" I ask absentmindedly, "Is it upstairs?"
"No, Mama," Evie replies, shaking her head, "not upstairs."
"Do you know where it is?"
"There, Mama," she replies, pointing to the ledge that runs over the radiator in the hall. I look at it, and at the tower of papers; unopened mail, magazines, and general detritus that lives there. I pick it all up to discover my phone lying underneath. I must have left it there the previous day and had completely forgotten about it.

But Evie hasn't; she's remembered.

We spin around, overwhelmed by the balls we're juggling, only to add another just because we can. Lacking the awareness that all the while our children are watching, sensing a disturbance that very subtly makes their parents a little less playful, a little more grumpy, sad, remote, or needy. Our children's resilience is something we parents rely on, perhaps too much at times. Uncomfortable truths may be to acknowledge how much they take in.

And so phones, credit cards, crucial items around which our daily lives depend start being lost. *Remember remember* the whispers seem to say, *remember remember,* because perhaps if you do, right there you'll find not more pain, but a peace that brings with it a much more resilient peace then the autopilot existence that can become your new normal when events such as separations take place that trigger old wounds.

⃞

tentatively

But amidst all the forgetting, something else is calling out to be remembered: the joy of dancing with others. On a weekend when Evie's with her father, I book myself onto a 5 Rhythms workshop to discover my inner Goddess and inner Whore, in hippy capital of this small island, Totnes in Devon.

My train's leaving soon, and Evie's upstairs with Camella. I've said goodbye, as it's Friday, and I won't see Evie till Sunday, maybe Monday, which until now makes it the longest I've been away from her. Our goodbye earlier had been rushed, and I sense that Evie hasn't really got that I'm going. Do I go upstairs and say a proper goodbye, but then risk disturbing her when she's potentially just about to fall asleep? Or slip out, and hope for the best? My gut tells me to say a proper goodbye to my child but there are other voices that say *don't do it. It'll only cause a fuss.*

I'm caught in that rabbit-in-the-headlights way and, as a result, I very nearly listen to those voices that say *hey mother! You don't know what you're doing! Walk on, move on, go away...* but I ignore them and head upstairs, pausing before I go in to bring my attention to my breath, to calm and soften and tune into the vibe of the room, which is all songs and relaxed and warm with the curtains drawn and dim light coming from the lights on low. When I open the door, Camella's face drops. I can see she thinks *uh o,h Evie's going to cry,* and I walk over to my daughter and kiss her on the top of her head.

"I love you, bubba, I'll see you on Sunday." She continues drinking her bottle and nods her head as in yeah, mum, I'm cool with it, we've chatted, peace out. And then I kiss Camella on her head and say goodbye, and leave the bedroom, closing the door behind me, my heart pinched in my chest: she's okay! She gets I'm going away and there's no resistance or sadness. I feel joy that it's all going to be okay.

If only I could carry that sentiment forward more viscerally...

☐

clearing

And now I'm here.

It's the first morning and I've headed out for a pre-breakfast walk in the woods. And even though I can hear the roar of cars zooming by not too far away, still I'm surrounded by stillness, and my body and mind cannot help but respond.

Raindrops rest on naked tree boughs, whilst birds call to each other. A moment ago; glorious song. Green ferns sprout from a mulchment of browning leaves, quite unmoving to the naked eye and yet of course in perpetual oscillation and unstoppable movement: a dance so subtle that, though it happens every nanosecond of our lives, I live most days forgetting to gaze at it in wonderment.

There's a thickness. Whereas normally it's me, singular, walking towards a tree - also singular - right now we all seem very much thickly souped together.

As I sit here alone, listening to the birds, wondering at being able to find that space within and of the possibility of being able to carry it with me wherever I go; to expand my mind from the micro to the macro and then perhaps settle somewhere in between, it seems to me that, though my relationship to that which is indestructible appears somewhat unreliable and disappointingly unassured, what does seem inevitable is that one day soon my daughter and I will be moving to the country.

mirrored

Later that day we sit at the table for dinner.

"It takes you a lot to be present in your body, doesn't it?" asks Ruby, a fellow dancer who's around fifty years old.
"Yes, it does. How can you tell?"
"Because it's the same with me."

We look at each other, ever so slightly hesitant; there being so many possibilities of where this conversation could go, whilst around us the others carry on their conversations. I want to say more to this woman, and ask her things like how and why and what? But instead, we look at each other, and I think maybe I kind of already know where she is, as she does I; conversation complete because somehow witnessing reduces redundant explanations. So without saying a word, we turn our heads, dip our spoons, and go back to finishing our soup.

🛛

release

The surprising thing about separations and divorce is how much pain they cause to erupt from places long ago thought healed. Even though you may have been bracing against their inevitability, when they happen, all the pain that you've stored so secretly throughout your life deep in the wells of your heart is dynamited open. The separation with Ben itself acted as a floodgate for a cornucopia to erupt. Like tsunamis finally allowed to pass through to where they want to travel: the sand at the end of the beach where they can sink through and return to the big wide expanse of nothingness that we call the centre of our very universe.

Which is to say that finally in a place where I don't feel the pressure to be stoic, I spend most of my time during the weekend wiping tears from my face. Towards the end of the workshop, Julie invites us all to sit in a circle. As a way of closing the experience, we're invited to take it in turns to stand in front of the group whilst the rest of us call out to that person all the qualities we see in them. It's an excruciatingly uncomfortable experience. When my turn comes, I don't so much stand, as wince. I've spent so much of the weekend with tears pouring down my face and I feel ashamed. Although the truth is that tears or no tears, shame was there to finally be felt. But it's a misaligned shame; there not being much else so repressed, and yet when released, that has such power to liberate and return me to a softness of body and an opening of heart. It's not until I hear one of the women name it that my shame starts to feel that maybe, just maybe, the tears have as much of a place on the dance floor as my naked breasts had the previous evening. So when someone calls out something about tears having beauty, this one I can hear. This woman isn't shaming my tears, she's saying she feels them too.

But I'm a British woman, so I try to make a joke of it. "So many!"
"Those tears were for us all, Laura. You cried for us all," says another. We British are not wholly at peace with hearing affirmations of our goodness; we've been raised too cynically for that.

Three years previous, I'd spent three months living in a tipi in France, unlearning everything I knew about yoga. During that summer, I took part in "pussy circles" where we'd stand in front of other women and talk about the parts of our body we felt ashamed about, and also the parts we liked. It was terrifying. But healing too, resulting in a kind of softening around the very brutal way that I'd always related to my body; namely acting as if it were a relative with whom I'd like as little to do with as possible.

But that summer, during a glorious three months of nakedness and six hours of yoga a day, of meditating and simple foods and life lived as a community of a haphazard sort, of exploring if open relationships were something that felt natural to me (yes, and no), and of sleeping in a little tipi for one under the black cloak of stars and listening to my yoga teacher talk about the interconnectedness of everything, and trusting the intelligence of our body, my body and I came towards each other once again, in a way that made me appreciate it's not all about the intellect and, more than that, our bodies house an intelligence that, if we choose to tune into it, can change not just the nature of our yoga practice, but the rhythm of our days.

After my go, I sit down amongst the other women, sending out my words of encouragement to the others whose turn it is. Notably, whereas the majority of us squirm when it's our turn to stand and receive words of recognition, one or two of the women simply sit and receive.

It's rather glorious to watch.

a cure

When the affirming finishes, Julie shares with us a story from her teacher.
"The only cure for the type of tiredness you're feeling is learning to stay awake!"
We're trying, dear Julie, we're trying.

?

extended stay

When I get home, the builders have moved in to paint over cracked walls and turn our bath, that's as big as a loo, into something more accommodating. As a result, our home has become a thing of dust with people coming and going, but never staying.

"Come and stay in Battersea," my mother says, sensing that our home isn't the calmest of environments to be living in. "We're fine, Mum," I reply.
"Lau, it's just going to get dustier and louder, and everything will stop working. Come and stay here. You can have your old room." So Evie and I relocate from north London to south London, to stay at my mother's home in Battersea where my brother Charlie lives.

We're meant to stay for three weeks. We stay for nine months.

remember, remember

After deciding to relocate to Battersea, in the hope that being in a home environment will somehow soak up some of the pain and provide Evie with a larger family as opposed to a reduced one, I put Douglas Road on the market to sell. It sells quickly, and afterwards I wonder if the new owners keep the canary yellow front door that I'd had painted, or the wisteria tree that I'd planted, or the updated bathroom.

One of the benefits of moving to Battersea is being able to slip back into a life that doesn't need too much thought. My family moved here when I was around nine years old, so memories and positive associations are scattered around every corner. But it also means negotiating ongoing politics of once again living under the same roof as my brother. A human with whom I seem to share some pretty gnarly karma. So that whilst Evie is delighted to be living with her uncle Charlie, I feel as if all that's happened is that I've moved from living in a home of tension with my ex, to a home of tension with my brother. It's a strange time, living back in my old room with Evie and then in my mother's bed when she's in the country.

One cold afternoon in November, Evie and I are heading back to the house when I realise that I've left my housekeys where we've just been. I grumble, blame, and curse, and then call for a mini cab to retrieve them. I'm told the cab will be around thirty minutes, so I take Evie to My Old Dutch, a restaurant that I've wanted to take her to for a while, if only because it's where great meals of my teenage years took place. So although the pancakes are bland, they're stuffed with such sentimental memories that my own gut is more than happy to chomp away. Evie, however, has a good two years yet till her appreciation of pancakes will appear, and so ignores the large spheres of moribund tastelessness, and instead picks at the cheese. After a while, I admit defeat and we head back outside again, passing a café where I pick up some banana cake, which we eat on the patch of green beside the fire station, under the jet-black sky.

Fifty minutes later, the cab arrives with my keys. I bend down, peering through the window and ask the driver if he'll take us over the bridge.

"I can't take you over," he says, his eyes blank. I consider pleading with him, as it's nudging 7 p.m. and it's cold as hell but instead pay him and turn towards the bridge to begin our walk home.

As we near the junction in front of Albert Bridge, Evie and I find ourselves behind a man who's perambulating at an exquisitely tortuous speed. Fine if you're a Zen monk, frustrating if you're a tired mum. He's absorbed in conversation on his phone and I feel pissed and annoyed as there's too much traffic on the road for me to walk past him. At the lights, he and another man take a shortcut across the street, which I can't do as I have the buggy.

Damn them.

A moment later our little MacLaren zooms to life. My daughter, pram and I perform a mother-daughter version of a James Bond car stunt as Evie and I skedaddle past two men who've been pitted as imagined competitors in a race they don't know even know is happening.

Passing them, I feel a mild sense of victory – ah ha! But as Evie and I make our way across the bridge, we end up going pretty slowly, so our fictitious fellow competitors overtake us anyway because we're distracted by the lights around us and the spectacle that's Albert Bridge on a November night. After all, it isn't any night, it's Guy Fawkes night. And it's not any bridge, it's Albert Bridge, a bridge I've walked over at all hours: drunken hours, sober hours, in love and out of love hours. Hours spent calling universities to find out degree scholarship results, and on my way to yoga hours, pushing stolen supermarket trollies with friends hours, and alone hours. And now, with daughter, we stop at the crest of the arch on the pavement, where I park the pram and crouch down to point at the river through the portals on the bridge. Evie's straining against her pram straps to get closer, to see more, so I lift her out of the pram into my arms and we stand here looking at the river and the moon just one day away from being full and at London looking her most extraordinary.

Fireworks start booming in the air around us. "Bubba! Bubba! Can you see the fireworks through the trees?" I ask, pointing at a tree behind where an effervescent display of wizardry illuminates the sky around us.
"Pink ones! Red ones! Green ones!" we cry, Evie's face a pure depiction of awe. After a little while the fireworks stop and a little voice whispers "More..."

As if in agreement, the sky above the east of London starts zittering with fireworks. They're soon joined by others in the north, whilst the moon looms high in the southeast, and aeroplanes and helicopters soar above us, as the stars twinkle and Evie watches her first fireworks. My heart's singing because wow, we almost missed this, so I send out a thank you thank you to the mysterious delights misplaced keys can bring to one's life.

"Fireworks everywhere!" Evie calls out. To others the simple sentences our children say may sound trite or irrelevant; to us, there's little else that can pierce our hearts so tenderly.
"Fireworks everywhere! Yes!" The bare necessities of life will come to you...

Whilst I point out more, a couple walks past us, turning around to watch them too. As strangers stroll by, I look in their eyes and we smile at each other; the sweetness of the moment giving me confidence, and that's such a sweet, lovely thing: to share a moment of appreciation with a stranger, to be standing on this heart-toucher of a bridge, with my daughter in my arms in the midst of all this movement and light and splendour. The hell and confusion of all that's been before slipping away into the cold grey waters of the Thames as dogs pass us, heading home after walking their humans in the park.

This is a moment I'll remember for a while, I think.

When the fireworks stop, we continue on over the bridge. Hearing more, we swivel around to watch as some more crackle and boom behind us. The view's even better here, because what was hidden before when we stood on the arch of the bridge is now clear and brilliant and bright.

I bend down to see Evie, her little open face imprinted on my heart, as we stand underneath the moon beside this river that swells and sinks so eternally. A night, or a gift that years later will seem as ephemeral as a whisper that I heard in the beat of my heart, but blessed with a day and a name:

Remember, remember, the 5th of November. Of that, I hope to be sure.

food glorious food

There're few joys more satisfying than watching Evie plonk a knob of butter on a door stopper of a chip, and then feast on them both.

Ketchup is so last yesterday.

parenting: a Zen adventure

One Sunday, Evie returns from a weekend with her father around 5 p.m. When she arrives, she's just woken from a nap, so that bedtime at 7 p.m. isn't looking particularly realistic. So instead of heading upstairs for our usual routine, after supper we head outside. Out here, the darkness swirls around us as if the world is closing in on itself, and yet, so much broader, expansive, wild and unimaginable than I typically interpret it to be. Mother Nature is whispering to us, in all her roaring resilience, and for once, we respond.

We walk over to the tree house, Evie carrying Basil, the cuddly stuffed dog we've just discovered hiding in an upstairs cupboard. It's a reunion, as the last time I saw him, I was seven years old. Seeing Evie with Basil, I wonder if this'll be the toy she becomes attached to. Right now in this moment, up in the tree house, he matters gloriously. And so he accompanies us as we head towards the tree house, me carrying a bowl of food, remnants of a supper mostly untouched.

When we arrive at the tree, it's blooming with light. Someone in the house has turned the floodlights on so that we can make our way up the steps easily. First Evie scrabbles up the steps, then I go, Basil tucked in the nook of my arm. Then back down to carry Bongo, who's desperately unsure about the whole procedure. He clings to me as we climb the tree, dropping awkwardly like a plump rock when we reach the ledge at the top. We go into the tree house and sit at the little table there. There're lights on, and I think of Mum; I hadn't known that the tree house could be lit up at night and the discovery that it can makes me appreciate my mother anew. Then Supper, Part II commences; an event my daughter ignores completely. As a result, Bongo is rewarded for his part in the adventure with five beef croquettes and a handful of steamed carrots.

Afterwards, a game commences. Basil's escorted outside whilst Evie retreats back into the tree house and closes the door and then *knock knock! Someone's at the door! Oh look, it's Basil! Come in!* And so on and so on.

Children are the most amazingly merciless Zen masters. The same dressing up sequence needs to be repeated ad infinitum. The same scooting sequence, up and down, down and up: *Elsa! Come back! It's me, your sister who didn't mean to make you freeze summer!* And each time: "beginner's mind" invited. As if although this is the hundredth, or perhaps ten thousandth time you've played this game, or heard this song, the joy is fresh each time, because somewhere in all the repetition, it's okay. As if the repetition is a conduit to something else; a portal that leads you to a tender-hearted experience of equanimous joy.

Then right there in the middle of the game, the lights go out. It's 6.30 p.m. and Evie, Bongo, Basil and I are up a tree in the dark. It feels wonderful; wonderful to be outside, and specifically, enriching and enlivening to be outside in the dark. And because we aren't marooned in the depths of the woods with bears, snakes and wolves prowling nearby, we're okay.

Nonetheless, hanging out in the pitch dark black has a limited appeal to my diminished imagination, hence the evacuation begins. First the pink plastic bowl's thrown overboard, followed by Basil, then down go Bongo and I, with him hoisted over my shoulder, and all the while me encouraging Evie to "Stay back, bubba!" behind the closed fence "because it's safer." But she's so interested by the whole spectacle of mum and dog going down the ladder in the dark that she stands there at the precipice of the entrance to the tree house, peering over the ladder. I come back up for her quickly, but before I can reach the top rung of the ladder, she's launched herself into my arms. We make our way to the swings, the silhouettes of which we can just make out in the dark night's bloom. Basil's placed in one of them; Evie's the mother, swinging her baby. She's gentle and tender with him.

The games that our children play, they tug at our hearts. They also tell us so much. Fears that're unable to be expressed come out during play, along with their worries, dislikes, sadnesses, jealousies - all of it, the whole messy *schebang* of being a human - translated in play. These little people emerge into the world with all their purity and goodness but slowly, through the wear and tear of growing up, emerge as adults, masks intact, hearts protected, play all but forgotten. And because we're so focused on keeping our own masks intact and hearts protected, we fail to pause to see that in times when we're telling ourselves that we're trying our hardest, the people we hurt, confuse and bewilder are not so much ourselves but these people we love and cherish most tenderly: our children.

impermanence

After the swing session, Evie, Bongo and I walk to the paddock to visit our equine friends: two donkeys, one Shetland pony and one falabella, or miniature horse. Mikey, the larger of the donkeys is the chief; Toggles, a wee falabella, is the one that packs the least influence but he's also the one Evie most adores. Then there's Smokey Joe, donkey number two, and Zotlie, the second equine, a portly but handsome Shetland. Generally, they're an absurdly rude quartet: a merry band of broad bottoms and irresistibly gruff demeanours. Zoltie, who at first you think is a foul-tempered bandit, softens as soon as he realises that you've the potential to be a chief too. He pushes his weight around, but like all chiefs who've become chiefs as a result of turbulence and chaos, once he knows that there's no need to do that, he relaxes, relents, and all this innocent sweetness tumbles out of him. A sweetness that you in turn can't help but be softened by.

As we near their fields, I can just about make out their faces. Hearing us approach, they come to the gate, whinnying and *ee-awh-ing*. They're curious, hopeful too, mistaking our presence for a second supper. But in place of carrots, we've brought hugs. We head over to their stable where Evie builds a sand castle in their shavings whilst I sit on the ledge and rub Zotlie's withers. He curls his top lip in delight. "He's laughing!" says Evie, as Zotlie carries on with his big top lip rolled back, exposing his grimy yellow teeth, the unbrought carrots forgotten.

We stay for a little longer, but as bed's now beckoning, I tug my daughter away, even though I'm sure she'd prefer to curl up on the stable floor to sleep with her "friends." We return to the house, me making good on a deal that Evie and I cut earlier: if she walked to the field, I'd carry her back.

And because these times aren't going to last forever, I do what I mostly always do: open my arms out wide and scoop her up.

P.S. Twenty or so minutes later, Evie's in her bed falling asleep. And Basil lies discarded on the bedroom floor.

⬜

Bongo

Bongo came into my life via an email, or to be more accurate: a life spent wishing for a badly-behaved mongrel to appear. Luckily though, the intelligence behind this life that we lead has a more humorous imagination than I, and so when it came to this longing being realised, I met a hound with more spirit, gumption and kindness than my musty old mind could have ever conjured up. And although old age has seen an improvement in his behaviour, take Bongo to the woods and that rebel spirit is released once more. Although he's also a mutt who knows how to chill too. Seriously so.

"That dog is meditating," Gregor, a friend of Mum's and my stepfather Burkhard's once commented, as we all turned to look at Bongo perched on the steps in their garden, staring into the black night sky underneath a full white moon. As it is, Bongo and I have spent more nights living away from each other than with each other, since he has spent the greater part of his life at my mother and stepfather's house.

When I do see him, it's increasingly with death on my mind. He's about ten years old now and has had various health problems over the last couple of years. One day, I tell myself, trying to prepare myself for the inevitable, Bongo won't be around.

If we do get the chance to walk together, whilst in the woods when we walk and when he wanders off into the trees, sniffing, searching, I'll use the chance to crouch and sit and watch, and then he returns to where I am, and I'll reach out and stroke him.

"Thank you, Bongo, thank you," I say. And we'll stay a little while longer.

When I drive away, with Bongo standing by the front door, watching my car pull away, guilt percolates: in the same way that a parent who, after dropping their homesick child at boarding school, drives away, reassuring themselves that it's the best place for them, ignoring the flutter around their solar plexus that's trying to tell them otherwise. It's only for a little while, they tell themselves, or at least until they can address the dramas playing out in their own lives. This is a lie, of course; children just want to be near their parents, and our dogs are no different.

⬚

affinity

When I was pregnant with Evie, I would take the dogs for a walk in the woods at the bottom of the field near *Halnaker*. I'd go as often as I could and when we did, mostly we'd stray off track. Because off track is where life, that pulsating, extraordinarily interesting life that's probably more readily available than we allow ourselves to believe is to be found.

Here, twigs are to be snapped underfoot, deer to be chased, smells to be sniffed, and tree stumps to be sat on. Here are badger holes to get stuck in, fallen trees to clamber over. And on those days when the sun shines and streams through the tightly cloistered network of trees, dappled light to enjoy. There are also discoveries to be made, such as the antlers I once found, alone, separated from the sum of their parts.

When I saw them, I picked them up, placing the antlers on the top of my head as if they had sprouted from my skull. And in that moment, my sense of the woods was changed. No longer was I a separate part of the woods meandering through, I was a part of it, and as a result my sense of the woods was expanded. I removed the antlers from my head to discover a tangible shift in my perception: *just human.*

I played with bringing them back again and again, exploring this sense akin to an ability wherein suddenly the movement of the forest was something of which I was keenly aware. The woods and I were no longer separate from each other; instead, the world around me was an extension of myself. When a deer senses someone close, it flinches because that intruder is intruding on a part of themselves.

As I sat there playing with the fallen antlers, every cell of my body rippled in response to finally being needed. These antlers were inviting me into a richer experience of another who normally passes me by. So I sat there a while, bringing the antlers to touch on the top of my head, and then bringing them away again, when the experience would drop away; human, woefully human. It was as if my physical form was nothing more than an apparition – that in the subtlety of senses, I could notice the smallest tremor of a leaf. With the antlers on, I was able to perceive much subtler things; without them, my sense, or at least my judgement of what was possible to perceive as a human, returned, and there I was a human walking in the woods, separate, a part unique to her sum.

Months later whilst walking nearby again, I looked for those antlers that I placed back down onto the earth. Were they still there? In a way, yes of course they were. Dissolved and returned to the soil beneath. What was once solid, now scattered and immersed in a way you and I are not yet, but of course one day will be.

Whichever way we go.

⬚

resistance

It's nudging closer to ninety minutes after Evie was meant to be asleep, and here I am sitting, wishing and praying for her to fall asleep. The minutes are ticking by, and still she lies there, wide awake. I grow fed up of trying to be soft and still, all I want is for her to fall asleep so that I can leave the room. I'm irritated and angry, internally lambasting all the elements in our lives that're beyond my control. My breathing's short, my asthma's triggered, and there's a soft wheeze in the room coming from my mouth.

I look across at Evie, sitting there in her cot, looking at me. And I see her, not yet three, with all these changes in her life. In the space of less than a year, her father and mother no longer live in the same house; to see one she must say goodbye to the other. As well as this, she's moved out of the home she was born in and is learning to adapt to a home that is not ours, simply a stop gap until I've made a plan. We start parenthood light with ideals, and then all too quickly we find ourselves heavy with the shards of our fragmented dreams that've smashed against the rocks like Icarus on his way down.

Apparently wise people talk about the importance of cultivating compassion for ourselves. The tougher of us, mid-flagellation, will snort in derision at such notions, and then whip ourselves some more over our failure to create for our children a childhood free from suffering. They don't deserve to suffer, we tell ourselves, but of course it is in suffering that perhaps our appreciation of magic increases exponentially.

Which is to say that finally I can see a need for something more beyond this rigid formulaic way of relating to my child. So that it's only when I acknowledge all that has happened to my daughter in such a short space of time that I get to see Evie, sitting there in her cot, and instead of imposing on her my ideas, plans and anxieties, I get that her inability to fall asleep is because she needs something else to happen first.

I move closer to her, and squeeze my hand through the railings of her cot, which she takes with one of hers. She lies down instantly, turning her head to look at me, and then raises her head and we nuzzle noses through the cot bars. My heart opens, my chest expands, and my wheezing stops right there. No inhaler needed.

Evie gives me this sweet smile as if to say *there, Mama, this is all I wanted, is it so bad after all?* Tears fall down my face, *not bad, darling, just hard*. Hard to stop and be and sit, and feel. And almost impossible to surrender to something, or rather someone who isn't even asking for surrender, only to be met and to be seen.

I look at Evie's soft, tired face, the wired energy's gone; something's released in her, relieved perhaps that she didn't have to climb out of her cot another time to come and say hey Mama, I need something a bit more than just "Go. To. Sleep." And then someone turns the light off in the stairway, so that though I can't see my daughter's eyes, I can see the soft haze of her as she sinks into sleep.

There are these moments that happen where a communication so deep takes place, we're left surprised by the very fact that words have been absent. Given the torrential speed that I live my life, where my adrenals all too easily tip into a ready for battle state that I take as confirmation that I don't need my sleep, because hey, look at me, I don't *even yawn anymore*, it can be hard to pause, soften and see.

70

Perhaps because it's too painful. There being a melancholy that infuses the unspoken parts of parenthood marooned in those places that appear between that lofty ridge on which we place these impossible ideals of the parent we want to be, and reality's uncompromising headquarters down here on Ground Zero, where we face the reality of the parent that we actually are.

Generally, I think of these two places as separate: one is impossible to reach and one's a depressing reality, but recently, I have been able to see this bridge and yes, it's faded from lack of use, so that tufts of wild grasses and the gnarled tendinous roots of trees are pushing through the cracks that grow ever wider along the cobbled path but nonetheless this bridge is there. This bridge that takes us from what is striven for and what is; not yet crumbled, just waiting to be used.

⍰

pigeon Deva

Evie and I have come to Battersea Park to feed the pigeons. Our pockets are stuffed with mouldy bread that turns out to be pretty edible. At least for Evie.

"There's one!" I cry, spying a pigeon a few metres away. Forgetting all pigeon feeding etiquette, we run towards it. The pigeon, unsurprisingly, flies away. We pause. We need to change our tactics. Dropping to our knees, we press our palms together and pray.
"Pigeon deva! Pigeon deva!" we call out, "Please send us some pigeons!" Nothing. I concentrate harder, peering over at Evie, whose eyes are scrunched tight in concentration.

I get more specific.

"Please Pigeon deva. Please would you send your pigeons to the little clearing by the river over here in Battersea Park?" And then we head over to the water's edge and wait. After a few seconds, we spy not a pigeon but a seagull flying through the air.
"Look! Look!" cries Evie.

We throw a bit of bread into the air, watching as the seagull swoops down to catch it. Then we throw some more. Word travels fast in the park because a moment later thirty seagulls come soaring straight towards us, and given the aerial gymnastics that these birds are capable of, we don't begrudge the pigeon deva her species diversion too much. Especially considering that more just keep showing up. So that instead of sky, the space above our heads is full of white flapping wings and yellow beaks, and our ears are full with the sound of their squawks and our laughter.

"So close," says Evie in awe, whilst a couple to our right stop to take photos. And then whilst Evie does her version of feeding the five thousand, I take photos. Looking to my right, towards Chelsea Bridge, I see more are on their way.

"Look Evie, look Evie!" I cry, in the manner of the woman who's just discovered a thousand Pegasus' leaping through the air! And whilst these birds may not be flying horses, it's the numbers that are currently flying towards us that are so exciting. And yes, the sky may not be black, but it's definitely altered as more and more arrive. Eventually we are surrounded by around fifty or sixty crows.

Such is the sense of you called, we answered, that I can't stop laughing. Evie's dancing around, arms out wide open, throwing whatever bread remains, face beaming with a smile. The crows aren't particularly interested in the bread; instead, they're lining up along the railing that protects passersby from falling into the Thames. And here I am, not so much picking up the shards after the crash of Icarus but marvelling at how our high points teeter and reshape themselves once parenthood becomes our new normal. Because here I am and I want to say having one of the most amazing moments of my life, but of course that's a ridiculous thing to say, but really, I am, surrounded by crows, my daughter and the river Thames.

I turn to the crows and say *thank you*, and Evie thanks them and the bread's beginning to run out, and so we are separating it into the smallest pieces we can. The crows are hopping around on the ground around us, watching us, as if waiting for more communication. I, too dumb and stunted in my imagination, have no idea what to say or how to say it, but am filled with this reverence that if we communicate we will be answered.

And now London is blooming with Christmas trees and lights and twinkles. "Why, Mama?" asks Evie, so that again I get to think about this man Jesus, and why he died and what he hoped to give us all.

Little questions + little moments = big things inside.

wing strengthening

Evie's starting nursery. It's a fifteen-minute walk through the park. Or should I say, *cough cough*, a three minute, um, drive away. For her first morning, Evie's nanny Carla takes her. On the second morning it's my turn. About half an hour later, the head teacher walks over and suggests that I "Come back in an hour."

"Evie seems relaxed and happy," she says. "She's settling in quickly. It'll be good for you to head off for a bit." But I'm hesitant. The original understanding was that I'd stay around all morning. The change is unexpected for us both.

As I go to leave, Evie becomes upset. Buying time, I take her down to the loo where we wash our hands, really slowly. When we return, neither of us is any more convinced by the suggestion of me leaving, so we fling ourselves guerrilla-style into the doll's house which stands by the door. Once inside, I grab a book and start to read. The head teacher's onto us though and, popping her head through the curtains, gently encourages me to leave.

I walk away with Evie screaming. I feel weak; I've let my daughter down. Why didn't I stand up and refuse to leave? It's only Evie's second morning; this is happening too soon. I immediately call her father: "Am I doing the right thing?"

"Give her the full hour," he says. The fact that he's relaxed helps, marginally. "The nursery will call if she doesn't settle," he adds. "Go and walk," he says.
"I haven't brought my coat," I reply. "I didn't think I'd need it."
"Go and have a coffee, take the hour."

I last forty-five minutes.

[?]

a lesson (part i)

When I return, the head teacher's waiting for me at the top of the stairs. I say something about it being important that I'm able to keep my word with my daughter, that the change was unexpected, and so I hadn't been able to tell Evie about it.

"I'm sorry," she says, "I didn't know that." And then she turns around and points through the door at Evie, who's painting at an easel. I walk into the room and over to her, crouching down. "What are you painting?" I ask. "Mama!" she exclaims, turning to me. "Your belly, boobies and body!" I'm very big and very brown...

When we get home, I apologise to Evie about things being different from how we'd planned them.

"I was screaming, Mama," she says, her face scrunching to emphasise her point, which only serves to make me think I'm a terrible mother for leaving, and should have insisted on staying the whole time.

Later that evening, I read a passage in a book that a friend has just given me for my birthday. It's by an Indian teacher, Radhanath Swami. I open it and read a story about a boy who finds a caterpillar struggling to release itself from its cocoon. The boy hates to see the butterfly suffer, and so runs inside to get a pair of scissors so he can cut the caterpillar free. Or at least that's what he thinks he's doing. What he's really done by cutting the caterpillar loose is to stop it from developing the strength it needs to become a butterfly. Because its wings didn't get the chance to strengthen in the struggle to free itself, when it attempts to fly after being cut 'free,' its wings lack the strength. Its destiny is diverted, its fate sealed. Struggle is crucial to freedom. In other words, the butterfly's fate is to remain earthbound rather than be heaven-infused. Plodding, not soaring.

As a mother, it's a continual process to realise that not only is it not possible to remove all pain from my child's life, it's not even necessarily that responsible to try and do so. And because we get confused discerning the difference between what's our pain and what's our child's, a great part of our parenting efforts can focus on just that: making our children as gloriously happy as can be.

So that yes, she was distressed when I left, but whether that was because she was picking up on my own feelings or expressing her own is something that I have to accept as part of the mystery of being a parent. We can never fully know what is really going on inside our children, only take in the information that we see, intuit as best we can and, wherever possible, learn to discern what is ours and what is theirs, so that when they do need us, we are able to truly support them. Which normally means not so much removing suffering from their path, but empowering them to find their own way through.

⬚

part ii (if only for a moment)

The next morning, something in me has settled. I feel confident in my daughter's ability to be alright, I trust the nursery, but most of all I feel confident in where I am as a parent: oh, such rare real estate! When I drop off Evie, before I can even kiss her goodbye, she's walking up the stairs, her teacher reaching out to hold her hand, so that they finish the stairs together.

The following day too, as we drive in, Evie calls out "Nursery!" As she strides up the stairs, she turns and blows me a kiss as she walks through the doors to see the other kids, ready to start her morning. This was her adventure, one we'd all been talking about for months. At two and a half years old, she's ready.

When I come to collect Evie later that morning, they're all out in the garden. I walk over to see one of the teachers calling out each kids name so that they'll come and take their place on one of those plastic ropes that nurseries use to keep kids together when they need to walk somewhere. Evie's at the front, waiting for her name to be called.

"Come on, everybody," she calls out, copying the teacher, her little chest broad with the joy of inclusion. She seems relaxed and happy, and as I stand there watching, something alights in my heart, flutters its wings, and finally takes flight. Because maybe, just maybe, we're going to find our way.

Travels With Love

longing, meeting, reality...

All the while he loved her and wanted her, knowing, or at least hoping with the deepest of longings, that one day, inevitably, they'd come together.

And all the while she loved him, and wanted him. Fantasized and dreamt about him, and spoke about him, and saw herself with him. Knowing, or at least hoping with the deepest of longings that one day, inevitably, they'd come together.

When it did happen, it was more natural and connected than either had dreamed.

And then the tide came in, the breakwaters kicked up a fuss, and everything that had been imagined, fantasized and dreamt about, thundered like a tsunami to the shore.

deserted in Devon

I've read somewhere that you're not meant to start a new relationship for two years after separating from the parent of your child. I've only waited two months. As a result, precautions need to be taken.

"Are you sure you're coming back?" Tom asks me hesitantly, standing in a car park in the middle of the moor.
"*Of course* I am," I reply. "We'll be ten minutes!" I call back, looking in the rear-view mirror at Tom watching us driving away, the grey December landscape stretching out desolately behind him.

I need to find somewhere with reception to call Ben, so that he can say hello to Evie. The only thing is that he thinks I've come to Devon alone, and although we're no longer together, I'm not feeling entirely confident about the etiquette of nudging closer to a new relationship so soon after ending a relationship with someone with whom you have a child. As a result, I've asked Tom if I can drop him off for a walk, and then Evie can chat with her father without feeling like she's hiding anything, and Tom can enjoy a moment alone, outside, on this land he so loves.

Twenty minutes later, the phone call has happened; the only thing is, I can't remember how to get back to the car park where I left Tom.

Shit.

After driving around for another twenty minutes, I finally find him, standing as if frozen to the exact spot we'd left him, a howling wind blowing his hair, his gaze low. When he does look up at me, his blue eyes have frozen into that glacial look that tells me more than words could ever say.

The anchor's been pulled in and the ship is gently drifting away.

gratitude

A couple of weeks after that trip, Tom heads to Mozambique to visit a project he supports. Halfway through supper on the first night there, he realises that despite being given direct advice to do so, he's forgotten to shut his bedroom door. On returning, he gives the room a quick check, concluding that it's safe. Around 3 a.m. however, he wakes, sensing something in the room.

Turning on his phone for the light, he peers around the room and sees a green snake coiled atop the chest of drawers on the other side of the room. He sits up and considers his options: edge out of the room and go out into the night, risking potential meeting of other snakes, or stay, and attempt to befriend the snake. He decides to do the latter and makes a prayer to the Deva of the snake along the lines of: You stay there and I'll stay here, and p.s. please let's not harm each other. Feeling relaxed, he settles back down under his duvet, falls into a deep sleep and wakes at 8 a.m. the following morning.

Over breakfast, he mentions to the others that he'd found a snake in his room. After eating, they all troop off back to his room and discover her in one of the drawers. Two brawny men yelp, as they leap back. "Dude, that's no ordinary snake!"

Tom's 'friend' turned out to be a green mamba; a temperamental creature whose bite is fatal.

That night, on heading out to supper, Tom closes his door. Although he'd initially insisted that we take things slowly, when he returns to London a week later and we meet, he makes love to me for the very first time. So, dear green mamba, fatal though your bite may be, it would appear that within you moonlights less the spirit of Hades and more Aphrodite. Without you, who knows how long it might've taken.

⏾

awkward

Tom and I actually waited for over seven years before we had our first kiss, after having met via an introduction from one of my mother's oldest friends, Adrian Rolt.

"I think I've found the woman for you," Adrian told Tom, an unmarried bachelor in his early forties who was forever being set up by his friends. "She's a little bit younger than you, and just as difficult."

My mother, a woman whose match-making abilities make Mrs. Bennet's look timid, invited them for lunch.

"You two sit next to each other," she said, and so Mr. Tom Bible and I did. And although I liked this man, and found him interesting, my heart was otherwise preoccupied with the man who would become Evie's father. Even so, I liked Tom. We had many interests in common – dream analysis being one of them – and during the lunch, he mentioned a Jungian analyst whom he saw for sessions in London.

"Please can I have his details?" I asked. An avid dreamer, I'd been looking for someone to work with since at least the age of three. Afterwards, Tom and I stayed in touch. And somewhere through the years, friendship turned to a caring for one another which, in turn, changed into something else. Which is to say that falling in love with Tom happened slowly. When it did, it was as confusing to me that it was happening as it was emotionally messy: I grew up believing in *The One*, and hadn't contemplated the potential of *The Two*.

⏾

unexpected changes

Skip forward six years and everything was very different. Ben and I were no longer together. And Tom and I, who'd developed a close friendship, hadn't seen one another for a year, since he'd taken himself back to school and moved to Devon to attend Schumacher College near Totnes.

To *study*, said he.

For *distance,* said my mother. Then with a bit of encouragement from one of my mother's friends, I call him.

"You need some light-hearted fun, Laura. Call him." And so, I do (although I'm not sure if light-hearted fun is what followed, for either of us). When we speak, nothing awkward is mentioned. But there's a dissonance in the conversation, the type of which I can only detect on account of how close we've previously been. Whereas before there was a fluidity and openness to our conversation, now there's a subtle friction, mingling with the excitement of reconnecting.

"I'm flying out to India in a couple of days," he says.
 "When are you back?" I ask.
"Three weeks," he replies.

My stomach sinks. We agree to meet when he returns, and say goodbye. After the call, I remain sitting on the grass at the base of the tree, frustrated with a vague sense that everything that needed to be said had been avoided. It was also a moment preceding a series of events that was to see my life change in ways that I'm still making sense of.

[?]

or almost

And then here I am, sitting on a bar stool in a pub in Islington, eating crisps. He's late. About twenty minutes. I'm trying to look relaxed, but my heart's pumping as if I'm that deer and this moment is the headlights shining on me, and *Oh Christ, floor why won't you open?*

Tom arrives all relaxed and jovial. Which only accentuates my silence. We don't have time for a drink and so walk to the church, inside which is the North London Steiner School, where I take Evie for weekly toddler mornings that start with candlelight and porridge, and a lullaby-singing German lady, and which has organised a concert to raise money for the school.

The church is lit with hundreds of candles. And as we sit on our chairs listening to music played live by the musician Nitin Sawhney and watch performances that include Lenny Henry, all I can think of is that my thigh is touching Tom's thigh and that maybe if we ever get married, this is where we would have the wedding.

Afterwards, we go through to this room which is all hallowed lights and way too surreal and romantic to be a school, and drink red wine and eat canapés, and sit and talk and oh god it's happening. After wondering about it for so long, there's finally nothing to deny, because I do. I love him. But whilst I'm at least a decade ahead planning our nuptials, Mr. Tom Bible is somewhat lagging behind.

On the car on the way back, as we curve around the roundabout near the Houses of Parliament, he starts talking about relationships.

"I sense that this is the year I'm going to meet someone," he says, with added emphasis on someone. An arrow's been pulled back, a target hit: my heart.

When we return to Battersea, I wish him *good night,* shutting the door a little more vigorously than necessary.

Then I turn and walk away.
⬚

movement

The next time we see one another is at a dinner for *Resurgence Magazine.* Tom and I sit next to each other and spend the evening talking intently to the people on our other side. In the car on the way home, my mother, who had also been at the dinner, invites Tom for lunch at *Halnaker* the following weekend, whilst I sit in the back with my cheeks burning like a teenager's. *Muuuum, if you ask him for lunch, he'll know I like him.*

Which ends up being a good thing. At least it creates a little more motion between us. Because he comes alone for lunch, which later he tells me made him think *maybe there's something here.* And he and Evie meet and even though they've met before, it's a meeting I'm kind of watching and simultaneously crossing my fingers that they like each other because you don't want to interfere too much, but here are these people whose orbits in this world I am forever spinning around, meeting each other. After going to the loo, I return to the kitchen to find Evie climbing up Tom's legs; their nook has been found. I exhale, and send up a thanks to the skies.

When I walk out to Tom's car to say goodbye, he invites me to dinner at his place the following week. I say *yeah, sure that would be nice* and then we say goodbye and I walk back into the house, unable to take the smile off my face.

⊡

progressing

I'm here, in Tom's man-cave in Battersea. We've just finished dinner and opening our hearts to each other, as we sit across from one another at his kitchen table.

Standing up, he walks towards me. "I would really love to kiss you," he says, as our conversation takes a pause. Suddenly I'm no longer confident woman sharing truths from her past, I'm the incredibly shy teenager I used to be, running to the sofa, where I perch on the edge like a woman sitting side saddle, about to bolt for home. Unperturbed, Tom walks over and sits down beside me, then leans forwards to kiss me. I lean back, kite-surfing the arm of his sofa. He looks at me quizzically. I look at him.

Oh Christ, Oh Christ, Oh Christ...

The more I try and relax, the more my muscles seize into a response that a chastity belt would give a hearty round of applause to. The atmosphere's becoming increasingly awkward, so that there's nothing for it except for the both of us to bring our lips closer and just go for it. Our first kiss, rollercoaster style. And so the kissing starts and it's a kiss that's been building for a fair few years, and it's finally happening and it's... oh Christ, I can't believe it, *it's terrible.*

And it just gets worse.

To make it even more painful, it becomes humiliatingly obvious that I'm not the only one struggling with the kiss. My pride is appalled: it's one thing not to be into a kiss yourself, quite another for the person you're kissing to be as disengaged as a monk who's been forced into a moment he'd rather not be in at all. But despite my best attempts, the effect is *nil.* Marilyn Monroe's Sugar may have finally caused a flame to flicker for Jack Lemmon's Junior, but it seems my kissing just ain't doing nothing for Mr. Bible. So we move to the floor to see if relocation enhances our flailing eroticism. I undo some shirt buttons (his, not mine), and make all the proper noises, but *niente.* And so after a few minutes of nothing, we give up.

I say good night, the both of us too humiliated to make eye contact, and then make the *oh-christ-this-is-very-close* walk back to my mother's, just a ten-minute walk away.

◌

second chance

A week or so later, we appear together on another date: a charity auction. Afterwards, we head across the square to a nearby restaurant for some food. We're joined by a friend and her new girlfriend.

Tom and I, moderately traumatised from the failure of our kiss, sit untouching on our side, whilst across the table sit my friend and her lover, all touches and kisses and, damn them, laughter. The eyes of my friend and her lover's sparkle at each other, while Tom's and mine look desperately at the menu. We try to touch each other nonchalantly, but it comes out all wrong, like two strangers picking dust off each other.

Afterwards, Tom drives me home and as I shut the door of the car, I walk away unable to muster up any energy to reassure the both of us that hey, maybe, just maybe we'll find our chemistry soon, too bedraggled by a thought worming its way into my mental space and niggling at my mind that *maybe dear, just maybe, the best years are behind you...*

thank god for tomorrow

So here I am, reclaiming whatever carefreeness I can: in the tattoo parlour in Oxford Circus's Top Shop. Because if it is true that my most carefree days are behind me, then so help me God, I'm going out with a bang. Or at least a little bling.

After paying the man with beefy, ink drenched biceps, I follow him into a small room. "Have you got a stud?" he asks.
"Um, no."
"Okay, right, these are the ones we have left." I peer into a box to see a line of nose studs the size of conkers.
"People normally bring their own," he adds, unhelpfully. "How long do I need to wear these until I can change them?" I ask. "Six weeks." I contemplate six weeks of conker wearing, potentially a rather long timeframe to be wearing such a large piece of gold in the nook of my nostril, but such is my state of asphyxia around the demise of my carefree days and ability to melt like caramel with the object of my romantic affections that I convince myself that six weeks is not long at all...
"Okay great, I'll go with this one, please," I say, pointing to the humdinger of them all, sitting corpulently in the centre of the box. Then I walk over and sit on the bed whilst the gentleman cleans my nose.
"Is this going to hurt?"
"Yes," he responds, bringing the machine close to my left nostril, through which the stud shoots, and there it is; my nose has been pierced with a conker.

I pay and then head out to my bike, take a photo of conker and me, and send it to friends. It's cold and I'm wearing a huge big coat and my nose is swollen and red. I look like Rudolf the Red-nosed Reindeer.

Except I'm a human, and I was trying to look sexy.

unexpected

A couple of days later, Evie's with her father for the weekend and I'm at home with the conker and my enlarged red nose, and I call Tom to ask if he wants to go see a film.

"Christ," he says as he walks in.
"I got my nose pierced!" I say jubilantly.
"I can see that," he replies, and then I get my coat, and we walk over Albert Bridge to the cinema to see a film that ends up being terrible. Which, along with the fact that the conker's ugly, my nose is sore and my carefree days are behind me, cause my head to collapse onto to Tom's shoulder, where it stays for the remainder of the film.

When we get back to my mother's, we find ourselves on the sofa in the sitting room. We lie down, facing each other and this time, instead of dissipating our chemistry, the build-up gently stirs our connection as we lie nostrils to nostrils, breath melting into breath, bodies pressed close, so that when we finally start kissing, we don't stop for two hours. When finally we do stop, I bring my hand to my nose: the conker's been misplaced. In the days that follow, it's not replaced.

a brief honeymoon

For our first (official), holiday together, Tom's brought Evie and me to Cyprus. We arrive and it's raining; we leave, and it's raining.

"We've never seen weather like this," we're told by the staff. On day two, it's so cold that I even catch a cold. One evening after Evie has fallen asleep, I go for a walk by the sea. Tom and I are arguing (our honeymoon phase seems to have passed quicker than a teenager's mood) and it's only out here by the sea that I can feel a space and tranquillity that Tom and I seem to suddenly be struggling to create when we're together.

nature: a good friend

I spent the greater part of my childhood at my grandmother Dean's home, *Delta*, in West Wittering, in the south of England. When young, I'd fall asleep listening to the sound of the waves pummelling the shore twenty metres away from my bedroom window. Each night that I spent there, I'd open the window to listen to the waves, soothed by the sound of them crashing onto the sand not too far away. This window opening became a ritual of sorts, where every step had its place: lights off first, then walk over to the other single bed in the room over which I'd crawl, then kneeling, dip under the heavy curtains, push open the window and listen as the waves roared hello. Then I'd walk over to my bed, which had previously been my grandmother's; the shape of her imprinted on that old mattress as she is imprinted in the belly of my heart.

Later, as a teenager, I'd often head down over the hills of stones to walk by the water's edge. Something inside me would respond instantaneously to the desolate grey landscape, so that when I walked beside the sea, I didn't feel nearly as separate and adrift as I did to the other elements of my life. The plod of my feet matching the rhythm of the movement and the withdrawal of the small waves, their rise and their crash and so on and so forth, for as long as the moon is high. The adults may be struggling to find a way to communicate, but nature never is.

Decades later, I sit alone watching the rise and swell of the ocean here in Cyprus, peering at and into her. I sense a mystery both relax and grow taut, as a volatility trembles in the background in a place I've forgotten was there. Given the depth and diversity our lives can experience, it's extraordinary the incredible inertia we can allow to take hold of our lives, in not only healing the darkness that our lives have known, but in reclaiming the magic.

The Dagara tribe in western Africa have another word for remembering: initiation. Where we fail to remember, our lives bring to us the people, dynamics and situations that force us to return once more, via processes that can feel a whole lot like initiations, to the very places that we've spent such internal effort to deny even exist. So that if we find the courage to face what most torments us, we may once more rediscover what most delights. The challenge of relationships is that amidst all our own confusions and befuddlements there too exist our partners. So that just as we may be too scared to walk on hot coals, so too may they be. Equally just as we fear the gold dust of our dreams, so too do they.

How many of us dare to honour our dreams and those inner tides and currents whose only threat is to drift us closer to events, people and places as meaningful to our hearts as we could wish for? If we only knew of the joy and the sweet bliss that lies there waiting for us once we respond to our most private longings, maybe we'd waste less time arguing and more time just getting on and living. But it's scary, so we walk away from those untameable seas and wild stretches of sand, too frightened to dip our toes in let alone take off our clothes and immerse ourselves wholeheartedly. Which is to say that I sit on the beach for as long as I can until I have to move; I'm alone and my imagination has started to bubble, so I get up and head back to our room.

⏿

the ocean speaks

"You love to throw stones," Evie says to me the following day, placing small pebbles into my palms, urging me to join her and throw more when I grow lazy and stop. And so we hurl stones and pebbles, rocks and silences into the waves; *plop!* being a particularly delicious sound, impossible to grow tired of hearing.

In the afternoon, we pedal a pedalo across the ocean, looking over the edge of the plastic boat into the water; so clear we could see to the bottom. Turquoise patches here, dark patches there; as always it's in the dark where the imagination awakes.

The following day, on a stretch of land unowned that we discovered on a road trip, the three of us are sitting on the sand, munching, Evie and I nude, the hot sand warming my naked skin as my daughter lies across my lap; tranquil, relaxed and content. A peace flares up in my heart; today, I remember.

Later, as I lie here next to Evie, I hear the ocean speaking as I soothe her with *shooooshes* to help her fall asleep. Like a conch shell, oceans find ways to travel and be heard, further than the sea-bed from which they arise, and we humanoids listen, entranced.

I read once that the Inuit's don't let their children laugh for too long in order to protect their children from that ethereal line where the laughing mouth is transformed into crying eyes; sadness and joy, the two inextricably linked. A mistake perhaps, as how often do tears allow us to slip into laughter rediscovered?

⏃

oceanly human

It's our last morning. I'm telling Evie about the ocean: the home from which we come. She turns to look at it, out through the windows, past the two nests the swallows are making in the eaves of the roof opposite us, to the place where trees don't grow, at least not on top of the ocean, only down below. I look at my daughter, a mermaid once, a human now, perhaps remembering that longing that first propelled us to land. Tailless, we flap about for memories of our first home, not realising our folly because it's not so far after all: we carry it in our tears.

When we cry, the salt of the sea is found in the salt of our tears, with just a lick returning us to a home once lived. From this moment on, if ever Evie and I cry, her little finger will find one of my tears, "Look, Mummy, from the ocean."

So that sadness can be allowed, if need be, instead of rejected and feared. It simply being a reminder of where we come and yet, it's not only our tears that remind us of our heritage, but something more mundane. I discover it when we return home, as I sit on my yoga mat in the bedroom at my mother's in Battersea, where Evie and I are currently living, and where I hear the ocean rolling rhythmically and increasingly deeply, in and out of the shore of my breath, as I oscillate between human and ocean, ocean and human and settle somewhere in between.

small request; big ask

Evie has a favourite game: the princess game. She's Cinderella whilst her playmate performs every other role, from the ugly step sisters to the fairy godmother and the Prince. It's a game that'll see her through her second year and a little into her third. It's a game I'm also desperate to do anything other than play.

"Play with me, Mama?" They're only four words to this request. Little, simple words, and yet they make me squirm and look for an exit.

"Just one minute," I reply, buying time. It's not that I don't have the time, of course I do; I just don't have the juice, or the inclination. Unable to shrug off the endless worries and heavy with exhaustion, I've become soaked in seriousness. I remember playfulness, have flashings of it occasionally, but generally struggle to embrace and play with Evie in the way that she wants to play.

Often, I say, "I'm coming!" And then five or ten minutes later, "Just a minute!" Finding two or three other things that desperately need doing, as I make my trajectory over to my daughter to play. Really important things, like a jumper to pick up and fold that then needs taking upstairs and placing in the drawer like I actually care about things like this, a phone picked up, a message sent.

Later as Evie grows older, her little eyes watch me. "You're getting distracted, Mama." "You're right, I am, I'm sorry, I'm here." And I am, ready to play; a haggard mountain troll, with a nervous twitch as my eyes look for the exit. Because I get the lakes, the open skies, the imagination set wild amidst the trees. Or, I guess what's more truthful is to admit how reductive I've become in my way of looking at things. Because whilst I see the value of heading to the sand banks at the nearby polo field and playing at Clawtooth Mountain under the blue sky, I struggle to find the joy in playing the princess game again and again and again. Which of course, for a period of sixteen months, just happens to be the Number One game of my daughter's heart. And whereas when she's older, I'll see the value of taking Evie swimming whenever she wants and playing Ursula and Ariel, or just mucking about in the pool, I'll struggle to sit with her for hours and play the Lego games. I've justified this, thinking myself too intellectual, too grown up to play such humdrum games. I'm taking her outside, I tell myself. I'm taking her outside...

The truth is more uncomfortable: I've just forgotten how to play. And because of this short-sightedness (it's not that something has to have value, but that the blessing and extraordinary privilege is simply in being able to spend time with my daughter in a way that brings joy to her heart), it'll probably only be when she's full grown that I'll look back, and perhaps down, when I realise how close the magic had bubbled after all, and how blind I was - far too often - towards it.

[?]

yearnings longings

It's a warm night and I'm walking over Albert Bridge, watching a couple take a photo of the lights shimmering on the bridge's boughs, an ache squeezing my heart. An ache, or a resonance of a deeply imbedded, so far out of reach, but of course not really at all, essential part of what it is to be human: the magic we crave, which exists no further than the pulse of our beating hearts. So that I don't even need to reach out for it, just simply to see the macro morphing into the micro, and an "Oh!" like the old lady in the film Titanic makes when she drops the necklace off the back of the rescue ship, into the ocean, because there it is, all this time, not so much out there, but nestled safe and protected right here in our beating hearts.

﹖

life's truths: simple & hard to accept

We're finally doing it: Evie, Tom and I are relocating to the country. It's now, or potentially, when?

"This is too soon," says Tom.
"Fine," I say. "We'll go. Come and visit."

Before we go though, there's a dharma talk being given in London by the Buddhist lama Khandro RInpoche. On the second night, unable to sort out any babysitters, I take Evie with me. We leave Battersea at six, after her supper, with her dressed in her pajamas. As I walk, she sits in her buggy, straining against the straps because to be out at night seeing "Albert!" is inviting her inner Labrador to wag her tail so bumptiously that the life force coming from her is enough to propel us over the bridge. And yet such is the velocity of the excitement that before we've reached the other side, Evie's fast asleep. A place that she stays, more or less, even as I shuttle her down the stairs and escalator at South Kensington tube and *schloop* down that long road in Islington to Rigpa, the Buddhist centre where Khandro Rinpoche is giving her talk.

When we arrive, I place Evie in the gift shop and then sit in the hall, where I can both see my sleeping daughter and listen to the talk; most of which goes over my head. Luckily for me though, being of a compassionate nature, Khandro Rinpoche ends by encouraging us to "Keep it simple." And I simultaneously exhale, relieved, but also *oh Christ, this is hard* because a part of me would have preferred it if she'd said pluck a leaf from the eighth branch that hangs on the land where the Mohawk dances, by the hill where the deer prance and the eagle will come to rest. Chew on this leaf twenty-two times and then go to your mother's house and hug her fifty-five times, each hug getting a little stronger in tempo, and do this whilst reciting the first monologue in Shakespeares's *The Tempest.* But because her message is so utterly elegant, I reject it, forget it and carry on with my ways.

Life's truths are often incredibly simple; it's us who seek to complicate them.

⏀

the naughty nunnery

Finding a house in Sussex isn't a simple endeavour: there not being much on the market. Eventually though, we find one. Albeit with an unfortunate name.

"Why's it called *The Locks?*" I ask one of the gentleman in the wine shop where I find myself drinking aquavit at 9.30 a.m. just before I go and see the property for the first time.

"It used to be a prison," he replies. Oh Christ, "a rose is a rose is a rose" and *a name is a name is a name.* I walk out of the shop, tipsy and glum. When I arrive at the house, the managing agent lets me in and I ask her about it.

"Yes, yes," she says, "it was a prison, for naughty nuns."

When I hear this, something lights up.

For a brief interlude in my life I wondered about becoming a nun. The devotion and focus appealed. I was disenchanted with life as a yoga teacher in London. I yearned for something that for me was encapsulated in the life of a nun. Or at least my idea of life as a nun. That trip to Cambodia in 2009 warmed this wish, but the one to India in 2010 blew it out; Himalayan caves are pretty foreboding temples after all. Nonetheless, whilst I lack the gumption to carry out that part of me for whom devotion speaks so true, at least maybe here at *The Naughty Nunnery* I can honour my inner nun. Maybe here, this funny cottage which used to be a prison for naughty nuns is where I can invite my friends and we can laugh together and cry together and touch one another's tears, and go outside to dance under the light of the moon.

Maybe, I tell myself as I nod vigorously at Samantha the agent when she asks if I like the house, it's all going to be okay.

⏾

the gift of loneliness

Don't you get lonely? Friends ask and still do in that unasked place where all the questions you're not sure about asking hover and make themselves felt.

Yes and no.

Yes, in that, oh women friends, oh women friends where art thou? But also no, because when I go into the woods, or open a window, and the bird song floods in, I do experience something in my body and bones, but it's not loneliness.

At least, not that loneliness that inverts and silences you so that you drift by looking vacantly out on a world unlived. Or that loneliness that leaves you wanting and longing and entering rooms feeling utterly separate from everyone else in it, as you hover above yourself, watching, hawk-like, in case you do something or say something wrong. I know that loneliness, but this isn't what I experience when I'm out in the woods.

Loneliness isn't an aspect of country living; it's become a characteristic of modern life and, in some extreme cases, its punishment. But loneliness is also a quality of our humanity that if we spend the time getting to know we may come to a richer understanding of what it is that brings us joy. Because if I understand my loneliness as a sign that points out to me the themes that most resonate to me and from which my life has disconnected, then maybe I'll be more open to acknowledging my loneliness instead of rejecting it every time it arises. Because when I do this, something else happens and it's the very opposite of that hollow doom that comes with a loneliness ignored. It's just that getting to a place where I have the guts to trust the essential nature of those themes sometimes seems an awfully far away place. This is just a mirage, of course; too often, we are our own jailors.

In the interim then, whilst we make our way tortoise-like towards the life we wish to lead, we find ourselves not alone, just simply lacking in imagination. Because even during the lowest of our days, when our lives feel desperately lonely, and dislocated from the themes that matter so much to us, actually we're surrounded all the time: by the spirits in our garden, by our ancestors whose stories still play out in the themes of our lives, and by the very aliveness with which every moment breathes. We move, walk, think, talk and take ourselves to be solid blocks. Then we sit, breathe, watch and feel, and understand ourselves to be trillions amounts of cells vibrating and pulsating together to make up this apparition called human.

Because even though we think linearly, believe linearly and invest our very spirit, soul, existence and relationships into linear, the timeless vortex that is this solar system we live in whorls and swirls; time being but a concept, one that, though we may cling to, doesn't stop it behaving in the way that is its very nature: leaping here, twisting there, so that memories forgotten suddenly nudge a moment apparently unrelated, and another day appears where we drift into a time we've told ourselves doesn't matter now, it really doesn't matter.

Except it does, always will and continues to, whether we like it or not.

None of us live lonely lives, and yet because we experience ourselves apart, isolated and doomed, we do. (Not all of us, just some of us). None of us live lonely lives, but in our forgetting, we desperately, quietly do.

Until a moment spent walking by a river, or sitting outside, or making love leads us to experiencing a chink in the looking glass where we see ourselves as fragments of a far greater whole, no more solid than a cloud drifting by in the sky. Frightened and unsettled by this, we pooh pooh the experience away, hurrying back to what is reassuringly familiar: all that we interpret to be linear, solid and permanent.

None of us live lonely lives, except some of us desperately do.

a confession

Relocating to the country has brought with it both a gift and a challenge. The gift has come in the form of Bongo, who's come to live with us, and the challenge: how do you entertain child and canine simultaneously?

Given that Evie and I both get fidgety if we spend too long sitting in a café, and what with a lot of toddler groups lasting all of forty minutes, and not being particularly dog friendly either, we've found ourselves spending a lot of our time in local churches. Because not only do many churches have designated play areas for children, but their pews offer infinite options for a child's imagination to engage with. "Teddy, will you marry Teddy?" So that whilst Evie plays, Bongo stretches out to snooze, and I get to sit and write.

And dear Jesus, should there be any chance you're reading this, please know that a part of me feels terribly conflicted about the small chance that you might find this pastime of ours wildly inappropriate. Because yes, whilst I'm sitting here, I do feel inspired to think of the sacred because these churches that we visit express beauty in the simplest and subtlest of ways. I think of Buddha, too. And I think of Mary and women and the loyalty of women and their path, and so yes, I do reflect.

But also, dear Jesus, you did get angry on the Sabbath when folks were working. And well, yes, I'm using the time to write, but single motherhood Jesus! It's hard! Seriously, I don't even think it's necessary to add in single. Motherhood in general Jesus!

We're all trying our best, Jesus. And I know churches are places to come and pray, and maybe being more Buddhist than Christian (although I definitely referenced you more than Buddha in labour dear Jesus, so maybe the conditioning's more Christian at least), if I was in a Buddhist temple and I saw someone come in with their daughter and dog, and tap away on their phone, I'd think it was sacrilegious. But I don't think so.

And it's a lonely world, dear Jesus. Play dates can be okay, but terribly distracting, Jesus. And ideally everyone would have an afternoon and really hang out where the mothers would really chat, but having a real conversation is hard, Jesus, *really really hard*. A combination of the children, Jesus, they don't seem to like us finishing sentences, Jesus, and mothers, Jesus, we're all so tired, Jesus.

I did try organising *Meditating Mums, Jesus*. It was chaos, Jesus! The idea being that one mum would look after the toddlers whilst the others meditated, but oh Jesus... the mess, Jesus. Spaghetti everywhere, Jesus.

I can only add that generally, Evie, Bongo and I don't visit on the Sabbath, but more on weekdays. But if we do go on the weekends, Tom's there too. So were you to walk in and see us, my hope is that you wouldn't be too incensed. We're fairly quiet: Evie busies herself giving sermons. She's quite strict, Jesus. A bit bossy, Jesus, but sometimes she says things that open our hearts, Jesus. She talks of the need of having a home "full of peace and harmony," Jesus. And we're trying, Jesus, we're trying. Most of the time, though, she's engaged in the conduct of marriage. Sometimes we sing our ceremonies and sometimes we speak them. Sometimes she marries teddies, others humans, once a daisy, and tomorrow, Bongo.

If Tom's with us, sometimes Evie will even marry us. And seeing as marriage is something that petrifies the both of us, for the moment at least, this is a game that enables us to feel into something that feels so very scary and yet (please don't tell him), doesn't feel too bad standing up there, holding hands and waiting to say "I do."

Although maybe Evie's cottoned onto a basic dilemma in my and Tom's relationship dynamic, because there was that one time when she refused to marry us. When we asked why, without looking up and continuing to read through the Bible in her hand as she stood in the pulpit, she muttered "Responsibility."

Jesus, we're working on it.

So, I hope that you don't get too angry, dear Jesus. Women and children and dogs, we like movement and like the Sufi's, we hold God in our hearts as we play.

Evie's third birthday

Favourite moments: The beginning.

Watching Evie receive Happy Birthday. Whereas most of us will shudder at the prospect of receiving too much attention, not so for Evie, who's sitting at the breakfast table, her face beaming, listening with rapt attention to every word Tom and I sing to her. Afterwards we go outside and plant her birthday tree: a Japanese acer. It has pink leaves; that's meaning enough for her.

"Mama, let's stay here and watch my plant grow," she says, leaning back into me, as I squat down on the floor.
"Yes, darling, lets." And so we do.

please

"Dance with me, Mama, dance with me." "No, I'm too shy!"

"Oh pleeeeeease," Evie stretches out both arms, reaching for me, "Please, Mama," and because it's only self-consciousness that holds me back and because this little mortal means so much more, I get up off the sofa that I'd previously hoped myself wedged on, here in this tent at Into The Wild Festival in East Sussex, and even though it's 3 p.m. in the afternoon and people are lolling about nearby and the light of the day is shining through and it's an awfully bare big stage in the middle of the tent, I allow myself to be led by my three-year-old daughter to the stage at the back of the tent, music coming through the speakers on either side.

Evie climbs up, whereupon her body begins to twirl and leap about. I climb on and dance beside her, awkwardly, as if a large heavy net were obscuring my movements; trapped in that place where you want so much to be free and not give a damn and yet such is the fear of being seen to make a spectacle of yourself that you invert your energies and play it down. Yet even though I am a diminished version of a whirling dervish, with my eyes averting contact, nevertheless joy pours through the shackles of my heart, so that right here, in the middle of the afternoon, in a festival in England, I'm dancing on a stage with my three-year-old daughter, embarrassed and touched, awkward and alive. Tears come to my eyes as I dance with Evie, who's as free in her movements as I am static, and innocent where I'm cynical. But nevertheless we dance, old and young, mother and child, dancing until I finally sit down, a flame having returned to my heart.

⏷

a song

Evie and I have arrived at my mother's "to see the donkeys." We've marched to their fields all *Here we are! Amuse us!* as I open the gate and let them into the smaller field with the lusher grass, which they charge into like a band of mutinying soldiers, then I sit back and watch as they munch.

Evie grows dictatorial; she has a stick in her hand and is playing at being a teacher. A few moments later when she's sitting on the falabella Toggles, she tries to make him walk. Being the hardy gentleman he is, he refuses.

"He doesn't want to go," Evie says, frustrated, her legs flapping at his portly circumference.
 "No, he doesn't," I say, watching her willing him on. Then she stops suddenly, looking down at his withers, atop which she places her hand to stroke him.
"This pony needs kindness," she says, looking up at me.
"Yes, he does," I agree. And then she slips off him, the stick gets dropped and ten minutes later or so, we herd them all "baaaack in the field..." (My favourite part, as I get to play at living on a ranch in Wyoming). When they're through the gate, we go to leave but my manners get the better of me. I turn back, and go towards our friends to praise them for their responsiveness. Or more specifically, for indulging my geographic whimsy. For whilst I may be rounding a herd of wild mustang, all these guys know is that that human is speaking a little louder than normal, and waving her arms in a vigorous, perhaps more-urgent-than-needed way. As a result, they're all sighing and licking their lips; apparently an equine way of processing an overload of information. Whilst the chief donkey Mikey rolls, I walk over before sitting down beside him to feel out how the roll is going to go. When he stops, I crouch down beside him and rub his face. He stays down, seeming to enjoy it, and then Evie comes over and tries to climb on top of him.
"Hey, no that won't be good for him," I say. She stops, turns and runs over to the far side of the field where my mother's left a bonfire of wooden jumping poles which Evie picks up and lugs around, carrying them with surprising strength. Following her, I get distracted by a big swoop of a branch hanging off one of the trees. I hold onto with both of my hands and then wrap my legs around it like a monkey. I'm not even sure that I did this as a kid. But as an adult, it's kind of irresistible.

Despite the enjoyment, there's guilt too. It's a Monday, after all. "Keep things simple," yes, but not this simple... Thing is, the other alternatives aren't that appealing (play dates can be a particularly cruel way to spend your time). Whereas right now there's an unfolding which feels as spontaneous as play dates can feel monotonous.

I know where my spirit really soars: out here playing rough and tumble with my daughter, as it does as I swing her around, her feet flinging around circle after circle, her smile wide open as she screams for "More! More!" But I'm a reduced version of myself and so grow quickly tired, returning Evie to the ground once more, and whilst she scampers off to play again amongst the wooden poles, I sing a song made up not of words but of noises that come straight from my solar plexus, imagining myself an African woman singing to her earth, in a manner I've never seen, only sensed. When the singing is done, I lie on the ground, the wetness making my t-shirt damp. My body's heavy. I'm tired. Maybe, just maybe, I tell myself, I might just be able to. If I do it really quietly, perhaps Evie won't even notice. And as my fantasy lulls me closer to a place I miss: deep rest, my reality shocks me awake to protect itself, as my three-year-old daughter launches herself on top of me.

Afterwards, we head back to the house, the freedom of outside countered by the habit of returning. On our way back, though, we make a detour, dipping down to the vegetable garden to pick strawberries, which we stuff, unwashed, into our mouths.

here, again

"Laura, do you have mould anywhere in your house?"
"Yes, in the basement."
"Right, you need to get out of your house, Laura. As soon as possible."

Seeing that what he's said hasn't quite landed, Laurens brings up a report on the impact of living in a mouldy house. If you have asthma, are young or elderly, then you shouldn't live anywhere near mould or damp, says the NHS website. We're two of the three, and so I take Evie home to pack a bag and, once more head to a home of my mother's, who lives twenty minutes away.

When I return a week later to pick up some clothes, the paperwork in my study, which is directly above the basement, is damp enough that when I pick it up it collapses, as if left out in the rain. As well as this, the paintings I have hanging on the wall have begun to curl, even though protected by glass and frames. As a result of the mould tests, which Tom's placed around the house, we're released from our rental agreement and, once again, my mother opens her door, because with few options on the rental market, and with Evie having started her new nursery, we need a place to stay.

"We won't stay long," I say, half believing it. We end up staying four months.

broth woman

It's a dark, cloudy November afternoon and I'm sitting here at my mother's desk. Evie's asleep and the dogs are sprawled out, wherever sprawling has led them. To the left of my computer is a glass of vegetable broth and to my right a tumbler of red wine.

However, despite the initial seductiveness of the wine (it'll be such fun! Drink!), it was a flirtation with a tepid life span, collapsing soon after first emerging. In other words, when faced with wine or broth, I'm going with the broth...

Now, broth is a very wonderful thing to make. All that's needed is a pan, some water, then heat. Followed by vaguely washed vegetables that've only needed to be haphazardly sliced, along with some ginger, coriander seeds and, because it's *very very* healthy, and because I'm generally *very very* addicted to those sorts of things, some kind of seaweed.

And yes, broth is stinky, and wine is not, but what a wonderful stink. What a wonderfully, deliciously, gazumptiously gumptiously stinky stink.

Which is surprising, because the wine looks so great. She's darker and plungier than the pale brown broth. Also, the aforementioned stink doesn't apply.

So here I am, sitting at my mother's desk, Evie's snoozing and the dogs are sprawled across the house. The broth has almost gone and I'm looking at the left-over wine, which looks vaguely like Ribena.

Which is a bummer, really, because I'd high hopes for the wine and me. It's such a sexy drink, such a grown-up drink and I'd so love to be like the Chilean writer, who drinks wine in the afternoon and can write and it's all fine. And I'd so love to drink a glass and feel inspiration pour out of me and to be absolutely brilliant with it.

But I'm not.

I'm me; broth woman. Just hopefully without the stink.

⬚

puzzled

Evie's discovered puzzles. For now, they're simple, like this caterpillar one which is numbered one to ten. All the segments are spread out on the floor and I'm sitting here beside her and she's working out which piece goes with which piece. She's looking for the first, she's got the second piece in her hands. So far, everything's going well. The two pieces look made for each other: what could go wrong?

Evie glides the two pieces together with an exuberant confidence that says I have this sorted, and then it happens: the fit doesn't come. She tries again because hey, it's so clear, right? This piece and that piece, they're made for each other. I mean the first even has the number '1' on it, and the second '2.' And this one has holes and this one has prongs that so clearly go into those holes.

Except they don't.

The joy dribbles away as cracks start disrupting that tranquil bliss that *One-Who-Knows-Where-Puzzle-Pieces-Fit* so likes to feel. A worry, a tremor, a question mark appears: why's this not happening the way it should?

Ah ha! Of course, the thought comes, I just need to try harder! So my young daughter starts putting some welly into it. Her face is scrunching up, her brow furrowed, but still the pieces are refusing to join. A pulse quickens, blood starts to simmer and a rumble of a dragon roar can be heard from not too far away.

She pushes the pieces away. "Urgh! Damn you, you bloody puzzle piece, why won't you do what I want you to do?" Or at least something like this, on a more age-appropriate level.

"You're so close, bubba," I say, "keep going. What about trying another way?" My daughter looks at me as if I'm missing the whole point. *Other way? Dear mother, can you not see there is no other way?* I move one a little and she moves the other a little, and then we watch in disbelief, fascination even, as these two pieces come together, just not in the way envisaged. Because not only are they fitting, but they're fitting so simply, so sublimely without struggle that somewhere a puff of breath releases, as muscles relax and a gaze softens. Could it really be this easy? Encouraged, she turns to the next piece, hope renewed, restored because this time she has a support person involved in the quest too. Perhaps I'll be there next time too. And so the process begins anew.

Or not. Because maybe this one time of seeing two pieces come together so without struggle was so awesome and beautiful and inspiring that she won't need to repeat the same mistakes. And so rather than exert effort, force, or that wonderful thing we humans are so inanely proud of: our will, she'll look for and sense the way that fits as it's meant to, with this feeling of ease and simplicity being the guide instead of the deterrent. And this bewildering thought guides me forward, through the quagmire, like a friend I hadn't even realised was there.

Kids' games: not just for kids.

waiting

I'm waiting, Evie's playing. I listen to her in the bedroom chatting with her toys and I watch that neurotic voice in my head that cajoles and bullies: we had a plan! It screeches, *what are you doing standing there? We're wasting time! Let's go!*

Because there was a plan. But then Evie needed the loo just as we were heading out of the door so here we are, upstairs, me waiting to put some clothes on my daughter who'd prefer to continue with this game that she's so absorbed in and that if I weren't so whipped by my internal dogma, I'd more readily see this moment for what it is: a chance to actually do some yoga. But it's late in the afternoon, the voice whines, there's not much light left in the day, we're never going to make it outside! I know this voice, it's not the pull that lures Evie and me outside because of a sense of rejoicing and enjoyment; it's the opposite of anything celebratory. Its tone is punitive, accusatory. It's the voice that makes outside good and inside bad, that makes sugar-free ideal and anything sugary *wrong wrong wrong.*

It's the voice that says *you should do this* and, *you shouldn't do that* and it's the voice that asserts this is the way and that is not the way and it's a voice that really goes full throttle whenever it gets the chance. It's a voice that causes me to dither and eventually wither under its consistent, persistent demands.

But today, *today* I ignore the voice and get down on the floor instead. At first, my movements are scattered, as my intention oscillates between let's do some plank and get all toned and oh phooey, I just want to do some yoga. But slowly, as I start spending more time in each pose and I start being led more by the enjoyment of what I'm doing rather than the neuroses of what will happen if I don't do it, my body relaxes and I feel myself slowing down as I allow myself to return to something that used to bring me so much joy, all the while listening to the soundtrack of my daughter immersed in a world meaningful to her. And as I stretch and move around on the floor, something in me is reminded of the yoga I used to do and the yoga I do now; I miss those long sessions.

After a little while, Evie comes through to the landing, carrying her toys, which she puts down with Bongo lying beside her. And I watch them, my daughter and dog, as I sit not far away, my legs in a v-shape, a mottled memory of a pose I adored when pregnant. Evie plays, chatting with her toys, as she sits role-playing a scene involving Arial the mermaid and Flounder, who in this case is a plastic black and white dog, instead of a fish as in the animation. I watch my daughter, my heart touched to see her playing so joyfully and animatedly. And in watching I have a moment undistracted, a sweet simple moment of watching and loving and feeling those feelings inside. When it passes, tears come to my eyes.

I read once that life is a hologram and we're all an expression, a part of that. I struggled for ages to get a tangible understanding of this. The problem is, my understanding never comes, or rather so rarely comes from being told something; it comes from experiencing something. Like now, watching my daughter and dog, where a disappearing is happening that's much more expansive than the state I normally entertain.

Typically, though I may be in the room with people physically, mentally I can be quite far away. To be really, truly in a moment is incredibly hard for me because most of the time my experience of myself is not of a thumping heart with limbs and muscle, hair and blood, skin and bones, but of an endless cacophony of thoughts, energy and buzz, quite disassociated from something more akin to the bodies and people that we are.

And so, I flitter between trying and then trying not to try and then a few moments and occasions of not trying at all because there's an endless stream of thoughts ready to carry me like a piece of driftwood down a current that it can be hard to avoid, especially when I'm swirling around in the middle, desperately looking for a plank of wood to hang onto. So here I am, like a drunk who wants to get sober, this non-present person who really wants to get present.

rest

The following Sunday, I take the dogs for a walk through the woods. Halfway, I stop and sit down, listening to the birds and looking at the trees. Piglet, my mother's Jack Russell, moans and whistles for me to throw her a stone. She's not one for waiting.

On the way back, we pass through a meadow trembling with wild grasses. Something about them is irresistible and I lie down amongst them. In 2001, when I was eighteen years old, I spent a week on a yoga retreat. On the first day, after yoga and breakfast, I went for a walk in the woods nearby. It was hot and dry, and I walked slowly, meandering through the woods, not knowing where I was going. Along the way, a wave of tiredness hit me. The earth pulled me close and I sunk down onto the path, coiled into the foetal position, and fell into a deep sleep.

I'm not sure how long I slept. But when I woke, I got up and headed back to the yoga camp. Lying here next to Bongo, a dog who's not one for coming too close, I inhale his closeness through every pore of my body whilst lying amongst the wild grasses, thinking of that sleep in the forest. Maybe, if I lie still enough, the same will happen again...

⬜

Eeoyore goes to the beach

Four and a half years of poor sleep does not a healthy immune system make. So that rather than warding off bugs, mine has morphed into an incredibly accommodating and welcoming host, for absolutely any virus passing by. In fact, it doesn't so much as welcome them in, as make it practically impossible for them to leave. *Hey guys! Come on over and in! This lady's got absolutely zero resistance! You can stay here FOREVER!*

And so here we are in the beginning of 2016, and I have another respiratory virus.

"Go to the beach," says Grace, my mother's house-keeper.
"It's too cold," I reply, inwardly thinking it's too far and I'm too lazy.
"It'll be good for your lungs. Go." I feel resentful towards Grace; does she not see how sick I am? I mope around a little, dragging my feet. And then I do what any noble mother would do: I blame my daughter. "She doesn't even want to go!" I say, pointing towards Evie.

But Gracie sees through the bullshit and so twenty minutes later Evie, the three dogs and I are on our way to the beach. When we arrive at the entrance of West Wittering car park, the wheeze has turned into a grumble because you have to pay £6.50 to get in and Christ that's expensive and I need to reverse because I only have £2 change on me and have lost my debit card again for the twenty-second time that year. *Poor lungs, poor me*, bemoans my inner Eeoyre, and then I see an office near the entrance and go in and asked for change for a fiver and the lady looks up and says "But the machine accepts notes."

"Ah."

So I get back in the car where Piglet, one of my mother's dogs, is beside herself with excitement as she gets a whiff of sea air and as we drive through the gate towards the car park, Evie calls out, her arms, hands and fingers pointing towards what lies ahead.

"The sea, Mama! Look! Look! You can see the sea!" My inner Eeore walks away.

After getting out of the car, and before I can put a coat, or anything remotely warm on my daughter, Evie's hurtling across the sand with Piglet not far behind her; her little arms circling like a sprinter's as she runs as fast as her body can move her. She suddenly stops, spins around and standing, calls out: "Come on, Mama!" and then spinning once more, gallops over the sand like a horse set free.

She leads us to a spot where the sand is soft, and starts digging a sandcastle with the dogs digging beside us, and even Badger, the most Eeyorish and anxious of canines is mucking in, occasionally stopping to grin at us in that goofish, surprised way of his that oozes goodness, and says something along the lines of, sometimes, sometimes life is good.

Aeroplanes roam overhead. "On holiday!" Evie cries.
"Yes," I say. Or at least I think I say, because sometimes the vocabulary of us parents doesn't need to amount to much. Although I struggle with this and generally say too much. And so, more often than I like, my words tumble out, trampling over my daughter's silences. But today, life offers me a respite, and for that, dear Gracie, thank you, thank you for nudging me to go.

So as Evie roams about, I just sit there, revelling in being able to watch my daughter, enjoying this rare moment of really seeing her, instead of being consumed by everything that my mind allows

111

itself to be consumed by, i.e. all the things that when that deathbed and me come together, I'm not going to give a shit about. So I sit here, watching Evie, whilst my eyes absorb the colours around us, like thirsty sponges, desperate for some sea air, my whole being humming with delight.

Each activity lasts only a short while, pulling Evie in before she scampers off somewhere else, to something else, such as hide and seek, which I'm called in to join and for which I throw myself onto the sand dunes, imagining myself a Marine (I've done the sleep training). Then as Evie climbs mountains of sand hills, I write, after which we draw numbers, letters and waves in the sand, Evie with her toes, me with my fingers.

"It's a one!" Evie calls out, her chest swelling with pride that she's recognised this number out here on the beach. It's not that one is followed by two, but that in this moment, she's recognising the shape of a one and seeing them everywhere and that for her, this is her world coming together; the extraordinary and unknown have started to slowly make sense.

Afterwards we throw pebbles for the dogs who, after a while, seemed content to hang around. Which is rare for Piglet, who normally pummels you with yaps to throw more stones, balls and anything vaguely aerodynamic for her to run after and retrieve, but today she's uncharacteristically Zen.

At some point, clothes are taken off; sadly, they're not mine, as I remain sartorially respectful and sit wrapped in layers whilst Evie runs around partially naked, albeit with her t-shirt on. The responsible mother in me is uncomfortable: what will people think! Put her clothes on, for God's sake! And the other mother, who I'm not sure is necessarily irresponsible, it's just that moments like this win her over, says her joy will warm her heart, let her be just a little while longer. As I sit and watch my sand-scattered daughter, so engrossed in what she's doing, life slips me another moment. So that instead of a mother watching her child, or Laura looking at Evie, the macro becomes magnetized as my 'myness' slips away and the moment sinks into itself.

Moments like this, when everything comes together, or falls apart, offer us a chance to forget ourselves. And so, our awareness of ourselves as a separate autonomous self slips away and instead there's this perfect moment of watching and seeing. And I think maybe I want to do this more often. Because I'm lazy and, well, the beach is far, and oh do I really have to go, but you know, some distances are worth it.

"Let's go to the water, Mama!" Evie calls out, and my first reaction is resistance. And then surrender, hell, I may even enjoy it. So we make our way to the water and as the dogs wade in, Evie jumps over the waves.

"I think the water's coming in, Mama." And this kind of astounds me. When and how does the concept of tides come in?

And I watch the movement of my daughter, the way motion calls to her, and I feel our separateness. And so here we are: Evie leaping and exploring and me, crouching and sensing into a stillness that challenges, mystifies and electrifies me, and yes, I know that children can be still too, but my god can they move.

And maybe this is the residue of the adrenalin, made all the more skittish by the pulse of anxiety that's been passed down from generation to generation in my family, or maybe what I'm witnessing as I watch Evie's exuberant camaraderie with life is something simpler: a human, experiencing the joy of being alive.

Times like this, it's easier to remember.

▢

searching

And then we head back home to Little Halnaker where we're still living. The rental market has meagre pickings to offer a family looking for somewhere to live and my stepfather, Burkhard, is unimpressed.

"When are they leaving?" he hisses to my mother. Since we've moved in, this has now become the way that he greets my mother each day. My poor mother, locked in the middle of understanding her husband's reticence at hosting her thirty-two-year-old daughter's family for such a vague, apparently unending duration of time, as "until they find a home, dearest," and her thirty-two-year-old daughter's need for a home, stumbles between us with increasingly anxious-looking eyes.

One morning, I wake to find the property section of the local newspaper at the end of my bed.

"Go on, darling, find something," Mum urges me later, a note of desperation in the way she articulates the word "find."

Meanwhile, Tom's started spending more time in London. "But you're so happy here in the country," he says, his tyres screeching down the driveway as he leaves for London - as every day starts to feel like Christmas but in all the wrong ways. As Burkhard starts spending even more time in his study than usual, and Evie, who seemed to pass through her 'terrible' twos with about four tantrums in total, is now having at least two meltdowns a week. Meanwhile, to help the sense of equilibrium really get to a boiling point, Burkhard has turned his attention to my parenting.

"Why's she using her hands instead of the fork?" he'll growl, incredulous, as we sit to eat at the table whilst watching Evie devour her food like a hungry wolf cub, all hands and no utensils.
"Why's her face covered with paint?" he asks, as she skips by, an interior designer's worst nightmare: thick slabs of fresh neon paint spread all over her hands, limbs and torso.
"Why's she eating the dog food?" he asks, his jaw hitting the floor as he peers under the kitchen table to find Evie lying next to Bongo, munching on some dry dog biscuits.

Unable to hold the tension much longer, eventually Mum starts walking towards me, hands imploring, smile jilted. "Darling, you know we absolutely love having you here, but we were just wondering... when are you going?"

Unfortunately, I don't have an answer. And whilst fervently praying and actively searching for another home to appear, the only thing to do in the interim is for Evie and me to head outside...
⬚

halcyon days

Because out here, Evie and I can oscillate between sitting here in a field overlooking a meadow and playing tumble and roll through the long grasses.

"Stop, Mama," Evie says. We do, and I look to where her pointed finger stretches: I only see grass, field and sky. A moment later, a fox leaps like a deer over the grasses, one, two, three, before disappearing through the bracken and cluster of trees that stand in the middle of the field where I used to nurse Evie when she was a baby.

Later, Evie sits bareback on Zotlie, a black Shetland pony with a stallion's butt and an incredibly glossy mane. I rub the jawline of Toggles, the smallest in the group, as the two donkeys munch. My bottom's on the ground, the earth's damp, birds sing as the sky soars, whilst I listen to the sound of teeth chomping grass.

We spend a great deal of time trying to figure out things that really, in the end, will prove to be dissolvable, impermanent, forgettable stuff, meanwhile forgetting too easily moments such as this and others that follow, such as afternoons when you're looking for something to do and you stumble upon a new church, whose garden is the perfect place to play hide and seek. Nothing apparently special, until at least you recall the joy that was singing in your heart as you watched your little daughter run to the back of the garden and throw herself behind a tree, before yelling out, "I'm hiding, Mama!" because you know that soon, one day, these moments will be the memories you sift through, wanting to reach out and relive them once more.

[?]

I capture the tadpole

I write this sitting beside a stream flooded with thousands of tadpoles; frogs not yet apparent. Drying mud cracking around my thumbs and fingers, my throat's parched, as a plane glides overhead. Nearby, the family dogs lie on the grass beside me, as I enjoy one side of my face being warmed by the sun. Evie's somewhere running around barefoot. And then she's back, poking sticks into the water, fascinated by the tadpoles.

Later, she catches one, the little black squirm nestled between the dips of her fingers, while she peers at it, bringing it close for inspection. Then she lets it go again. As I sit typing on my phone by the rocks near the stream, Evie comes and scrambles over me. Snot smeared across a deliciously chubby cheek. I'm still typing, she's still scrambling. And then we pause: two monkeys sitting, doing what monkeys don't particularly do on a Saturday afternoon in Sussex, sitting and watching the water of the stream run by.

⏾

Fair-weather canine

Sometimes though, I head outside alone.

Like tonight: Evie's asleep and I'm here, walking the dogs in the wood, watching as the sky turns all milky greys and dark sapphire blues. It's started to rain, not enough to finish the walk, but at least speed it up a little. The rain's replenishing, not quite *Singin' In The Rain*, but it's triggered some kind of eternal anthem to set off, the notes of which are maybe too indistinguishable to remember.

As the dogs and I continue on our way, my eyes begin to lose their way as my feet find theirs. There's something liberating and also relaxing as they develop their own confidence; the surer they become, the more my mind relaxes and settles, as the possibility of danger - danger being the only reason not to go out at night, because it's not exactly bad for you, and it's not exactly dull – reveals itself to be a worry that my mind doesn't have to clasp onto, because I have the ultimate alert system with me: the dogs.

When we get to the top of the field, at the end of the woods, my hand comes to my mouth again and again, as I whoop and whoop again out to the cold night air: a welcome to a time of night not particularly special or noted – after sunset, not yet midnight, nor dawn or sunrise – and yet despite the rain, which has grown heavier, and the wind, which has grown stronger, god it's uplifting. Night. Sinking black enveloping, I'll be staying for a while dark night. Looking out to the south, the only light that I can see is our local town: Chichester, emitting a hazy light, mottled by the fog. There're no stars; the clouds have taken them hostage.

A wind picks up. I turn around just about able to make out Piglet, who's easier to define because she's white, whereas Bongo's harder to see because he's dark; a black dot on your vision who, when you blink, makes you unsure if it's him or not. In the end, the only thing that distinguishes Bongo from the dark mist, is his movement. And this sense about him: here I come, I come, here I come to you. And then that movement suddenly stops.

"Bongooooooooo!" I call, my voice ricocheting across the land. There's no response and apart from the pulse of my breath, for a moment I can't even hear the wind. I stand, waiting for him.

I'm done, missy. This is not for me.

In other words, this is it, the end of our dark night expedition. Bongo's stopped: the walk is over. Because whereas the rain does nothing to dampen Piggy's perambulatory devotion, Bongo's a fair-weather walker of a canine, and tonight, lady, his parked bottom tells me, I've come far enough. But it's not far enough for me, which is unusual because normally night walks, like night dives, night drives and generally being out alone at night-time is something I try to avoid.

But because fear says pay attention, and maybe he senses something ahead, I go to him and we retreat slightly, curving to the right, and take the shortcut back home. A home that lies somewhere ahead because right now, though I can't see it, I can feel it; the feeling of which is keeping my feet moving, one step at a time. ▨

curious

The following night, I go out again, taking myself to the far end of the wood, wanting so much to be okay with the darkness but I'm not; it scares me. I cannot find my grounding amidst the rising fear, nor do I even know where to look, and as the sky starts darkening, causing the trees to collapse in on themselves as visibility fades and the birdsong grows faint, I turn for home. A walk that slips to   a run which stumbles into a sprint: the bogeyman may not exist, but tonight I'm convinced a relative is not too far away.

And yet, there's a place that exists that even as I gallop back with the dogs by my side I can feel myself tapping into. Even though I've freaked myself out by coming out at night, and I'm sweating and my heart's thumping, something's coming alive. As I run, I feel its pulse; one that's sending out a howl of *I'm here*, as I sprint, imagining myself a wolf, flying through the woods because she's finally found her pack.
⏹

Little Oaks

And then we find a home.

My brother, noticing that luck is not on our side, calls a friend who'd used a property finder, Philip, to find him and his family a home. And although Philip only deals with properties for sale, as a favour for the friend, he calls around his contacts. Two houses come back as available to rent beginning in January. Later that afternoon, it's dropped to one. The next day I drive to see it.

"I'm not so impressed by it," Philip says.
"Why, what's wrong with it?" I ask, because whereas Philip sees a lack of aesthetic, I just see a house free of my family. A potential blinding that means I overlook that the median age of our neighbours is about eighty-three.
"We'd love to rent it," I say.
"Great," he says.

And then in the first week of January, Evie and I move into our fifth house in three and a half years, to the home of Little Oaks.

⏾

feels okay to me

I've come to Halnaker to pick up a few boxes and collect my house plants in the greenhouse. When I walk through the door to get them, there they are, and beside them sits a pair of antlers.

"Are they yours, Chris?" I ask Chris the gardener.
"Nope, don't know who put them there." I pick them up and put them in the car and then leave them in a box by the front door with an umbrella. After a few weeks, I return to them, and after cleaning them rehome them on the kitchen table.

"That's disgusting, Lau," says Mum when she comes for dinner one night.

Feeling ashamed, I take them outside and place them under the tree where we do our rituals. Or at least do for a while, till this becomes something we forget too. Every time a dog comes to visit, though, the antlers get masticated, so they're now sitting on the little wall that runs along the patio, although their significance to me speaks to me still, if only with the touch of a secret most clandestine. And although they don't look entirely comfortable in their new home, where they sit tilted and slightly awkward, I've yet, like with so much in our house: the wonky pictures hanging on the wall, the lamps with no lights, to do anything about it.

Because something in me is not yet ready to fix them.

⬚

inevitable

Bongo and I are on a walk, across frozen fields that take us up a hill, the steepness of which makes my heart pound and where once we're at the top of we discover the remnants of a castle once lived in: ruins that appear to make up a circle of sorts. Not yet knowing their history, the discovery of them feels clandestine.

When we start our return back to the car, I watch as Bongo picks his feet gingerly across the frozen puddles, his head hunched low. It's been a cripplingly cold few days. I'm wearing trousers that don't so much repel the cold as inhale it. And as Bongo has Cushing's Disease (which means his body struggles to regulate his temperature), he could do with a good sheepskin coat wrapped around him, too. I encourage him on, but my asthma's causing my lungs to grow tight, so eventually I stop talking and just focus on putting one foot in front of the other.

When we're back in the warmth of the car, I suck on my Ventolin to ease my wheeze then pour some of Bongo's food into a bowl along with his medicine, and then we have our supper. Mine's a loaf of rye. I bite into it: huge big soul-warming bites and turn off the car lights to look up through the windscreen at the lip of the moon. When we finish, I turn the car on, and we head home.

As I move the car towards the main road, I can't stop shivering. My teeth crash against each other like waves beaten by the storm. Then as I move away from the farm shop where I'd parked, without warning, a memory erupts that I didn't even know I had, and as it storms past my vision, a great crashing of grief rips across my chest. And there I am, an infant in her cot whose cries for someone to open that door are giving way to a bleak hopelessness: why does no one ever come?

A couple of days later my cold's progressed and I'm struggling to breathe. I'm not able to take Evie to nursery and so text her nanny Stacey, who helps out a couple afternoons a week and who would've been picking her up at 12 p.m. at nursery, to come to our home instead. When she arrives, Evie doesn't want to leave my side.

"It's fine, it's fine, just stay," I reply, unable to offer anything in the way of direction. Stacey calls the local GP for me, as I can't get in the car to drive to him.

"I think you might have pneumonia," he says an hour later after checking my chest. "You don't want to let it get much worse before you go to hospital," he warns, looking at me with a pinched expression. He then writes out a prescription for steroids and antibiotics, and leaves me with a Ventolin breather. Stacey goes to pick up the prescription and when she returns, I take one of the large steroid pills straight away and then walk across the landing to run a hot bath, walking in the way you walk when you're sick and even your thoughts have silenced, so you can direct every bit of energy to the simple tasks like walking, putting the plug in and making sure the water's the right temperature.

But the bath and I are not to be.

Mum and Tom are here now, and as I make my way back to my bedroom at the pace of a disorientated snail, Mum walks in behind me.

"I think you need to go to hospital, Lau," she says, looking at me with worry; something I take note of.

In the months that followed my father's death, I began waking regularly around the hours of 1 and 2 a.m., with lungs that were struggling to breathe. No matter how bad my attacks were, my mother always remained calm. However anxious she may have felt, all I remember is the feeling of leaning into her relaxed and warm body, as we sat up on my bed in my uncle's house where we'd moved when we'd lost all our money and sold our house after my father died. And it was the gentle and soothing rhythm of her voice and the warmth of her presence that would always restore my breathing and allow me to sink back down and fall asleep. Where was that presence now?

Its absence creates room for doubt to trickle in, so I relent, say okay, and someone goes to call the ambulance. As I wait alone in my bedroom, the strength required to stand slips away, and I collapse onto my knees by my bed. Sinking down, a wail lifts out of my chest. It's a bleak wail, a mournful wail, a wail that's not to be stopped, like a ghost finally transitioning to another realm, simply passing through as it transitions from my solar plexus via a tight-fisted punch in the middle of my chest. It feels surreal in its unexpectedness, so too because there it is again, this hollow feeling of pure grief sweeping over me as a question hovers: why does no one come?

As I sink lower towards the floor, I give up trying to be strong, and pretending that I can juggle the dramas playing out in my life with characters who seem intent on unsettling and disrupting wherever and as much as they can.

This is my SOS, of sorts. I only wish someone was around to hear me.
⏃

defeat

When the pre-ambulance woman arrives and walks into my bedroom, I say "I'm an asthmatic, a neurotic. Please, whatever's happening, don't tell me. Just be positive." And she totally gets it. So that even when I'm hooked up to all the breathing apparatus that she has, and I can see that my oxygen levels are steadily lowering bit by bit, I believe her words, not the evidence.

"You're doing fiiiine. Well done, Laura," she says, speaking to me as if I'm a child, which in some senses of the word I am. I've regressed; the adult's checked out, the child part that's been ignored, pushed aside, is reappearing. I'm thankful for her tone and her kindness, and grateful to be able to completely hand over any semblance of being in control. Even over this thing that we're meant to all be able to do - breathing. Except as it turns out, for some of us, at least, it's not so automatic after all. When the ambulance finally arrives, her mask drops.

"Where've you been? This was a code red," she snaps, updating the man and woman team of my statistics. Then the three of them help me downstairs, and even though I don't feel any strength, the motivation that my three-year-old daughter not see me in anything that might distress her gets me up and I don't know if I'm going to be coming back and all I can think is, *fuck, I've got two days to do my will.*

"I just need to say goodbye to her," I say, moving towards the sitting room, and as I do, Mum and Stacey block my way.
"Don't. She'll get upset," Mum says. "She's watching Peppa Pig." Tom comes towards me, "We're more worried about you right now, Lau. Just come into the ambulance."
"But I need to say goodbye to her." No one moves.

I want to fight, to tell them all to bugger off, to say but what if this is it? But I don't have the juice, or more specifically, I doubt myself too much, maybe I will distress Evie more than reassure her. Maybe they're right and I'm wrong. So I give in, walk out the front door and climb into the ambulance and lie down on the bed. Tom's by my side, and as we head to A&E something in me relaxes.

a heart reopens

When we get to the hospital, I'm given a bed and told to wait for when the doctor can see me. We wait for two hours, during which I have an x-ray and a blood test, and then retreat back to the curtained cubicle to lie on the bed and wait. The lights are glaring and because it's late, I put on my eye mask and attempt to sleep. Meanwhile, Tom sits beside me on a chair that looks ergonomically designed to leave him in hospital; a way to keep the beds full, perhaps.

As I lie there, I practice an asana, or pose, known as *savasana*, the corpse pose. This pose has become my yoga practice. Traditionally practiced at the end of a yoga practice, these days it's all I have the juice for. It's also the way I compensate for the lack of sleep at night and my inability to nap in the day, as I've slipped into the all-too-convincing tired but wired feeling that insomniacs succumb to. And it works, because twenty minutes in this pose revitalises me in such a way that I can get to the end of the day feeling even a little bit exuberant; death is revitalising after all.

Whilst I lie on the hospital bed, sensing into the sensations around my right toe, top of the foot, ankle, calf, shin, kneecap and so on, the muscles in my body sink into a deep relaxation, whilst the traveling up and down my body gives my mind something to focus on. As the thoughts settle, someone appears who I haven't seen for a while: my grandmother, Dean not Jean. I feel her close by, and a series of memories rush through my mind; ghosts wanting to be remembered. I try to direct them towards a more coherent message: my memory has it all wrong, says the voice in the head, these aren't the ones I need to see. *Which ones would make more sense?* But there's feedback: Laura this isn't for you to control, this is for you to see.

So I stop attempting to direct and instead relax and watch, and it's kind of confusing because my mind's still there, interfering, trying to work out why this scene? This scene isn't significant, why am I being shown this one? But at one point I surrender again and instead of trying to figure it all out, I simply take it in. And then the memories stop and at the end there's a message:

Let the love in...

It's not a bad idea, so I lie there on the hospital bed with Tom by my side, feeling into and inhaling this love. The love of everyone in my life who, as I do them, loves me: we love one another. But it's one thing for us to always be declaring our love for others, another to allow ourselves to feel quite how much we are loved too. Then the doctor comes in.

"You don't have pneumonia, you can go. But you need to continue with the antibiotics."

Afterwards, we take a taxi to my mother's, which is only ten minutes away, and I go my to my old room, where I stay for four days, taking the antibiotics, eating meals brought up to me on a tray and watching bad rom-coms. Evie's with her father for the weekend, and Tom looks after me, as I remain in the room, not wanting to be anywhere else.

more practice needed

In the days that follow, letting the love in becomes a practice, if only temporarily. Mostly, or really only when I'm putting Evie to bed once back at our home here in Sussex, *Little Oaks*. As I sit on the floor whilst she's falling asleep, I breathe in this feeling of being loved, thinking about all those people who I love and in turn feeling their love coming back, which causes stupendous yawns to stretch my mouth wide open and my entire body to grow heavy.

Evie occasionally responds, ripping a yawn or two of her own in symbiosis and then sinks into a deep sleep. Considering Evie also struggles with her sleep when she's unsettled and also leans towards the wired not tired way of being, I'm paying these yawns attention.

badger killers

Evie has a long purple worm of a balloon that she's asking for help to blow up. It's too long and thin for my lungs to contend with. We need help.

"Let's go and ask our neighbours," I suggest whilst getting breakfast ready. But now it's later and breakfast has happened and I've grown lazy, so that walking around our neighbourhood to find someone to blow up our balloon isn't that appealing.

"Do you want to go now or," I say, thinking I've found a way out, "we can go later when you come back from being with Stacey?" referring to Stacey, Evie's nanny.

"Now, Mama." *Damn.*

As we leave our house, Evie asks: "Are we walking, or going on the bike?"

"Walking, bubba, our neighbours are people who live near us," I say, as I take her hand and we cross the road and walk towards the house opposite. As we get near, we slow a little.

"I feel shy," I say. My constant paranoia that my daughter is able to grow into a woman who's not ashamed of certain emotions is encouraging me to express the ones that normally get overlooked. Evie, thankfully, totally ignores me. As we near the front door, Evie takes the balloon. She's excited and crouches down to see through the glass door, and we both bang on the door. Richard comes quickly, opening the door, a question on his face.

"Hello?"

"Hello. We were wondering if you might be able to help us blow up this balloon?" I say, holding up the purple worm. A look crosses his face. Oh Christ, it's pity, I can do most things, but please, not the pity. I want to respond with something witty, something convincing... *Lonely, no, not I!* But I pause and look at him, yes we really are here, and we really do need your help. He's game. Taking the balloon, he begins to rub it between his palms. Evie's staring up at him, silent, watching, expectant. I see the wetness at the end of the balloon. "You might want to wash it a little."

"She's not infectious, is she?" Richard asks. I shake my head.

"Well, no problem then." He brings his mouth to the balloon and blows. Nothing.

"Hmmm, this is a hard one." He tries again. "We're going to need a pump. If you go around, I'll meet you in the garage." Infectious we might not be, but house entrance, for now at least, seems off bounds. So Evie and I walk around to the garage to wait whilst Richard comes through the house.

The garage door opens and we walk in. It's stuffed with stuff: a car, a lawnmower, a wetsuit hanging. "Do you surf?" I ask.

"No, I used to sail. But that's a woman's wetsuit."

"Ah. You're garden is huge!" I reply, embarrassed.

"Yes." Richard finds his pump.

"What's your wife's name?" I ask.

"Judy."

"Judeeeee!" Eve says, her face contorting.

"Come," Richard takes us through the door to his house. I feel embarrassed, as if we're imposing. His wife is brought out of the sitting room: a glamorous woman with short bobbed hair. At first, she's reserved, cold even, and then as Evie and I back out into the garden, she comes forward, and suddenly we're talking about star signs.

"Richard's a Leo, I'm a Sagittarius." She tells me one of her kids is a Leo. I tell her that Evie's a Leo and I'm a Capricorn "with Leo rising."

"What does that mean?"

"Constant conflict."

"Ahh..." she says sagely and we leave it at that.

Richard returns, the purple worm still dangling from his hand. Its fate is to remain limp.

"We'll wait for Tom. Thank you so much. Tom's back tonight." I think I've mentioned this three times now. If I say it enough, then I look like I'm okay. When really what I want to say is, sometimes at night I get scared. If I'm tired enough and I'm walking around the house, locking up, my imagination hurtles to the bogey man and I imagine men coming into my home and wonder if I would hear them if they came in the night if I was asleep. If I was asleep... *Please come over to our house anytime you like,* I want to say. But don't.

"Is Tom still upset about Brexit?" Richard asks. "Tom's not one to get upset. But he is worried."
"Oh, it'll be fine."
"It's probably more the environment that we need to worry about more." God, I sound like Tom.
"Hmm, perhaps."
"Oh no, don't touch that," Judy says, pulling back a rifle.
"What is it?" Evie asks. "A... a rifle."
"What's it for?"
"Ummm, for getting rid of things that need to be got rid of."
"What did you shoot?" I ask.
"Um, a badger."
"A badger?" I screech.
"Um, no a mole."
"A mole? Not a mole?"
"You couldn't shoot a badger with an air rifle."
"We need our wildlife. There's hardly any left."
"Yes, but you should see what they do to our garden."
"But that's what they do! They're not enough of them. We have loads of mole hills." Then changing tact: "But how did you shoot them? That must have been hard."
"I didn't shoot. I dug and used a spade."
"Right." Smiles. But I've drifted; am I desperate enough for friends that I can hang out with mole killers (or was it a badger)?
"Right, well we'll get together, and we can discuss Brexit and moles."

Judy backs away. Evie and I head home. The purple worm wrapped around her wrist. As we cross the road, we see Stacey. As we come through the gate, I look down, there's an earth worm poking its head into the thin lines of mud in between each tile.

"Go and get a stick, bubba," I say. Evie brings one back. It's a bit bendy and thick for worm picking up. Stacey passes one over.
"Can I help, Mama?" Evie asks, placing her hand over mine, and we pick up the real-life worm.
"Can I carry it?" she asks, and I pass the stick to Evie and then, using my foot, etch out a hole for it in the soil. She places it in, and it wriggles away.

never that far away

The following week, Mum comes over. "Are you alright?" she asks. I looked exhausted I know. I'm a *single mother*, I want to say. Tom's in the States. We just moved house, *again*. We live alone. I don't sleep. What do you want me to say?

Which means I say, "I'm fine, Mum."

"Come over, Lau."

"It's alright, Ma, we're fine." Mum looks at me unconvinced. The inference is that it's odd, us being alone, just a two. *It's not odd, Ma*, it's hard, I want to say. Hard because so much of my parenting comes out of the fear of not being there for my daughter, for her growing up experiencing an absence where her mother could've been. But also the truth is, when I get away from my family's judgements about what is normal and what isn't, the truth is, when Evie and I are home and discovering each other in little moments, life isn't too bad.

"Maybe we'll spring clean your room tomorrow, bubba," I say to Evie later. She whips her ahead around: "Yes!"

After, Evie falls asleep easily, which means I have some evening to myself. Which means I can go to bed at 8.30 p.m. on a Saturday night and not feel guilty about it. The sky's black. My body's pooped, and I feel a peace flare up in my heart at last.

the threat of change

It's a bank holiday in May. The three of us are meant to be in Devon, but such is the current stalemate that Tom and I are in that when I suggested he go alone, there was suddenly a flash of hope in his eyes.

"Okay." And then, "If you're sure?" The question mark seemed hesitantly included.

He left later that afternoon.

The next day, a Saturday, over breakfast, Evie and I map out our day, because sometimes, knowing what's coming next doesn't only calm just the child, but the parent. After breakfast, we head straight out to the woods for a treasure hunt. We take Judy, our mouthy Australian puppet, who's just like Mary Poppins, only more crass and less helpful.

There's a particular place that I want to show Evie which requires a fair bit of a walk. I'm curious if we'll get there. Hopeful, too. So far, generally, whenever I go to the woods, it's only because there's someone who can look after Evie whilst I'm gone. It's precious to have time alone, but with things that we love, there's always a part of us that can't wait to share them with our children. Be that riding horses, discovering a particular country, or the joy of walking through the woods.

Along the way, we collect treasure: a chickling's feathers, some flowers, a rock, some twigs, listening to birdsong, and holding hands as we walk. At times we slip into silence. After a while, Evie looks back from where we've come, "There's going to be a long walk back," she comments. To boost morale, we resort to *Twinkle Twinkle Little Star* to reboot. Halfway, in a space between the avenue of trees that line the path, we stop for a water and chocolate break. Judy's been terribly efficient and brought muffin cups which chocolate mulberries are placed in. Evie liberally helps herself to them.

As a result, my portion is a reduced version of itself.

After our refortification snack is finished, we continue, discovering a dragon's tail clinging to a branch of a low-lying tree. We're not sure what's happened to the rest of the dragon, perhaps it's shed its tail, just like a stag sheds its antlers. I pull it away and give it to Evie, who walks with it dangling from her hand, trailing along the ground. And then we're here: a vertical walk that takes you up to the south downs way. It's my favourite walk, the combination of the intensity of its steepness and the sense of accomplishment and peace one feels at the top. But for now, simply to be at the base of something so loved is enough. Evie and I potter about twenty metres up, where amongst the bluebells we meet Rosehip and Evie.

You see a tree, my daughter seems to say to me as she hugs a mossy Rosehip, *I see a horse.*

I crouch down amongst the indigo floor, watching as Evie straddles one of the tree ponies and goes for a gallop. After her adventures, she comes over and nestles in my lap, and asks me to tell her stories. First, *The Three Little Pigs,* then *Sleeping Beauty* followed by *Little Red Riding Hood.* There not being anywhere else I'd rather be in this particular moment, the telling of them seems a joy, as simple as it is self-perpetuating.

When the last story has been told, we find a spot away from where we were sitting and pee, then make our way down the path towards our car. Bang on schedule. At the end of the path, we touch the pink arrow on the public byway sign and then get back in the car. At home, Evie gets her TV time, and I get my writing time. Then lunch, followed by chill time. Then outside again.

"Play with me, play with me," Evie implores.
"Would you like to build a mandala?" I ask her.
"What's a mandala?" she asks.
"I don't really know," I reply. Then remembering a book a friend recently gave me, I run into the sitting room to grab it, and return pointing out photos to Evie.

"It has a centre, and everything spirals out from that centre. Look, look here," Evie peers over at the book, unsure, or unconvinced her mother really knows what she's doing. I attempt to direct the order of play, and she follows me as we search the garden for ingredients, returning with decomposing leaves, dandelions, daisies, and primroses.

"You can eat these!" Evie calls out, holding a dandelion leaf aloft. We place the leaves in our mouth and then spit them out again. They're bitter, maybe better on a salad, drowned in dressing. Then we return to our mandala. I'm controlling, Evie's hesitant. "No, like this, see it's like a circle." Then we find a flow and work together with concentration. Afterwards we kneel back, appraising our work. Evie's looking at the mandala, and she's rocking, and then turning to me "Mama, can we destroy it?" she asks. As if sensing the missing element to our efforts: to dissolve all evidence of them.

I pause, disappointed to lose something so pretty so quickly and then catch myself. "Yes!" I respond. And we both reach out, ripping out the carefully placed twigs, and brushing away the leaves with gusto, like hungry cats demolishing a plate of butter melting in the sun. I imagine myself a Buddhist monk moving her hands across the sand to destroy the intricate painting we've spent hours creating, only with slightly less discipline and perhaps a little more attachment to the nature of the illusions that shuffle their way across my view. Then onto the trampoline where we play tag.

"I'm so tired," I say, and she smiles that smile, the smile wakes me up and on we play, all the while me running in and checking on the roast chicken, which cooks in about thirty minutes, and we go in and Evie stands on her stool and rips the skin from the chicken, devouring it whilst I make my first gravy following a Slater recipe, which actually tastes miserable (I forgot the wine) and then we go to the table, and Evie's pouring liberal amounts of gravy everywhere, although she mostly ignores it, focusing instead on the chicken.

Later, my mother and stepfather arrive; they were meant to be here for dinner, but are late, which means that an already tired Evie moves into hyper mode. Bongo's been living with my mother again, and comes for a visit.

"I miss Bongo," Evie says as we stroke him by the kitchen table.
"Me too, darling, me too." And we talk about what we love and miss about him.
"He gives me licks and he jumps up on me and gives me greetings." Because Bongo's greetings are an extraordinary event that make Christian the Youtube Lion's hello to his two friends on an African plain look frugal.
"Come home," Mum says as she leaves. "We're only fifteen minutes away." They're twenty and the five minute reduction of the time spent traveling to hers carries with it a message that, though unspoken, is not silent. *Better to be with others Lau, it's not normal to be just you two.*

Thing is, though, I reply, practicing my telepathy, getting to hang out is something precious.

Don't you love the time you have to yourself when she's with her father? people ask. You force yourself to, I want to say. But I don't, because the longing to reach out to other women is so strong, and earnestness and genuiness can be so off-putting, so I smile and say *oh yes, the lie-ins are good.*

And here, on a weekend together, knowing that next weekend we won't have together, or every other weekend after, Evie and I have a chance to hang out at Little Oaks, which has become our home, "our dear little home," as Evie calls it. What I'm trying to say to my mother, or rather just wish she realised and got herself is simply, *every single moment I have with my daughter is precious, mum.*

I don't know if it's simply the fact that Evie goes away every other weekend, or during holidays for longer visits, or because my father died when I was a child, or even that somehow the gift of meditation is *anicca, impermanence.* Also, if this relationship with Tom isn't going to work out, which right now is very much a possibility, then being a single mother is something I need to feel into, and maybe even just plain accept. Because there're days when truth is yes, the aloneness of the whole thing scares me. But there're also days when the preciousness that exists in the space between Evie and me carries me through. And for someone who's been addicted to change and spontaneity I'm finding an awful lot of peace in repetition. So that the child who thrives on repetition and the adult who struggles, actually there's a blessing here for me, and it's this: to find the peace in the sacred moments that arrive from a simple life.

I don't need to worry about showing Evie technology and films; other people and her own innate curiosity will do that. In my heart is a love of the outside, and an irritation at the lack of creativity and open-heartedness that leads to a life lived where the television becomes the solution for all of life's ills, from boredom, overwhelm and even for those for whom intimacy feels so terrifying a thing. So, I let Sunday play out as Saturday played out. Rather than obsessing about needing to diversify Evie's entertainment, instead, I seek to provide regulation for her nervous system; Evie doesn't need distracting, she needs connection. All I need to do, and indeed want to do, is hang out with my daughter.

On the Sunday, we start the day much the same, except this time excitement is bubbling so much in Evie's imagination that she doesn't eat much breakfast, but instead helps me pack the picnic and off we go, with our mouthy Australian puppet, and instead of boring, this walk has elements of a ritual: a beginning, a middle and an end. When we get to the entrance of the walk, I lift Evie to touch the pink arrow on the wooden footpath sign, and so commences the start of our walk. Beginning, Evie finds a stick which she grasps with her hand, poking it amongst the hedgerow as we make our way along the path, listening to the birds. "Blackbirds, Mama," she says, after pausing and looking up at the skies. And then on we go. She's more confident on this walk, clambering up the banks on either side, looking for treasure. When we get to the spot where we stopped previously, I ask if she wants to eat there, or continue to Rosehip and Evie.

"Continue, Mama," and so we do. Somehow we end up talking about snakes, and I obviously overdo it because Evie's asking about where they live, and we make a prayer to the snake deva to send them all away.
"What colour do you feel about snakes, bubba?"
"Brown."
"Is it a warm feeling, or a cold feeling?"

"Cold."

"A comfy feeling or an uncomfortable feeling."

"Uncomfortable." We make a prayer to the snake deva: please send your snakes away. Then I point out to Evie that it's actually perfect for snake catching as it has a fork at the end, so she's alright, she's protected already.

"When you kill a snake it will be dead forever," she says.

"Yes, that's why life is so precious."

"Continue, Mama."

And so we do.

Reaching Rosehip and Evie's spot, we sit amongst the bluebells, whilst my forest exploring daughter eats the rest of her breakfast. She finishes with a chocolate macaroon whilst sitting on my lap as I tell her stories. Her father calls halfway and Facetimes with his daughter. Then we eat a little more, chat a little more and she's in no rush, and in the end it's me who's cold from a damp bottom on the earth and off we head back home.

And this pattern isn't just soothing to Evie, it's soothing to me. In between it all, I've had time for housework, cooking two proper meals, meditating, and the previous evening, engaging in adult conversation with my stepfather for an hour. In the absence of certainty around my and Tom's future, something else is expanding, although it's a precarious thing, and my unconscious is a hardy species of thing so it does its best to undermine it whenever it can, but when I do feel this thing, such is its strength that I'm convinced I'll never forget it: trust.

I'm not sure that it's a trust that's directed at anything specifically; its roots are budding after all, not yet established in that way that no matter how hard you tug, there's nothing on the planet strong enough to take them away from the soil through which they weave. It's a trust rather like a winding path, spiralling through the woods whose destination remains to be discovered.

Our lives are little, and yet larger than we allow ourselves the joy of contemplating. We don't so much lead them as find ourselves at one end of an ever-unravelling carpet, doing our best to launch ourselves atop the part that rolls free, because a free rolling carpet feels a dangerous thing. Who's to say it's heading in a safe direction after all?

⏃

in our hands

At the end of the walk, I lift Evie to the sign post to end our ritual by way of making a thank you, a something that says that was nice. And then as we're getting in the car I'm listening to some serious squawking of birds. "Blackbirds, Mama." And I'm like *yeah yeah, what do you know*. And then I look up and there's a whole sky of the creatures flying and squawking about their nests.

"Do you want to see them?" I ask. And she nods her little head and I lift her out of the car and we walk towards the blackbirds, which I'm not convinced aren't crows. Isn't the blackbird song meant to be beautiful? Along the way, we head up on the bank that runs alongside the road and have this mini adventure that feels like a full scale legitimate adventure involving spiky thorns and steep clifftop crevices, as we negotiate our way through a bramble bush to get closer to the birds' nests.

"Mama, why don't we just go down there?" Evie points down at the road and we go down, nearly falling, and I grab her and we laugh and she's right: why on earth did I take her the way we just went? And standing there in the middle of the road, we look up and there they are and after a while I turn to go, Evie in my arms, "No can we stay, it's so beautiful, Mama," and she says this to me twice before we head home, two pink flowers picked from the roadside in my hand. "What are these?" Evie asks.

"I don't know, I've never seen them before," I reply, as her fingers curl around them to keep them close, for at least as long as until we get home.

a leap

We're heading to Clawtooth Mountain. Not so much the home of Arlo the dinosaur, as a hill of sand by the polo fields about a fifteen-minute bike ride away. After meandering slowly, we arrive to discover that Clawtooth Mountain has bloomed: more sand has been deposited, the sight of which causes Evie to rip off her shoes and shoot up one of the banks, whilst I crouch down, planning to use this time to write.

Nice thought.

"Come on, Mama!" Evie calls out. I look up to see Evie rooted by two mud-festooned feet which instaneously shift my priorities. My shoes and socks come off and a moment later I'm leaping off a mountain peak into the crevasse below. It's a great big leap that, once landed, makes me look up, and *phrwoooah, I want to try that again.*

Soon my heart's pounding and the sand is everywhere. But it doesn't really matter. I'm lying in   a nook on the sandbanks, wedged between two vertiginous hills, with Evie standing at the crest of one. "Jump!" I say, joking, but of course sarcasm is a detriment of mind lost on a three-year- old, and so she leaps into my arms as I lie about four feet below her, and we roll along the sand, and I'm laughing and really, I can't stop; the pure joy of being with my daughter along with the rambunctious simplicity of running up and down some sandbanks, creating this bubble of delight.

Afterwards, Evie runs around, whilst buffered by the sandbanks around me I practice hand stands and dolphin pose, neither of which I can really do without a wall, but here with the sand the fear evaporates and why oh why do I forget this? Why do I forget this basic wonder of getting out, and going out to simple places where we can frolic around, so that the life juice that's currently a little depleted gets a boost in great plentiful heaps?

Sometimes what's most precious to us we feel almost guilty about if it in any way doesn't fit whatever mould it is that we've interpreted to represent the way we have to be. It's incredibly fulfilling, then, to find our way back to those moments, people and places that most nurture and sustain us, and that bring with them the kind of belly laugh that only really happens when our nervous system fully relaxes, returning us to our bodies, so that for a moment at least, we say to those near us, not in words, but through our simple embodiment of this structure that we call us, hey, I'm here, I'm with you and there's nowhere else I'd rather be.

[?]

loved, and yet inadaquate

One afternoon, I take Evie to a local softball class. Whilst the class runs, the parents peer over the balcony to watch. I'm looking over whilst chatting with Guy, the father of a boy in Evie's nursery. After a few moments, Evie comes running to stand beneath the balcony, then looking up calls out: "I love you, Mama!"

And I call back to her: "And I love you!"
And Guy, who I'm talking to, turns to me and says, "My son would never say that." I feel a mixture of things, and after a few seconds of feeling awkward I say, "Yeah, but I had to pay her to say that." "Ah well then, I'm too tight," he replies.

And I feel so cheap for having said that. I'm so touched that Evie said what she did; it was so sweet and genuine and I regret having had responded like that to Guy. I feel like I've diminished my relationship with my daughter, when instead I'd have just liked to have said how grateful I am for it.

We parents do funny things in our attempts to be accepted and liked by other parents. And in the end, whether we are making fun of our children, reducing the significance of our relationship with them, or wildly exaggerating it, all of this comes from the same space: a sense of inadequacy. Our ability to remain true to what they mean to us then rests on one thing: that we get not only how much they mean to us, but how much we mean to them.

A week or so later, I'm in London to attend the launch of the Women's Equality Party in City Hall. There're so many of us pouring in that the woman standing at the door, who's meant to be checking that everyone has tickets, is simply waving us in.

"Go on," she says with a smile, as if the gates to the selfish giant's garden have finally opened.

Afterwards, my friends and I go for drinks somewhere that's meant to be super cool and hip, but there's only us and another table of people there, and although they look suitably cool and hip, so too do they seem desperately aloof and uninterested. The Labrador in me wants to howl to them: wouldn't it be so much more fun if we could come together and have a real party, rather than behaving like we don't see each other in this huge magnificent room with one lonely bar man looking forlornly out at sea?

But of course, I don't; focusing as I am on looking super cool and hip.

When we all head home, earlier than I'd hoped for, I get in a black cab who soon engages me in conversation, thus reminding me that yes, Uber may be cheaper, but black cab drivers have an uncanny ability to moonlight as your therapist, delivering pithy instructions a Zen master would be impressed by. I tell the gentleman driving that the reason that I'm looking glum is because I recently moved out of London to live in the country. *I don't come to London much,* I say. *I miss my friends, get excited about seeing them.* The drinks had been a bit stilted, I said, lots of talk, when something in me just wanted to drink excessive amounts of tequila and then head to the nearest dance floor.

"Sometimes you just need to confirm you're in the right place, love," he says, looking back at me in his rear-view mirror. And there it is, just as I'm wondering if I can handle the isolation of country life: release, from a cab driver, on a Wednesday night, in town.

⏰

mothers: the hardest friends of all

It's been about eighteen months since we've moved to the country, and it's taking a while to find other mothers who're available to hang out with; at least as much as we'd like to.

"You can go and say hello," I say unhelpfully one afternoon to Evie during lunch with my family, as she tugs my arm and asks me to come and say hello to a mother and daughter sitting at the next table, as if I'm able to do this easily to strangers I don't know. I feel that pull of Britishness in the centre of my chest, but then I look at Evie, and I want her to grow up carrying this trait of openness with her for as long as she can; in other words, I'll be damned if I'm the cause of any inherited social reticence.

"I'll go with you," I say, and so we get up. "Hi, my daughter would like to say hello," I say, not brave enough to admit that by 'my daughter,' I mean 'we.'
"She's gone unusually shy," the mother replies, her chin gesturing towards her daughter.
"Yeah, well, I guess we came up and she wasn't expecting that." So Evie and I chat a little more with the mother and her daughter, and we're getting on well enough that I think of suggesting a play date, but I've gone a bit OTT recently organising play dates with other mothers, which can take up more time arranging and then invariably rearranging, because one of us has forgotten that we already have a plan on the date that we'd agree to, or something comes up, like a child is sick, or someone is arriving, or a piece of work needs to be done, or something else entirely.

So I don't. But I want to.

⯑

making friends

Luckily, I have a daughter who gives me more than enough chances to make up for lost chances. At the hotel from which we rent Little Oaks, and whose pool we are regular visitors to, if there're other families swimming there, Evie'll tug my arm, "Mama, can I go and play with them?"

We always go, mostly, I think, mostly. "Hi, my daughter would love to say hello," is my opening line, and Evie will smile this huge smile and introduce herself and then we start chatting, and even though sometimes the other kids may resist at first, soon they'll all be playing together. Something about the way Evie just gets on and plays; she'd prefer it if people joined her, but if they don't she just gets on and plays in such a way that soon other kids join in, no matter the age difference. Some even turn into friends – like Lucy and her mother Niamh. So that if we see their car parked outside, Evie will run towards the pool, arms waving by her side, "It's Lucy, Mama! It's Lucy!"

At the beach, we've gone up to a family; a mother, a father and their two kids. "Hi, would it be okay if we join you?" I ask, after a prod from my daughter as we sit there on the rocks with me trying to make this trip fun, but it's high tide and the dogs are all going off in separate directions and I'm beginning to regret coming out here.

The whole family look a little surprised and then say "Of course," and we sit, me lumpy and awkward whilst Evie immediately introduces herself to the two kids, and slowly we start chatting. The woman is reticent; shyer, or something.

And I wonder, if I was there with Tom, and Evie, and a woman and her daughter came over, and asked if they could join us, what would I think? Would I feel threatened? Or welcoming? Because maybe it's a strange thing this walking over and introducing ourselves, and asking if we can join, but Christ it gets lonely, and life's short, and I'd rather try and make friends, or even just connect for a little while than not.

And generally, folks are pretty friendly. Generally. At other times, I'm thinking that maybe *sang-froid* isn't just a French thing.

🔲

a longing

And then here I am: in France, for a friend's hen. It's the first morning after our first night out. Everyone's still asleep. I get out of bed, dress and head outside to the garden to make feeble attempts to meditate, and then move my soporific body through positions vaguely resembling yoga. Vague because the tequila oozing through my pores is dulling rather than enhancing my somatic sensitivity, and the hangover kicking in means my postural integrity is somewhat questionable.

Eventually, the pull of the city gets the better of me, and I head out to get croissants but really to see Paris as she wakes; insomnia finally comes with benefits, as rather than lying in bed trying to sleep, the excitement of exploring quiet streets pulls me out of bed. Because street roaming in the pre-dawn hours is about as splendid a thing as can be. And whilst this isn't exactly pre-dawn, it was at a time on a Sunday morning when most are still horizontal.

My plan is simply to keep the sun on my face; as a result, despite it being early, such is the strength of the sun that I can remove my jumper whilst sitting on a bench, overlooking a square just waking. A man comes forward asking for money. I say no, feeling conflicted. The man retreats, although his eyes remain on me and I can feel his gaze, waiting, just in case a change of heart occurs. I watch a Japanese man with a thick wad of hair cross the road, taking a long drag of his cigarette, letting out a collapse of smoke that reminds me of a 1970's hippy; birds chirp, buses pass and the metro rumbles below.

A mother cycles across the road, her unhelmeted daughter sitting behind her, whilst a waiter walks between tables crowded on the pavement at a café opposite the road. Despite our distance, he notices me and I notice him and even though I'm wearing sunglasses, our eyes meet, which, well, it feels kind of nice. And because we're a funny breed, we humans, having these eyes that we so rarely use, when another human has the balls to simply look and then go on with their day, the impact is a surge that comes with having been met, or perhaps simply acknowledged.

I get up and walk on some more, coming to a park, in the middle of which storms a fountain splurging to the heavens. A pregnant mother, father and their toddler walk nearby. I move off the ledge that circles the fountain so that the daughter can walk past. I smile at the parents. A brief rise of the corners of their mouths are made, maybe a flicker of eye contact; the child has made it safe.

In London we do our utmost to avoid other people's gaze when walking past them; here in Paris it's sought out, or at least this is my perception, my idea about Paris. The city where lovers wrap themselves around one another, no less inhibited than branches on a tree. We Londoners are frugal with our eye contact, because when is a smile just a smile and when is it an invitation for something else? Or maybe it's because we're so busy. Too busy to chat and definitely too busy to look one another in the eye. But also maybe lurking underneath all that busyness is a little question: am I good enough to be seen?

Well, I'm definitely lonely enough, so rather than looking down or away when someone is looking to connect, I've begun to look in their eyes and feel okay. Or even better than okay, because when you really look into another's eyes and they look back to meet your gaze, a communication takes place where words aren't needed and it's a communication that can lift you to the stars, reminding you as it does of all that is most burningly magical about being human: that who you are and who I am is no different really at all. We all herald from the same place and if we ever forget where that is, all we need to do is look another in the eye to remember.

For a long time the look of another really looking at me was an experience I always ran from. Whether a lover making love to me whose eyes were searching for mine, or simply a woman (they were mainly always women) whose eyes saw me and watched, and whose gaze I couldn't return because nothing in me had the comfort of soul to look back. And then life happens to you and the very thing you used to avoid you start to actively seek out. Inspired by people, such as a woman whom I passed one night when Evie and I were living in Battersea and I was visiting Tom. I'd parked my car and was walking on the pavement nearing his house. She passed me, I passed her, I looked at her, she looked at me and we held each other's gaze. When I got to Tom's door and waited for him to let me in, I looked over my shoulder, and the woman and I caught each other's eyes, because she was looking over her shoulder at me; the moment felt sweet, and it inspired me to try some more.

Because here's the thing: smiles stay, so too do frowns, although at this moment in time, it's the smiles I remember softly pulsing in my chest. And though I'm not sure I would be able to remember the face of the woman were we to meet again, maybe I don't need to; such was a moment of connection that it's not the specifics that count. Something deeper and more resilient is taking place. And it's wholly restorative too. It's the kind of thing we humans thrive on and pine for when it's running frugal in our lives: the chance to see and be seen. Not for who we tell ourselves who we are, nor even who we hope one day to be, but simply to be reminded via a look from another that in us exists the universe and so, too, does it in each and everyone else.

In a way, our children are so beautifully connected to this – hence the audacity of the child who dares to stare for second after drawn out second at a stranger, and then still some more. So too the older child who, upon staring at someone, will either determine that they are a kindred spirit, or vocally declare, "I don't like this person, Mummy." And perhaps that conclusion rests on something very simple: is this person going to respect the universe that exists within me or, in their ignorance of their own magic, will they tread all over mine?

⏃

Icarus falls

There're couples who never fall asleep on an argument, and there're couples who never get on a plane or drive away from one another when they've had a disagreement.

Tom and I are none of these couples. And sometimes, we'll do all of these things simultaneously, just to prove a point.

?

amour, armor, ah... no more

"You drive me mad," I say to Tom as I stand on his sofa facing him, my hands resting atop his shoulder. "You drive me madder," he replies, his face a grimace or a smile, there not being much in between. With not much more to say to one another, I head out to the park to walk as she wakes, walking against a changing backdrop as the morning light shifts from pale to moody to bright, the air from fresh to warm. I take comfort in the feel of my feet plodding over an uneven terrain that makes my feet feel naked. The soles of my shoes made obsolete. I stop to lean against a tree, into which my back sinks. One spine held by another. I walk around the pagoda that overlooks the River Thames om *mani padme huming* and then get distracted taking photos of the Buddha.

He's just so big and gold.

I lean against the railing and watch the river flow. She's loaded with plastics and waste: our gift to nature, forget us not! I watch runners run; immaculate men in tight neon shirts, and neat little show pony legs, knees lifted high as they canter down the pathway that runs alongside the river. As I walk, a man with knee-high black socks runs so close to me, in a pace akin to a walk, that his shoulder almost touches mine. There's a relaxed air about him, but his nearness to me sends a frozen chill throughout my body, so I redirect and turn towards the river where nearby a mother stretches her legs against the railing separating the path to the water, whilst her son waits beside her, holding his bike.

Rollerblading women glide past, their yapping spaniels skipping behind them. I watch people sitting pertly, like little chicks on a small boat making its way down the river, and I watch men stretch brown legs with no socks on, in trainers that're more fashion than ergonomically interested in the integrity of their feet, knees and spine. People run alone, together, slowly, quickly, tidily, messily and every now and again, joylessly.

Later, I meet a friend Piers and his son Hubert. We head to the playground. I buy a Twister lolly for Hubert, and say you know this is the kind of thing I would criticise Evie's father for: "And then he gave her a Twister!"

We laugh, but inwardly, a tear drops. There's a well inside each of us that sometimes some memory, some sentence, some sight or smell, stirs in a way that a wave of it will rise, causing old tears to slip out of our eyes before our hand comes to wipe them away. Too often, I reprimand my tears for appearing, or else I try and persuade them that now is not the right time for them to fall, can they come back later? But if I'm honest, maybe this right time is a little reluctant to emerge. Until something in me gets that there's more benefit in tears that fall - which is me admitting that my heart is moved or grieves losses it wasn't given a chance at the time to accept - than there is in showing a dry face to the world whilst in private a heart cracks once more.

☐

yet another

After I say goodbye to Piers and Hubert, I carry on walking. Sadness moves inside, unsure yet if it'll be allowed. When it finally believes and releases, its warmth floods me, and a yawn erupts across my face.

It's a good yawn. A full yawn. The yawn I love to hear Evie do just before she's about to fall asleep. The ones that lets me know she's relaxed, content. Afterwards, I lean against a tree, watching as a couple ride by on a pair of Boris bikes. The woman in front dangles out her left hand, her wrist soft. The man, who's cycling a little bit behind her, peddles quickly, darting out his hand to tap hers before speeding by. They both let out deep laughs that relax the belly and open the throat. Real laughter that when I hear it my own heart roars with a howl of contempt for all the monotonous dramas and complications that Tom and I seem to be sinking deeper and deeper into. Treating our hearts like wild animals whose lives are to be played out in a series of prods and pokes. Each one of us wishes a change in the other; it's a change we can only ask of ourselves.

Wild animals can always be tamed, and trained to behave in ways pleasing to their owners. Wild hearts learn to open and close, sending out feelers to sense if the savannah is safe. But no matter how externally well-behaved either learns to be, whether as a matter of brutalities experienced, humiliations suffered, or games engaged with the spirit of the heart, the spirit of the wild animal remains. So whether we place them in a zoo, or in a lifestyle to which they are wholly unsuited, a lion's roar belongs to the jungle, that place where whole ecosystems thrive and support each other; a place too where our hearts are natives, where they're a part of nature. Not better than it, not greater than it, but as essential as any root, any river, any plant or animal, cloud or ray of sun, and plume of oxygen. It thrives because it coexists with others, just playing out their tune.

Meanwhile two human beings continue to try. They try for different reasons. The whips used to cajole desired behaviour are slightly different, but they try. One tries to be tidier as the other tries to relax around family life. Or we both pause and go, *you know what I'm hiding?*; I'm hiding behind the mess, or I'm hiding behind the need for everything to be as I need it to be. I'm hiding behind complaining and criticising, when all I want to do is love you. I'm hiding because I'm scared.

Motherhood was never meant to happen in such isolated terms, nor was our relationship with our lovers. Our culture is one that neither understands what it is to parent nor what it is to be a child. We are the poorer for it, and our relationships the more challenging because of it.

⬜

a gift

It's the walking into the main room that does it.

Tom's gone to get a brochure, and I sit down and look around, and even the Italians are wearing expressions of wonderment. Sitting down I feel the woman who introduced me to this place, as if she were here beside me, holding my hand. Her presence and grace are as tangible as the collective sense of awe in this magnificent room. Look where we are, darling. Isn't it as fabulous as you hoped it would be?

Tears fall as I nod. Because it is. I grew up listening to stories about this place. About what it was to listen to opera in this room from a woman I loved so much, and with whom I felt such a profound connection, as she became like a second mother raising me alongside my mother after the death of my father.

I watch all the faces pouring in. All with an expression of wonderment on them, apart from one man, who's sitting dourly in one of the boxes, a bored expression pixilating his face. I'm curious: will he crumble? Perhaps not, and then just as I turn to see Tom walking back in, something softens uncontrollably, and a smile escapes from his face.

Just like the rest of us. The magic's finally got through.

▢

oh go on, stand if you want to

Quite soon after we return, Tom and I are taken to the Royal Opera House to see Tosca. English audiences are terrible: we've been so convincingly conditioned to believe that being polite is the most important thing of all that where we could be standing, unable to resist our bodies desire for appreciation in motion, we remain static. *Rigor politis.*

So, we sit and we don't move, because to be a good opera attendee, at least on British soil, it's all about not moving a muscle. Years before in Palermo, in Sicily, sitting with a friend, an elderly gentleman seated in front of us stands, carried to his feet by the singing. His right hand moves as if conducting the orchestra. Peeking up at him, I see a tear navigate the lines of his face. No one asks him to sit. Nor looks away embarrassed at this public display of senility. His appreciation is the very opposite of losing one's mind, it is simply that the largesse of his open heart is throbbing so large as a result of the music that the rest of us cannot but accept him as a part of the performance. Our hearts touched, too. We British outwardly place so much on manners, inwardly we howl for the moon. Thankfully, my Australian/Scottish boyfriend couldn't give a damn about any of that, and so kisses my cheek and holds my hand and places his hand on my thigh. Small things perhaps, but ones that make my heart tingle and skip as a result. Although whether or not I imagine it, I feel the disapproval of the elderly gentleman on my right. And because I'm a heavily conditioned creature, such is my social anxiety about behaving in the wrong way in the most important of places that I move Tom's hand away. Luckily, he's a resilient fellow, and his hand returns shortly afterwards.

Tosca's aria is exquisite, and hearing her, I'm moved, deeply so. This sense that this was really a rather splendid and rare moment to hear a singer like Angela Gheorghiu sing like this and sitting here, watching her, I imagine that I shall remember that moment until others come to replace it, or else I grow old, and now not yet knowing what I shall forget, perhaps this is one of those memories that shall fade. But for now it remains, tangible and alive in my chest. So that as I write about Tosca's aria, although I can't remember the exact words she sang, I do remember sitting there in the red plush velevtness of Covent Garden's Royal Opera House, and the sense of the listening in the room and thinking this is it, this is a moment I shall treasure because it's so damn beautiful and exquisite. After Miss Gheorghiu finishes her piece, we, the audience roar our approval. It's a hearty roar, and even though I wanted to stand and clap, after peering around the rest of the opera house and seeing everyone sitting, I remain sitting. It's an error I look forward to remedying on my next visit.

⏑

Evie's got chicken pox. We're in Verbier, Switzerland, and have delayed our return home until she's passed the contagious period. We head to the local doctor to ask for a letter we can send to British Airways to get a refund on our original tickets.

"But you can still travel," our Bulgarian doctor replies.
"Well, no, we thought that if a pregnant woman or an elderly person were to catch it on the plane, then it can be very dangerous to them."
"Ah, *ppf!*" he replies with a wave of his hand, "this is the evolution of chicken pox. Your daughter only has, let's see... how many spots can you see? One, two, three, she has only three spots on her face! Cover them with a bit of makeup, *e voila*, nobody knows." We stare at him in silence.
"No, I don't think you understand," replies Tom, "this is a decision we've made and we're asking you for the letter." The doctor scrunches up his face, looking at us with disdain. "As you like," he says after a pause, "If you wait outside, the letter will be ready shortly."

After being passed our letter by a dour-looking receptionist, we walk across the road to the pharmacy where the women there give us wonderful Swiss herbs and that pink ointment you put on the spots to dry them out, to stop them itching. My homeopath sends me some suggestions of remedies, including stuffing oats in a sock and then letting that soak in the bath, to soothe Evie's skin. This alone works wonders, creating a cream so soft and gentle that I stay by the bath after Evie's out, rhythmically squeezing the sodden pair of tights, as if milking a blackened cow.

As our days pass, with Evie house-bound, a rhythm develops. We don't have many toys out here for her, I've brought some books and some of her horses, but other than that there isn't very much. At least not compared to the oh-god-we're-so-not-frugal amount of toys we have at home. During the day, Evie's allowed to watch one video a day, with maybe an extension of some Peppa Pig if I'm hankering after more time to write. Although on one of those days, due to some attempt to teach action and impact, she isn't allowed to listen to any stories on my phone or watch a video. And she's utterly fine with it. In fact, she's thriving.

"When we get back, let's simplify," I say to Tom one night. "Not only Evie's world, but ours too." He agrees, and we talk about simplicity and the times in our lives when we followed the simplest days, which hummed with fulfillment and joy. Here at his family's cabin in Verbier which they've had for forty years, it's incredibly simple, frugal even. There're only a couple of pictures on the walls, one of which Tom drew when he was eleven years old, and which is still sellotaped on the walls. But really what is here in abundance is wood: wood walls, wood floors, wood stairs, wooden beds, wood on the roof, wood on the ceilings, and wood on the doors and outside frame of the building as well. The effect created is one of soothing, the natural material acts as a relaxant to mind and body. Our home that we're renting in West Sussex is stuffed with things. So many damn things – mostly all mine.

So, it's funny because I get lost in this idea that to go away we need to go to a hotel that's stuffed with things for the kids to do. Yet we're slowly discovering that what helps our little family thrive is going somewhere where we can be outside, somewhere where we can meet other families so Evie has kids to play with, and Tom and I can meet others too, with whom good conversation can be had, and that's it. We don't even really need that much good food. We can't go out to restaurants at night, so it's simple food, cooked together and probably on rotation, sitting in the same place, night after night after night. Or at least that's what we're experiencing here.

145

a question

Having said all of that, despite the peace and contentment that Evie seems to be showing, Tom and I are struggling to get out of a habit whose grooves we've all too quickly settled into. That old soul corroder: squabbling.

It's only when I storm up the hill near the chalet after Evie's gone to sleep one night, and go and sit by this mountain stream that's booming down the valley where I sit and look out, my pulse thumping as I lean against the rocks, that I have the space to ask: what the hell is going on?

Recently both of us are chafing at the bit to bolt. Outside dynamics are hard, days can be challenging and nights are spent not sleeping. A general recipe for a highly successful and harmonious relationship. It's only here, outside where I have the space to nudge a little closer to this impulse to leap into the future and plan my life away that instead of acting on it I can inspect it, come close enough to it that I'm able to find this small question, trembling in the shadows, it's face down in case anyone seeks to engage, so that I need to bend down to actually hear what it's saying, and when I do hear, I'm surprised. Because behind that charge to just end the relationship, behind the conviction that it must be easier to do this alone is a question: *is he going to leave me*? it's asking, *is he*?
⍰

breathing elementarily

I'm walking up, up, up, I don't know where to, only that the joy of being able to be outside, and walking in a way that's making my heart thump, is a joy. And then the asthma comes and with it too the anxiety: I can't breathe, I can't breathe. But there's another voice: relax, stop, pause. *Be Still.*

"Laura, when you're having an attack, is there any way that you can explore giving space to it, to observe it?" asked my cranial osteopath during one session in London. So because I have no other choice, seeing as I don't have my Ventolin (a respiratory hopefulness), I try this approach, so that rather than reacting when I feel the tightening of my airwaves - oh shit, an attack – instead, I watch it and then right there amidst there, amidst the tightness and clamping sensations around my chest, there's my heart, not cowed, but surprisingly resilient and thumping with joy.

Because no matter the tightness that's clamping around my oesophagus, nor the phlegm that's pouring out of me as my airways inflame, nor my increasingly shallow breath, or the dizziness that I feel as I walk, amidst all of this turbulence, something else stands true, like a wild horse standing atop a hillside, knowing she's free, not trapped.

I can hold this, not so much a voice as an internal conviction. Or rather, something that I'm a part of can hold this, creating space within the intensity, helped unquestionably by the mountains around me, the fresh water streams tumbling past me, and the birds soaring above, like a mother singing lullabies to her child; I'm the more peaceful for it. Although always there remains that internal battle over my ability to breathe, ready to take off at the slightest provocation, uneasy sensations included.

Reality often requires a phenomenal amount of effort to centre myself in. To stop the endless spiraling away of my thoughts tumble-weeding after one another, I need to go slow, to recognise that these images and ideas wailing, beeping and farting in my head create impacts on how I perceive and relate to the world around me. Suffice to say that the effort that goes into many of the things that I'm meant to be able to just do, like breathing and sleeping, drains the effort normally required for other things, like working, exercising and generally spending the daylight hours living like a normal human being.

And yet, maybe the asthma's not all bad, because here I am, forced into a stop by the asthma because I don't need to rush off anywhere, I can just be with it. I'm also distracted by the fact that my bladder is about to implode and so my focus on my narrowing airways is momentarily taken up with looking around for a boulder or something that I can crouch behind. I spy a large rock, about fifteen metres away but because of the intensity of the asthma attack, it's that little bit out of reach. Instead I sit, contemplating a full bladder and diminished lungs and the not being able to do much about either and so I get out my phone and start to write, the sun warming my left cheek. Eventually that soft exhale, the breeze, chills, although I remain squatting down, typing away, watching, observing, writing and slowly, over I'm not sure how many minutes but slowly, my breath is restored so that I can walk further up the path to pee behind the boulder, which is beside the storming stream that torrents by, and beside which I stay for a little while longer, listening and watching, soothed and restored.

⍰

147

if only

The next afternoon, I have a phone call with Vicki, a very expensive American nutritionist who helped Tom's recovery after an operation to remove a brain tumour some seventeen years previous. Vicki's based in New York, and we're speaking about the results to various tests that I had done prior to coming out to Verbier.

"Laura, your body produces hormones to relax you and to help you sleep. It also produces hormones that help your body wake up. At the moment, your body's struggling to produce either. Laura, you're exhausted."

Despite the fact that it's been three years of consistently little sleep, when a good night is maybe four or five (broken) hours, and a bad night, well, no sleep at all, it's only when I hear Vicki say those words that I feel bulldozed with a tiredness that the adrenalin and cortisol pumping through my body had been working hard to keep at bay. I want so much to exist apart from this tiredness, or rather the hopelessness and despair that engulf me as I contemplate another night of lying in bed unable to return to my body so I might fall asleep.

At the heart of this inability to sleep is a feeling that it's just not safe to do so. Convincing my brain otherwise seems to be a work in progress. Because most nights it takes an enormous amount of effort and use of various techniques to get back to sleep once I wake. Typically, I wake every couple of hours and then spend another hour or two trying to get back to sleep. And as with when you have a bad back, or are pregnant, when people hear you have insomnia they know just the solution. Unfortunately, I don't think I'm too far from the truth when I say that, apart from giving myself a new brain, I've tried every falling asleep technique there is. Some things work for a bit, but such is the power of the unconscious that soon enough, whatever technique has worked for a while is relegated to a scrapheap with a large sign reading *Dream On* flashing in an ominous blue light (terrible for the melatonin production). There is one thing left, though, and because it's so impossible, it's the one that needs some paying attention to. So recently, as I lie in my bed, what I turn my attention to is a somatic prayer that my mind will learn to cultivate *the serenity to accept the things I cannot change, the courage to change the things I can, and the wisdom to know the difference*, and that once I truly get this, my body will finally be able to let out a yawn, stretch and fall asleep.

In these "little lives" that we lead, there's a line, so subtle, so fine, so gossamer-tinged in its essence that most of the time I stumble over it, clumsy-footed and cloudy-eyed as I stagger about, caught in endless energy-sucking dramas that can waste a lifetime. And so another night passes with minimal sleep, and really there comes a point where you realise, either I make a stand for this to stop, or it continues ad infinitum. Recently, I've been trying to make that stand. Or rather, less stand and more a position that's horizontally inclined.

But I'm a work in progress, so that right now, in absence of a good night's rest, it's to the outide that I come to not only be restored, but reminded. Reminded by a flowing stream, an endless sky, time-whipped mountains and the wind exhaling on my face. All of which causes my mind to still, my view to expand and adrenalin-pumped body to relax; all things that I look for from my meditation and yoga practices, but which out here happen spontaneously.

If only I could feel this in bed.
⏾

A request, (slightly larger)

The following morning, Evie has a request. "Mummy, I'd like a baby brother and a baby sister."
"When?"
"Tomorrow please."
I'm trying my best, my darling, I'm trying my best.
⏑

returning

I've brought Tom to the Lake District, a belated Christmas present given in May. A gift given with the intention to hang out, except following some disgruntlement with one another, he's gone one way and I'm heading another; two 'gone out for a walk' signs flapping in the Cumbrian wind.

There's a stone plinth at the top of the valley, standing near some other magical and ever so slightly fantastical sight: a waterfall tumbling down. The journey towards them is boggy, and soon my dilapidated trainers are wet through. But this time, I have my essential item with me: my inhaler, so that when my chest starts getting tight because I lack the patience to live a lesson learnt, I fall back on habit, take a puff, and carry on.

Halfway up, I need to pee, and so I find a stone to squat behind. Squatting to pee is an especially enjoyable thing to do. Especially when you've the freedom to stay a while, like I do right now, and appreciate the view whilst the sun warms your bare thighs, which makes me want to take all my clothes off and lie here naked in the warmth. Unfortunately, such is the ingrained horror of acting in a way that'll upset the herd (despite the very obvious fact that the only other herd animals out here are slightly hairier and smaller in stature), I pull up my pants and trousers, turn, and continue heading towards the plinth. And even when the desire to turn and pound my chest like a gorilla sweeps over me, I resist, lest those invisible ones think me peculiar and have me taken off the mountain.

When I make it to the plinth, I drop my coat and jumper at the base, and then walk up and around a large oval slab of stone that reminds me both of Pride Rock, where Simba's introduced to the world, and the place where the Queen of Narnia stabs a knife through Aslan's heart. Walking around it, I find a spot in the sun, where I sit and look down at the valley; the view's extraordinary. Tears start to fall, memories flooding through contrasting with the realities of what exists now. Afterwards, that wonderful thing happens when I stop the resistance and allow myself to cry: softness comes, caressing my body with soft purrs, reminding me of a state I used to know well but, being of a human nature, have forgotten so vividly as to render any memory of it redundant.

Sitting in not too dissimilar a position to the one in Verbier, absorbing an ancient world around me. Two walkers stride past me, imparting a brisk hello. My eyes follow them, and I notice that they're following a path that leads back down to the road that will take me back to Tom.

I get my coat beneath the plinth, and as I do, I see another black sheep and behind him the waterfall. How easily I stray from my original motivation! I walk towards it, coming close to a nearby sheep who seems calm enough. It's okay, I say to her. And she walks a few feet away before stopping to chew some grass again, seemingly unbothered by my being there. Her companion, however, located several feet back, is not so confident; her belly expanding and contracting quickly. I back away, eager not to scare her more.

When I arrive at the waterfall, I pause. Not out of reverence but trepidation. It could be dangerous after all... Standing about four metres from the waterfall, I watch the water cascading down hungrily; how I want to be brave enough to go nearer. Trepidation not reverence and yet curiosity too. So that something in me exhales, and a trust emerges. I step forward, hitching myself over the rock, edging my way over to where the water's tumbling by. The water's so clean, the kind of purity you long to see here in England but so rarely do. There's a clarity and a freshness, and I'm reminded about something I read the other day about nature writers giving in too often to nostalgia; but my god, seriously, how can you not sit by something like this waterfall, in a landscape

151

so wild and ancient, and NOT feel nostalgic?

Eventually merely sitting beside the water isn't enough; I need to taste it. Stretching towards it, cupped hands to capture some and then reverse to bring fresh waterfall water to my lips. I feel like I'm breaking a code by drinking this water. Yet, how the hell have I got to thirty-three without having drunk fresh spring water? And yes, maybe there's a whole gang of sheep above the crest of the waterfall that I can't see, but there's so much hormones and detritus in the tap water that we drink anyway, that how can a bit of sheep piss be any worse? I take a tiny sip, then press the rest of it to my forehead and cheek; a sort of ritual to say *thank you, I'm remembering, and I'm here.*

Amidst the freshness of the water, I taste blood. I've cut my right hand twice on the walk up. One cut was at the base of my middle finger, another at that ridge that rises up at that swell of skin and muscle that comes from the base of the thumb. They're only little cuts, but I guess it's only a little sip. I try again, this time I taste minerals; a taste that's almost exotic it's so unfamiliar, but my god it tastes good and the tasting of which fills me with a reticence about returning to the life I live down there.

"I could've carried on," Tom tells me when we're both ensconced back in his car, looking forlornly out at the valley around us. Silence follows. What is there to say, after all, when you're both craving a freedom that your relationship is struggling to allow?

⏃

reconnecting

"Are you in love with me?" It's a question that could sound playful. Instead I just sound needy. We're at a local restaurant having supper and such is the rocky ground our relationship is currently traversing; it's a question whose answer I'm lacking some serious confidence in. Tom stalls, goes to speak, and then is silent again. My heart drops. Then he starts speaking, or rather launches into an awkward argument that skids and slides whilst trying to put forward its central point: what an impossible thing it is to claim one's love, and really, when one looks at it, what is this thing, being in love?

I would have been happy with some BS, I want to tell him.

Hurt hurtles like a tsunami to my heart, everything in my defence mechanism screeching at me to *Close up! Close up!* And I'm tempted to, really tempted to, but just for once, I don't. I resist the armour, say no to the battle, and instead, breathe into my heart, so that instead of closing shut, it starts to open, further and wider than before.

I hear Tom say something, and relief sweeps over me. "Oh! Is that what you feel? Do you feel *real* love for me?" Oh, Christ, he's panicking again, in fact I think his eyes are beginning to roll around like a man possessed. The eternal bachelor in him is no doubt bellowing at him to just get the hell out of there, just as my anxiety queen who carries this lock to my heart and that she's desperate to use, is getting all fidgety because where she likes me best of all is constricted, not soft and relaxed. My stomach falls, and again that tsunami comes crashing towards my heart, screeching at it to *close up! close up!* All the while sending smaller waves to the rest of my body to *shut down! shut down!*

And yet my body resists.

I'm sitting here, watching him talk, and tears come and instead of wiping them away, I let them fall. I am not ashamed anymore. So instead of just getting on with the dinner, and *phoo phooing* it all away, there's this humaneness of sitting here across from this man I love, who for whatever reason doesn't want to say yes I love you; in fact he's retreating so fast I can see tyre marks from under his chair. He starts to speak, and whilst I listen to him, this strange calm descends: it's all okay. I'm brought back to that place I knew as a child, and that I've felt only fleetingly as an adult, of a place that because of this, and because of that, I grew up to believe didn't exist; to rediscover it brings fresh tears to my eyes. Because despite all the shit we say to each other, and all the shit we do, it's still there, a state so vulnerable, yet bewilderingly tenacious, waiting to be rediscovered. Reminding us that it's not what happens on the outside that matters; it's the connecting to the exquisite beauty that our hearts live every single second; we've simply to allow ourselves to recentre our focus.

Relationships reopen old wounds whose scabs are not yet healed. Lacking consciousness around it, we demand love from our partners. Maybe it is not theirs to give. Instead, if we are able to cup this hollow pain in our hands and blow it soft tender kisses – in the manner that we kiss the foreheads of our children, hoping to impart to them how much we love and care for them - then we have the chance to not only finally find the love that we've always craved, but to tap into its very source: not so much those who sit opposite us, but something closer, and from which we only need to tune into our breath to feel more fully: our very own hearts.

the tests we set for our partners

My father suffered from vertigo, as well as extreme asthma. To overcome the first, he climbed to Everest's base camp. On that trip he wrote a diary, which I'm told he'd write in each evening whilst drinking a glass of whisky. A diary that when he started going out with my mother he passed to her and said, "If you'd like to know about who I am, then read this." She tried, but found his writing obscure. When my father came to my mother, she told him she'd found his handwriting too hard to read. He took it back, and it was never mentioned again.

When my mother first told me this story, I always interpreted it as a failure on her part to better understand a highly private man who was, for a rare moment, reaching out and saying help decipher my heart. Now, though, I see it not so much as a failure of my mother's, but an unnecessary test from my father: if you read this, you'll understand me, if you don't, well then you don't love me enough to even try.

What would it have been if she had simply asked him to sit with her and read it to her? And what would it have been if she'd discovered him sitting there before she'd even asked?
⏾

renewal

"I'm angry," I say, my hands are clasped, my gaze is looking down. Both feet on the floor. Tom and I are in a therapy session. My body's shaking and I'm finding it hard to steady my focus, to hear anyone's words.

"I know you are," our therapist says, a recognition, or perhaps a concession that allows whatever resistance I had left to give way, so that the rigid anger that sits in my chest moves quite unexpectedly to softness.

When the session finishes, that softness has replaced the wired state I normally identify with, so that I can actually feel my limbs as Tom and I make our way to the tube. We hold hands, with me walking a little behind him, feeling a woman vulnerable. It's a welcome sensation, as the fighter in me takes rest for a moment. I enjoy the feeling of Tom directing our movements, of trusting his kindness, shown in the gentleness and strength of his hands.

I feel safe, raw and soft, infused with a pale blue sky feeling, along with a stiller mind. I wish, how I wish I could hold onto this, instead of walking around in the manner of this hard, bold confident person who inhabits my skin too often and whose constant on guardness is exhausting, kicking as she does to the furthest reaches of the galaxy that playful innocence and soft, yet internally powerful presence that I associate with being a woman in blood and in heart.

Later that night, when we're back at home, we make love. Lying beside each other, two naked bodies, skin against skin in such a convincing way that my sense of myself, and all those exhausting priorities and defences that I cling to, disappear.

Of course, as soon as the disappearing happens, I reach across the sensual abyss, and retrieve them back. And quickly.

Once back in my grasp, I reprimand them for sneaking away like that. A life lived without defences: that's only heading for trouble.

▨

learning to make love

I've enjoyed being known as someone who likes sex, confusing this as a sign of being a confident woman, when actually it's not entirely true.

Truth is, I'm still learning.

In fact, recently I've felt more novice than woman who knows what she's doing. I catch myself moving in the way I've seen people move in films, and I'm just hoping and wishing that I've got it right, because please don't let me be a fool and get this thing wrong that we all spend so much time talking about, but never really soar to the source of.. That would be humiliating indeed. But sometimes, something happens that feels a lot like happiness. Unsure of where to go, I hold on to this identity of mine that I'm so loathe to let go of, lest all this happiness simply be a trap. But somehow a relaxing has happened, and I realise this self on which I've so much hanging has gone on walkabouts again. This time, I'm scared. I'm so close to slipping off a precipice that I can't control it. If we really merge, what will be left of me? Of my world and life with its plans that I've so protectively planned out for me, myself, and I?

And so, this goes on, until one day, I hope the merging feels a safe place, a place where no reprimanding or clinging needs to happen. Until then, I'll eye my lover suspiciously: does he know? Can he sense it? Or worse, is he even responsible? And in those moments when I decide that he is, the drawbridge goes up, the foot soldiers come out, and my heart hardens; a little, a lot; it's the same thing.

Occasionally, rare moments appear when I decide that it's okay to trust, and even enjoy this merging, which leads to a sweet softness permeating the air, followed by a joy that skips over to my lover's joy to melt exquisitely into each other. The sunset they leave from that merging, that disappearing, feels gentle, kind and balmy. My skin feels alive next to his, and my limbs want to wrap themselves around him, as my thoughts slip away; the moment is too infused with tenderness to need them.
⏾

rediscovering fun

Tom and I are staying in Santorini, in Greece for a weekend. Evenings are spent eating supper in bed watching a film, days lying by the pool with sporadic short walks in the day. Our hotel even gives us a choice of pillows. I go for the hardest.

But despite the conditions around us, there's a seriousness to the way we are: too much talking, arguing and analysing. On our second day, we're in a restaurant and we're kind of miffed because the food's bad and we're being overcharged, and then we start talking to this couple beside us, who're in their sixties and from Hanover, Germany.

"I've been pregnant for fifty years, and I'm still waiting for something to emerge!" the gentleman roars across the small room to us after we introduce ourselves.
"Oh, you're a double L!" he sings.
"Actually I am," I reply, "My name is Laura Louise."
"Ah, well then you're a quadruple!" Hi garrulous charm fills me with a longing. Here is the lightness I crave.
"You British have always been wonderful gangsters. Us Krauts; so efficient!" When I tell him that my German stepfather has missed more flights than any other person I know, he responds: "Ah yes! 89.9% of Krauts are inefficient. Only a small portion efficient!"

His wife sits smiling; there's a feeling between them of deep friendship and affinity. We don't so much as have a conversation with them as listen to a one-man show. But it's a good show, a warm-hearted show, and I sit and nod and listen, my ears eager for more.

Tom's a little less enthralled; perhaps the image of us two on a weekend away in Greece hadn't included a seventy-year-old German man and his wife, and so we pay and leave. But as we're meandering down the cobbled path I say: "Wait, I have to say something." And run back because sometimes magic needs, if not to be embraced, at least acknowledged.

I find the couple standing outside the restaurant.

"I so enjoyed meeting you both," I pant. "You made my heart so happy. I'm so inspired by how you are with each other – I just wanted to say this." They listen with the grace of elder years. The grace that doesn't take compliments – or insults – too seriously. Realizing instead that here is a woman who, for whatever reason, needs to say thank you. I also want to say that they encapsulate everything I hope for Tom and me to grow into with each other, that their easy camaraderie with each other is what my heart is longing for.

And I can't remember the specifics of what they say in response, but I remember the essence: words soaked in kindness and I want to stay chatting with them but can feel Tom's irritation and so instead I ask them how they make it work, relationship, how have they managed to stay such a unit, with such a sense of fun after so long? The question is long, winding, and ever so slightly desperate.

"We've been married for over forty years and the only difference is that it takes me a little longer to duck when the rolling pin flies across the kitchen," the gentleman replies.

We all laugh. And then silence, looking at each other. My tail wagging. I want to hug them both, but instead pat my heart, and say thank you again, and then lacking for some reason the appreciation of impermanence and the sense that god knows how long I have left on this planet, I say it once more, instead of doing what I really want to do, which is reach out to both of them and give them a huge big hug.

☐

patterns

We're on a walk in the woods, Tom's by my side, two images have merged as one: amber light on brown tree trunks, russet-coloured leaves shimmering like Polynesian girls' skirts and a purple butterfly fluttering by the foxgloves.

I wonder why she's there. Or even, more realistically if she's even there at all. As I look at this butterfly, somehow mesmerising as it flaps it wings inanely, again and again, again and again, and again.

It's an uninspiring rhythm, one that I want to get away from instead of falling into, and yet something inside, some internal wail is mirrored. Some neurotic anxious call that's longing to be heard, terrified that only a pair of deaf ears can hear it and so, of course, doubt its voice, leaving it to flap forever stuck in the same place. It's only when the weather changes and when the soft breeze turns into a gale that freedom becomes real. In other words, only a wind can set it free now. A wind that blows the reassurance of the breeze away, restoring the butterfly on a course.

⏾

restoration

It's Tom's birthday, and I've brought him to a small bed and breakfast nestled in the foot hills of the Pyranees. It's a trip of love-making, snoozes and walks, afternoon snacks of figs, black Muscat grapes and discovering the joys of Serrano ham.

When we arrive, it's late on a Thursday. We're greeted by Herve, who set up the hotel with his wife Sophie. She'll be back tomorrow, Herve explains, and then in an apologetic tone shows us the sitting room. Our room's not yet ready, would we mind waiting here?

Supper is thick, chewy ham and a slab of cheese. At first the ex-vegan in me hesitates, because I eat beef, chicken, venison and fish now but not pork, not the piggies. But it's all there is, and I'm so damn hungry that I reach for a piece of the forbidden fruit and my god, is it good. So that whilst Tom and Herve chat, I sit on the sofa eating this salty ham, thinking of pigs as I chew and of an article that I'd read once that said that these animals have the intelligence of a five-year old child. So, I'm thinking about this whilst eating this ham, holding it in both hands in a reverential silence, my taste buds weeping because it tastes so damn good, and because I'm as hungry as a vulture, ferociously so, I eat slice after slice, simultaneously rejoicing and apologising. Rejoicing because the cells of my body are coming alive and apologising because *oh my, the guilt.*

I come from a family of people with a few vegans of the militant kind, some floating vegetarians and then the rest of us, who are guiltily ordering meat and hoping that one of the vegans or floating vegetarians don't find us and for the love of god if one of them should ever ask: "What are you eating?" lie as if your life depends on it. Because although I was a vegan when I became pregnant with Evie, oh dear kale, I've drifted...

"Where's this ham from," I ask Herve. "Is it local?"
"It's Serrano ham," he replies. "It's not even the best."

Not even the best...

Then Tom leaves the room to go to the loo and I'm looking at the plate with the remaining pieces of ham: one, a small stringy piece, mostly tendrils of fat and a larger, more succulent piece. I know the piece I should take as I've already eaten most of the ham, but I reason that I've never before eaten Serrano ham, and most probably won't again (true, as it turns out, although I did gorge on Palma ham for a good couple of months following this trip). Which is to say: I take the larger piece, followed up with black tea in small porcelain cups so thin I can almost crack them with my teeth.

Later, I'm still ravenous and eat some segments of apple from the garden, which are slightly fuzzy. I chew them slowly, as opposed to sprint through them as I usually do. Next, I eat cornflakes piled up high to the rim of a bowl swimming in thick white milk with a small heavy silver spoon. I eat every morsel, all the while lying in our bed, then glug the thick creamy full fat milk from the glass jug; a vegan no more. I finish with a slurp of water. It's one of those meals that, were I to eat it at home, it might feel lacking; fuzzy apple and cornflakes not being particularly substantial, but on holiday my mind relaxes away from the rigidness that normally clamours for air time, such as what I should eat and shouldn't eat, so that here, this simple meal feels decadent and sublime.

After his walk, Tom comes back and we talk, getting lost in our words as we are want to do; lost and then found. Through the darkness of the room, a thumb appears; his to my cheek in the dark.

160

"You cried?"
"Yes."

Then we make love, as if together naked in bed for the first time. It's delicious and healing and I fall fast asleep afterwards. During the night, we both wake. It's below freezing outside and although I have six blankets and duvets piled on top of me, (possibly seven), they've slipped so that my back, exposed, has chilled. I fall asleep again. Then it's morning. We're bleary, slow, eyes paunchy, baggy, billowy underneath the lashes to touch; skin giving way to pressure, to gravity, to time...

We get out of bed to meditate. Or at least I try to, as my asthma and hay fever kick up with the dust in the room, so that I sneeze and sniff the whole way through. As I do so, Tom looks at me, with kindness, not irritation. As a result, some internal stiffening relaxes and for the final eight minutes or so the sneezes drift away like clouds.

Then breakfast: black coffee and the cornflakes again. We drink apple juice from the garden, chilled by the fridge. It's all delicious, and my taste buds are roaring with delight. Then Tom, who speaks fluent French, gets stuck on the phone speaking to the restaurant where we're having lunch, and who've lost our booking. So that though this is a weekend I've organised for his birthday, he speaks in tongues, and I don't, so he's the one left to negotiate with someone who sounds fairly unnegotiable. Whilst Tom sits marooned on the phone, Herve shows me around. I'm drawn to these black and white photographs of Paris, New York and London that have these little lights sparkling away in them.

"Who's the artist?" I ask, reading the name that's written at the bottom of the photograph. Herve shows me more, then the light dawns: he's the artist.

Afterwards, Tom and I start our drive to lunch. The Sat Nav says we'll arrive around 12.37 p.m. But every time I look, instead of getting closer, the time's drawing away from us, as 12.37 p.m. morphs into 12.42 p.m., which extends into 12.53 p.m.

Most of the time Tom drives as if he's a Formula 1 driver; his driving terrifies me.
"I'm a mother!" I screech as he storms the roads.
"And I'm a good driver," he'll reply, tension tightening his tone.

The reason that our journey's taking longer is the stops we keep making. First to say hello to a lone horse in a large field who, on seeing, we park and walk over to stroke his face, pat his withers and breathe gently into his nostrils.

Then on, on and up to a land where the ice has turned to snow, green to white; The Selfish Giant's garden untouched. We're told later that here there're two inhabitants for every one hectare. And as we drive, winding up the roads, another car passes us in the opposite direction with the driver waving her arms up and down; the sign to slow down. As we turn the corner we understand why. Cows and their young are walking down the road. We stop so I can take some photos. A little further behind the first group, we see more, beside which walks a man.

He's extraordinary looking: sturdy, tall and strong in the way that you just don't see in the cities of our world anymore because men have morphed into a triad of forms: scrawny, thin and bottomless; paunchy, smooth and soft, or buffed, hairless and tight which is to say that it's quite rare to see a man simply owning his ruggedness. As if this is the very thing men are so keen to disregard. This man was none of those things and it wasn't that he was necessarily attractive, or maybe it's because I'm so damn snobby and 'civilised' that I can't admit it, but that he had a quality about him that was attractive in it's rarity. As if he slumbered amongst the trees and stretched his arms to touch the leaves. The broadness of his physique and the intensity of his stare were as refreshing as they are rare. Man now seems diminished. And we women, harder. And as he walks by, I feel both awed and embarrassed. Not by him, but by my own actions: I've trespassed.

Something he lets me see by neither returning my smile, nor even bothering to frown. Instead, he simply stares a penetrating stare so that as I sit there in the car, my iphone in my hand, I sense that I've been rude; taking photos of his cows without asking. In some places on this planet, some tribes believe that when you take a photograph, you steal a part of their soul. Paul McCartney refers to this on the introduction to My Soul, a song he sings on Nitin Sawhney's album *London Underground*. Something about the paparazzi taking all these photos without asking: is this okay with you? I think he's asking for compassion, or maybe just perspective. I don't mean to say that the gentleman we passed thought this, more that in our iPhone snappy world we can forget our basic courtesies, and so risk overlooking others feelings in the face of our need for likes, respect and recognition.

When we arrive at the restaurant, Bras, our noses red, nostrils cold, we're taken to the kitchen and I watch a man sharpening his knives, not aggressively or hurriedly but simply there sharpening the blade; a Zen master could not have asked for more. Then we eat in a room lined with huge glass windows, looking out over blue skies stretching over oranges and burnt coppers; autumn setting the world alight. Lunch is nine courses. We choose the vegetarian option, and ask for our wine pink, and some ice please; a request that makes the sommelier shudder.

Somewhere towards the end, I meet a pear comfit that rivals last night's Serrano ham for sheer incandescent joy. Then tea: I slurp Tom's mint tea, then, after a few sips realise that I prefer my order of Earl Grey, ask to swap. It's a three-and-a-half hour lunch, and along with another couple, we're the last to leave. Afterwards I think that, though it was wonderful and delicious, I'm okay with a hunk of bread, a chunk of cheese and a view. But several months later, after the digestion has completed its course, I think wouldn't it be nice to do that again.

⬚

heartlands

part ii

The following morning, we breakfast on Greek yogurt in minature glass bowls. No honey. Not because it's absent, but because the cream yogurt is so full, tender and creamy that none is needed. After we finish, Tom and I remain at the table talking with Herve and his wife Sophie, who's returned from her trip to LA, where she was visiting their daughter.

They're inquisitive and friendly and though I barely speak a word of French, we make our way through an attempt at talking about why people write, why people love and what it took them to build this hotel. Outside, it's raining and although the surrounding village isn't particularly pretty; inside more than makes up for it. Tom and I sit at the table and drink our coffee. The breakfast table we're sitting around sits fourteen.

"Let's come back," he says, looking at me, "and fill it."

🔲

162

two kings

Later, we head out for another lunch, and then on the way back stop beside a church. After looking inside, we walk out to the ugliest graveyard I've ever seen: a tiny cement space where statues of tortured witches and trolls clutch, with tentacled hands, onto a hodgepodge of grave stones, as if attempting to suck any tendrils of life left lingering from whoever is buried below.

"Look!" Tom calls, and I follow his gaze to see a bull standing atop a hill. A king surveying his land.

Twelve years previous, in 2004, my family and I travelled to Rwanda to see the gorillas. After trekking for a couple of hours, accompanied by armed guards (we were near the Congolese boarder, and tourists had been captured recently), we came across a family of gorillas chewing the cud.

I forget how many there were, maybe fourteen. What I do recall was the quiet intensity of our guides request for us to keep our gaze low. "Do not look them in the eye," he said.

After we'd hung out for a while watching the gorillas, we retreated back into the forest. We were soon joined by a mother and her baby.

"Look down, look down!" he cried. We stood still, our eyes fixed on the ground. The mother seemed relaxed. Her child was in a playful mood, unaware of the inter-species rules of decorum, rumbling and tumbling amongst us as his mother watched on, really watching and allowing this play to unfold. Whilst we, the enthralled, were just grateful to be allowed.

As we stood here, amongst the trees, the little gorilla started playing with my brother's legs: ra da bum, ra da bum went his little arms and hands on Charlie's trousers and calves.
Ra da da bum, ra da da bum.

Who was more delighted, human or gorilla, was hard to tell. After a minute or two, the mother made a gesture, and the child returned to her mother, and off they went trundling through the woods. As we started to slowly back away, the silverback, who'd been watching us this whole time, stood. He was sitting amongst a thick cacophony of leaves and branches, and it was atop this, about ten metres from where we stood, that he towered above us and then, curling his fingers into fists, he brought them to his chest, beating it like a warrior beating his drum: *Ba Doom! Ba Doom!*

The message was clear: *This is my domain. You humans are simply being allowed to visit.*

And now years later, a bull stands tall on a hill in the Pyranees. Two different animals, albeit brothered with the same spirit; they're both Kings of a lost world.

As Tom and I make our way towards the hill, the bull looks at us with inquisitiveness. He's less fierce than the silverback, seemingly without a tribe, he has less to protect perhaps, but as we walk in his direction (his is the best view around) I pick up a fallen branch lying along the way.

"What's that for?" Tom asks.
"Protection," I reply.
"He's peaceful, it's fine."

"I'm still carrying this. Just in case..." Letting my sentence trail off as if I know something Tom doesn't. But he's not fussed; he's incredibly relaxed around wild animals and nature, (it's we humans that cause him anxiety). It's this relaxed nature of his that's one of the most attractive qualities about him; it's also one of the most worrying. As we walk, Tom's body is languid, open, whilst mine is tense and shrouded with suspicion. I was frightened, and although Tom insisted he was accepting of us, I still clutched to the stick, just in case he changed his mind. And yet, Tom wasn't wrong; there was a peace about the bull, so much so that when we peeked over the crest of the hill after a while spent making love on the other side, we were surprised to see that the bull remained, albeit lying down. Not so much a voyeur as an appreciator of the sounds of joy. And as we made our way to the bottom of the field again, and turned back, there he was once more, standing and watching, before turning and walking away.

⬚

longings

We're back home at Little Oaks, and I'm lying here in Tom's arms, moving as moving tends to happen; our love-making already conditioned by the grooves habit wears. At one point though, something stops me and instead of going along in the same way that I usually do, I relax and settle into this this rhythm appearing between us; not so much the dancer, but the danced.

Too often, I'm bewitched by my own thrusts and contortions with life, misinterpreting them for confirmation of the way things are, so enthralled as I am in the myth of permanence. Instead, here I am with Tom, making love, and I feel that woman who wants to make love out there under the stars, except she's emerging right here in our bed; the very place that this woman within likes to declare rebellion against. Maybe it's not so bad after all.

For much of my life it's been normalcy, along with the continuation and sameness of things, that I've so resisted: motherhood included. It's a surprise then to find that contentment can be found not only by traveling to places that I've never been, but right here in our bedroom, in the arms of a man I've known longer as a friend and am more recently discovering as a lover, so that an eroticism sparks in such a way that I almost feel as if we were out there, under the stars, making love in a place only recently discovered. And although it doesn't completely pacify a longing whose discomfort at being so silenced is growing, it does at least soothe her.

⏹

gentle man

A popular modern myth runs like this: wives, women and mothers are always too tired to have sex, whilst men, husbands and fathers just want it all the time. This is an old story, an untrue story and in need of a good updating.

Having said that, for a great part of my and Tom's relationship I've become the no person, but not always for the same reason. Sometimes I say no because I'm tired, and sometimes because I'm too anxious about something else, too cut off from my body to allow any airtime to anything remotely libidinous. But really, these are just surface reasons.

Mostly, if I say no, it's because I feel lonely, isolated and worried. Mostly, if I say no, it's because I feel disconnected from myself and too remote from Tom to be able to find a way back to him. Mostly, if I say no, it's because I don't want to be someone's release so that they can simply fall asleep more easily. And mostly, if I say no, it's because there's a tremor in my nervous system so that despite being so physically close to one another, really, I feel terribly far away.

But sometimes I say no because I'm frightened by how much I want to say yes.

Right now, I'm lying there, hoping just hoping that instead of being hurt or taking it too personally, that this man I share my life with will instead reach across the trenches and be as tender with me as is possible. Because more often than not connection is craved; it's just that words can be poor tools to use to create it. Especially when storms may be raging outside that require so many words to put out, so that sometimes they're the very last thing you want to use. Instead, you want a pair of arms to come and find you, no matter if you say go away. You want that mouth not to tell you about their feelings and emotions, but simply to place a kiss atop your head, or the middle of your brow and then slowly, slowly as your limbs melt towards one another, resistance relaxes because something vitally important within you feels safe. It's only after this sense of safety occurs that you find your limbs wrapping around one another, so tightly and powerfully that as the kissing starts to happen there's no sense of you and he but simply this sense of being kissed and because the sensation of that is so powerful, you don't need to go to your head to create a fantasy to speed your body along, because for now, at least, what's happening in the moment is enough, so that finally, two can become one.

Two Become Four

coffee: sacred

We're on holiday in Portugal in the summer half term of 2016. It's breakfast, and I'm drinking my second pot of coffee. Except this morning, there's zero effect. Not even a slight rise of the heartbeat. Given that sleep remains illusory, exhaustion and I are so intermingled with each other that I'm on the edge, surfing another cosmos. It seems that whereas before I could at least rely on the sexiest drink in the world to get me by, now, not even coffee can reach me.

But it smells and tastes so good, and starting the morning with a cup has become a ritual I'm resistant to give up.

"Are you sure you need another?" Tom asks as he sips his decaffeinated, soya cappuccino.

I don't so much as look at him as growl in reply. He doesn't ask again.

⬚

I wish I'd spoken for the trees

Evie and I are having lunch in a *Pret* in London, and whilst she doesn't really eat, I read her The Lorax. Which for today at least, is our current favourite book of all time.

I look across at Evie, as she decides which morsel of food to eat next, and I see her there, and all that is innocent about her, and finally the truth of the Once-ler's signing off to the young boy, that "Unless someone like (him) cares a whole awful lot, nothing is going to get better, it's not."

When we become parents, our worlds narrow and expand simultaneously whilst other lives play out separately, and yet wholly connected in a far subtler way. Even though we continue to be distracted with whatever dramas are requiring our attention, the truth is that we cannot parent separately from what is going on in our world, on an ecological and wider social level. An absence of kindness at home, like those wasps whispered to me, is probably not only an indication of my own absence of kindness towards myself, but perhaps too of a greater malaise, my lack of engagement with consistent acts of kindness towards others.

And maybe this is the motherhood that has the power to speak to those of us for whom the anodyne modern version of parenthood just doesn't cut it. The version that says do this alone, or in cafes, or is played out on the internet. Do this perfectly and most of all, do this do this do this do this. Maybe this version of motherhood sees more of us on the streets campaigning for the world we'd like to see, for the changes we'd like our families to experience. Because yes, we're all tired and who has the time, but also, what is it to get to the end of life and look back not with a heart full of my god I lived, but my god, I just got by on comfy?

It occurs to me that I am reading *The Lorax* as a desperate attempt to fill my daughter's world with a meaning I worry is lost in the life I am giving to her. Not so much a life filled with travel and meeting people and places of other cultures and life realities, but one that where my very freedom to be the mother I want to be feels restricted.

Part of this is the absence of having the freedom to travel with her as I long to do, and in what feels a void, I have only words. *Trust your heart* I tell my daughter. *Trust your heart, even if an adult is telling you something, trust your heart*, I say to her. Not only so she develops confidence in her ability to explore and investigate and say hello to the world, but so that she develops a relationship with the part of her that will lead her to so much magic. Challenging magic perhaps, but the magic that, once touched into, makes everything else feel but false currency. However, they're words that come with an uncomfortable niggle, as I know that I'm not fully living my own life's instructions.

At least, not yet.

drifting

"Your fruit!" the waitress calls out.

"We forgot!" I call back, wading back through the bath-warm sea towards her. I sign the receipt, and then lift the large plate above my head, and walk back towards my family, sitting aboard a floating jetty abut fifteen metres from the shore. The figs go first, next the watermelon. And then we sit and watch the sun sink into the ocean; having watched it rise in England first. It's the summer holidays of 2016 and we're in Greece for ten days, at a hotel where our fellow guests are mainly other families.

At breakfast, a father goes to get more food, leaving a squirming toddler sitting awkwardly in his high chair whilst his mother's eyes remain glued to her iPhone. The father is gone for maybe five minutes and not once does she look at him. Her son wriggles whilst she sits motionless, with only the movement of her eyes flickering this way and her finger swiping up and down; a glamorous lizard waiting for something to amuse, distract and entertain her. When her husband returns, she lifts her eyes momentarily, as awkward as the child in the face of such non-relationship. At the return of his father, however, the child looks visibly reassured. At dinner, one family sits with the kids watching something on an iPad, whilst the parents stare vacantly at each other with large glasses of wine standing between them.

During the day, there're those families who take up station by the pool and those that prefer to stay by the sea. Occasionally a few drift between the two; it's with the drifters that we find our way. Some families, however, hang out all day together, with no evidence of any iPhones being deployed. Admittedly, these families are rare; there only being one that I see who do this: the mother's pregnant with their fourth child and the other three are never far from playing like mermaids in the ocean.

The oldest of whom Evie falls in love with, but they're such a tribe, we don't end up hanging out with them too much. Instead, Evie befriends eleven-year-old Sari, and her eight-year-old brother Linus, as well as a Flemmish girl Phillipa who's a similar age. As a result, we see increasingly minimal amounts of Evie, who returns for meals and if she wants a hug, otherwise it's Tom and me attempting to find our way back to each other, after momentarily having drifted.

a pause

If only we could behave a little more freely. But tonight, whispers of that wildness I miss can be felt tangibly wafting around us. Sensing it, something inside of me is purring.

So that whilst the sun sinks in such a way, we grown-ups are being pulled towards the shore with our cameras and phones held aloft, our hands outstretched and eyes entranced as we try and capture its beauty; as if walking towards our deity. (Although whether that be nature or Instagram, it's hard to tell). Kids call and shout to one another, as they play free of the usual herding and interfering from their parents. There're some running on the pier, others swimming over to the floating jetty, a few lying on the sun chairs deep in earnest conversation, whilst a brother and sister race along the sand, and new friends wade in the ocean amongst the floating lanterns.

It's an ocean that pulls you towards it. For the first fifty or so metres, it never reaches above three feet, so that it feels utterly safe to let your child wander in and out, as if discovering their own version of a secret garden. Behind us, Evie and Phillipa are leaping across sun beds, though neither speak each other's language, apart from each other's names. "Evieee!"

"Feeee-liiiii-pah!" It doesn't stop them having fun.

Years ago, when I was twenty years old, I spent a pay check earnt working as a runner on a magic show for the TV production company, Endemol UK, on a ticket to Guatemala. Whilst there, I became friends with an Israeli man, Elik, who invited me to join him as he travelled up to Mexico. Once there, we hung out in Tulum, sleeping in hammocks in wooden huts, through which mosquitos would feast on our bottoms whilst we slept.

One afternoon, on a walk by the sea, we came across three Italians carrying a large fish from one of the fishing boats. We stopped and chatted, and they invited us to eat the fish with them that night. Later that evening, we sat around a fire, eating the soft barbequed fish with our hands and drinking beer from bottles. We spoke about god knows what but what I do remember is how much we all laughed, how good the fish tasted, and the feeling of it between my fingers and the joy of sipping beer from a glass bottle.

Even so, what made that night so special wasn't the fish being so good, or the circumstances so spontaneous, it was something else: none of us spoke each others' language. Elik spoke English, but not a word of Italian. I spoke only English and the Italians only Italian. And yet we sat around that fire chatting, laughing – in the same manner as the breakfast with Sophie and Herve in France. Maybe the yearning to connect with others is so powerful that if it's there, small fry like speaking one another's language really doesn't matter. Especially when there's a more timeless language to enjoy: laughter.

Watching Evie and Phllipa play, and even occasionally argue, despite not speaking a word of one another's language, I was reminded of how little we need other than an open heart to connect with others, and yet, for so many of us, navigating our adult hardened years, how hard and remote even that has become.

Thank god then for the hooliganry that abounds in the most childlike of us, always ready to remind those of us who keep forgetting what magic burns inside.
▢

don't tell Tom

Evie's been upping her request for a sibling.

"Mummy, when am I going to have a brother or a sister?" and, "Mama, you've neeeever given me a brother or a sister before." I'd love to give her a brother or sister, both if I could, but there's someone quite crucial in the whole process who needs some persuading first.
"How many would you like, bubba?" I ask Evie. "About twenty-two, Mummy."

Ah, best not to tell Tom then.
⏹

wishes

Throughout the summer of 2016, Evie's request for a sibling comes at least once a day. Friends who've been hanging out with her tell me that this is what she brings up regularly when they're with her. A yearning for a sibling has taken hold of my daughter. Then autumn comes and we're in the middle of September and Evie comes close and looks at me and asks her question.

"Just wait and see," I reply. She apparently takes note of the different response because it's the last time she asks me. And then one day after the first trimester has passed, Tom and I tell her that we have a baby brother or sister coming, and she looks up at me, and wraps her arms around my belly and kisses me. In the initial weeks afterwards, Evie talks to my belly, telling stories to her baby brother or sister.

"This is for my baby brother or sister, Mummy, not for you." And then she seems to lose interest in the physicality of what's growing inside, but nevertheless at nursery, and with others, it's the first thing she wants to tell them: "I'm going to be a big sister!"

But Tom's concerned. "I think she thinks that this baby is going to come out fully ready to party," he says to me. "I don't think so," I reply. He looks at me, full of doubt. And because doubt spreads, one afternoon, some days later, when I'm lying on my bed following a Peter Pan flying session and Evie's kneeling near my belly, I ask her: "Bubba, you know when babies are born, it takes them time to learn to do certain things, like they can't even lift their heads at first." She nods.

"Yes, Mummy, but they can see and hear." "Well yes, yes they can." "Mummy, where do babies come out from?"
 "Um, well kind of down there," I reply, gesturing to the lower part of my body. Evie stares open-eyed at my belly button. "Out of here?" she asks, pointing towards it.
"Um, kind of no, more like around here," I say, gesturing around my pubic bone. Again, she stares at this part of my body, transfixed. And I watch her innocence. I often think Evie is so innately wise and knowing, and yet here I see, over this matter at least, how totally innocent she is, and I vow to do a better job of giving her the verbal and emotional space that she needs for this innocence to remain unruptured.

[?]

173

the art of striptease

I'm three months pregnant, and having a striptease lesson.

My first lesson with Jo had been ten years previous. Realising that I was in love with a man for whom faithfulness wasn't a particular interest, I wanted to do something that would retrieve my sense of feeling good about myself, by myself.

"What are you doing at the moment?" Jo had asked me, as I sat hunched in a chair in the studio she rented, changing into my just bought lingerie.
"I'm at law school," I replied.
"I can tell," she said, "it's the way you move your body."

And now here I am, back on her website. I go on, there's an offer, which is actually two days past its sell date (oh please don't let that be a transferable symbol), and before I can think too hard about it, I click and pay for a private session. And then do my best to forget all about it.

Which I'm struggling to do. So I email Jo, can we speak on the phone at some point? Of course, she replies, when suits? And so here I am about to call the woman from whom I learnt that sexiness isn't how perfect you are, but how sexy you feel. Tom's just taken Evie to nursery, and I'm sitting here on the floor, dialing Jo's number. I tell her that I had a session with her about ten years previous.

"God, I..."
"No, it's okay, I don't expect you to remember me. But I remember you. I just wanted to speak because I think, well, I just wanted to touch base because some things have happened over the years, and whilst I loved the session with you, I just don't know if I'm going to be able to do a striptease like that again."
"Laura, we can do whatever you want. My job is to help women feel relaxed, and at ease in themselves. You don't need to do a striptease, you can just come here, we can chat, we could even just focus on how you feel and move in your body." Jo's voice, a feline purr, relaxes me and I remember her closing words to me at the end of our first session together. I'd just finished my routine that she'd spent the afternoon teaching me and for the first time in my life felt turned on by myself. As I put my clothes back on, I mentioned that I was excited to show my boyfriend.

"No, Laura," Jo's strong voice pulled my gaze from tying up my laces of my trainers, upwards towards her face. "What I taught you today was for you. If your boyfriend is lucky enough to see it, so be it. But this was for you." There was a soft potency about her manner, as she invited me into a world I could sense but my just-twenty-something self was still struggling to inhabit: a state known not so much as self-respect, but self-appreciation. The kind of thing that we can learn from life, but god it takes time, and at which we are seriously helped in our efforts by hanging out with those whose own life path has taught this to them, no questions left. And yet it's something I've become adrift from again. Hence this call with a woman who I'm hoping is going to help me retrieve it once again. "What do you suggest?" I ask Jo, sitting on the playroom floor at our home here in Sussex.

"I suggest," she replies gently, "that you stop trying to control yourself, stop thinking about it too much. Don't bring your greys," she adds. "Look, I don't know what's happened in your life recently, but it sounds like you've lost your confidence." I nod vigorously.

We chat some more and then I say, "There's one more thing I forgot to say, I'm actually three months pregnant with my second child."

"Oh, how lovely!" she says.
"Thank you!" And then I make a weak joke about needing to find a bra and suspenders big enough to fit the pregnancy bloom.
"Laura, I've worked with women of all sizes and body shapes. I've worked with women who have no breasts, or have had operations. This is about empowering women."
"I know, I felt that in the last session." A pause. "Life's so multi-dimensional, isn't it?" I say. "Because I'm guessing you started striptease because of a genuine interest in it, and then here you are empowering women by helping them learn to accept themselves."
"Look, I don't know if we get another life, but I do know we need to live this one. To do what you want to do," Jo says, and then goes on to say something wonderfully life-affirming that I can't remember the specifics of, but the essence was: trust yourself... I want to say something about her voice: it's so soft, womanly, sensual and lovely, but of course I don't. She might think I fancy her, I worry. Missing the point that even if she did, Jo's the kind of woman who wouldn't give a damn. Some people have seen many things, and some people have become too sheltered for their own damn good.

⬚

appreciation

And so here I am, in a studio in Camden, changing into my underwear as Jo changes into hers. Or rather less underwear, more a sartorial sense of humour, which includes a pair of suspenders, some stockings, and a very, very small bra. And I'm just a little bit pregnant.

"Watch me first, okay?" Jo says as she turns on the music and starts the routine.

Jo is an abundance of flesh; the generous side of curvy. Watching her, I'm as captivated as I was the first time, except this time, being a decade older, although necessarily wiser, but at least a little more relaxed in the okayness of finding another woman sexy, I'm able to sit and enjoy watching this woman who's the opposite of everything I grew up believing women should be: i.e. discreet. Instead, Jo's a finger-licking, pouting, fluorescent silk goddess who doesn't so much move as prowl. She moves with a confidence that says yes, I know you find me sexy, because well, I find myself pretty irresistible too.

I know that I have breasts because my mammary glands are of the larger variety, for which I have to wear scaffolding to keep them leveraged at a decent level. I know I have breasts because people comment on them, or at least they did when I was in my twenties, and I know I have breasts because I fed Evie for twenty-one months with them. Other than all that, though, I'm largely removed from them. I come from a boarding school culture where one girl for whom puberty came earlier than the rest of us, and which gave her a beautiful pair of breasts, was relentlessly teased for the way she walked. "She sticks them out deliberately," some of the girls would whisper, looking down at their own flat chests. I took note, and when my own arrived, ignored them as best as I could. Jo, however, is all hands over hers, lifting one here, licking one there. I'm kind of fascinated and appalled.

Fascinated because here is a woman who knows her body so within her own right that it's hard to take my eyes off her. Whereas last time I was awkward and self-conscious, maybe it's the pregnancy hormones, but I'm sitting here and watching Jo strip, and Christ, my mirror neurons are jigging a dance in appreciation, because how often do they get to observe a woman who's so at ease in her sexuality, and whose every movement is so somatically assured? Because here is Jo, the generous side of curvy, with eyes that watch and direct my gaze to where she wants it: on her, her body and her movements. She's teaching me by showing me.

And appalled, because somewhere out there, shaking in the horizon, is my turn and oh please *don't make me do that...*

This, I could do more often: the watching. Whereas the stripping, I mostly suck at. I move as wooden and awkward as a woman trying to be sexy, but still desperately stuck in her own head. And although Jo's sticking with me (kind of), I can see she's beginning to lose faith, which is just a little bit humiliating. I want to tell her that I'm trying, but trying doesn't equate to relaxation, and I think that relaxation and sexiness like to hang out. In some places, I sense it: that place where my ego's grip on my body slips away and instead of this ridiculously impinged situation where my mind contorts my body awkwardly into what it says is acceptable behaviour, my body takes over and instead of a running commentary, I'm enjoyment bubbling over.

Unfortunately, most of the time I'm still this British woman in her head, who was taught not to expose her breasts, and that our bodies are things we clothe - and then ignore, dear teacher, not wear fluorescent panties and stare lasciviously at mirrors that we're pretending to be our boyfriend- and I'm trying to move in a confident way and to access that part of me that can do this; but *oh Dita, yours is an art most elusive.* And yet, I have two hours here after all, so I'm not giving up. I strut provocatively towards my boyfriend, a fifteen-foot mirror towering in front of me, pausing before following my teacher's command to make soft gentle eye contact with him.

"Not like that, Laura!" Jo booms as I stare at the mirror in what I hope to be a suitably demure expression, "you'll scare him!"

And then I turn my gaze to look longingly at the left strap of my dress, which I slowly begin to remove, whilst again peeking a glance at my boyfriend, who's looking just as awkward as I feel. Keen to get away, with a swivel of my hips I turn and walk to the other side of the room, appealing to my inner Jessica Rabbit to help me out here, as I pause and look over my shoulder, and back at my mirror boyfriend, feeling as unsure of my femininity as Jo is assured in hers.
⏎

timing

No matter how much you may fetishize wooden toys and dream of your home looking like a Rudolph Steiner classroom, in this world we live in you can be assured that your child is going to find her way to plastic, and if you're a mother to a daughter, Barbie.

"Bubba, you know Barbie's bodies are very different from women's bodies?" I ask my daughter one night as she sits in the bath playing with about twenty-seven of them. Evie looks up at me, a blank expression on her face.

"I mean, look at me," I say, in a voice I'm desperately trying to make all nonchalant, but even to me, sounds mildly tin-like. "I've got wobbly bits around my waist, hairy bits around my lip, and I get spots and things like that." Evie continues looking at me, a Barbie in both hands. I continue, hopeful. "And well, if you look at Barbie, her body's all tight and narrow, and hard, and well, my breasts hang down a bit, and I'm more squidgy and well, women's bodies, we're a bit more like this." Again, the blank look.

"Squidgy I mean."
"Mum. Barbie's. A. *Toy*." She says this slowly, as if she's speaking to someone who's missed the main point of the whole thing.
"Oh, okay darling, just as long as, well..." I'm losing my sense of this. Evie's looking at me quizzically, and then she goes back to playing with her Barbies, and I go back to picking her clothes off the bathroom floor, the sense that maybe I'm trying to teach the right lesson to the wrong person.
▢

feral body

I'm lost.

I've come for a walk near the woods where we live, down a track I've only just discovered. I can't find the bridge that I'd crossed to get to this mud-sunken field that I'm now wading through. Following the sound of the trickling stream, I come to a stack of trees whose roots have twisted into labyrinths. I've no idea where I'm going, other than I'm following this sense of wanting to get even more lost; only so that I can enjoy the delight of being found. Not by another, but by following my sense of where a path leads.

I crouch atop the bank, which runs only centimetres above the not particularly deep - but deep enough that I don't want to fall in – stream below. I want so much to leap to the other side. Instead I stay balancing on the roots of the trees, as a memory that has yet to die out, of the woman who I might have been many moons ago, or at least from whom I descend, flickers into my thoughts. I feel this woman still taking residence in everywhere that counts: my gut and my heart, though I lack the courage to follow her spirit more in my life, she doesn't desert me, instead she remains close, for when I remember. Till then, maybe it's her who's keeping me awake at night. Too long I've drifted from so many aspects of life that are meaningful to me as I try and etch out a place in a situation I feel trapped by.

Standing on the edge of the bank, I make an involuntary prayer to the Deva spirits: please, guide me across. When I finish the prayer, the long nettle stretching out from across the other bank curves to the right, as if moved by an invisible hand.

I pray again; the nettle stays still. I don't feel brave enough to leap; the water's cold and the idea of falling in and making my way home drenched this fresh October night has limited, if any, appeal. I move the nettle with a branch to see if it makes a difference. It doesn't. Then standing, I take of my coat and jumper and throw them onto the other side of the bank. Now I have to cross: my housekeys and phone are in there.

Just as I'm preparing to launch myself across the metre or so wide stream, I hear a crackling sound, as the mulch that I'm standing on gives way. I back away, just in time to avoid a full earth slide of miniature proportions, as the ledge onto which I'd been crouching gives way.

I back away, weaving around the tree to my left, looking for another jump point which, of course, was there all along, two metres away from me on the other side. Here, all I have to do is step across half a metre or so of stream, over the tangled roots, half expecting them to wake and wrap themselves around me. Then clomp over the nettles to retrieve my things and through the undergrowth and bracken to head home. A home it takes a depressingly short time to retrieve; it's hard to get too lost these days.

As I make my way back, I sense that woman prowling inside. Not so much running free, but walking, alone, wondering what's gone adrift. I attempt to supplicate her with occasional howls of joy, and to some extent these are enough to cause a wag of her tail, but what she really wants is to run loose in real wildness, to make love in the fallen leaves, to make a home out of mud and twigs, to sit with others around a campfire that roars, to howl, sing and cry, and share stories with others. I swear mud beneath the fingernails pertains to this spirit. It's why I'm loathe to remove the dirt from my fingers, if I'm ever lucky enough to be engaging with nature in such a way that some finds its way stuffed up there; maybe if I let it stay, the thinking goes, alchemy's bound to happen and my life will be transformed.

reconnection

Sometimes alchemy happens when we least expect it. The following day, Tom and I leave for Italy, as I'm taking him to Italy for his fiftieth. When we arrive at the hotel, we're told to wait in the car park and are soon picked up by a mud-splattered jeep; a glorious contraption, stinking of musty cigarettes and so filthy inside that when we tumble out ten minutes later, we look as if we've been dancing with hippos.

When we enter the hotel, the owner, Marcello, greets us. "There's half an hour left of the spa," he says. "Go. Supper is at 7.30 p.m.; there'll be a bell."

I've forgotten my bikini, so wrap a hand towel – the only towel that's available in the spa - around me. Which, with encouragement from my tightly-held hands, just about covers my bottom. Luckily, we're alone.

The heated plunge pool is dug into rock, the light electric turquoise, the walls tower above us, the water's two degrees not yet hot enough. Tom walks in behind me, down the steps, butt-naked, his towel in his hands. I feel frozen: we're away for his 50th, this is clearly an ideal place to make love. In fact, it couldn't be more romantic: staying high up in the Umbrian hills, soaking naked in a stone pool, alone.

Yet we've been arguing, and I'm not able to let go of some of the things Tom has said on the way here. He leans over and kisses me gently. I freeze.

"I'm sorry, it's too soon. Or quick, or something," I say, feeling guilty. I didn't want to upset him. "Do you mind wearing your towel?" I want him not to be offended. To get it. To get that maybe he can ask me questions instead of expecting instant physicality. I wish he didn't so quickly feel rejected. That maybe he could sit next to me, to understand. Instead he moves to the other side, turns on the bubbles, then stands.

"I'm going to check out the sauna." He leaves, and I exhale. In this aloneness, I feel something in me relaxing, the alchemy, it's starting to happen.

A woman in a black swimsuit comes through the door, stepping down into the pool. I sit there with my tiny towel wrapped around me. Five or so minutes later, Tom comes back in. His towel's barely there. I feel embarrassed for the woman, is this awkward for her?

I look over at Tom, wanting to meet his eyes. To say, hey look, it's a good thing we're not making love, we would have been interrupted, but he won't meet my gaze.

No one says anything. The bubbles bubble. The silence's strangely soothing. I feel myself relax. The woman leaves, Tom and I remain.

"I'm going to go and do my practice," I say. Meaning to meditate.
"Okay."
"Are you coming too?"
"Yes."

We get out, and I stand under the shower's hot water for a couple of minutes, then stop, remembering the small sign in our bedroom encouraging us to "Use water sparingly," and quickly turn it off.

We head back to our rooms together. The bedrooms are so small – the hotel used to be a monastery – that each room only has a single bed, so that Marcello has given us a spare one for free. In my little cubby hole, I sit on my bed and try going through my practice, reading the Buddhist mantras, but my eyes are dry and tired, so I close them and meditate instead, which causes another decimal of relaxing to happen.

After a short while, I stand and get dressed, finishing with my boots, which need lacing. And it's here that another part of me emerges, a part who I felt yesterday in the woods and who's being tempted out of her hiding place, here in this monastery, where all light is by candlelight, and rooms have only what's necessary in them, and around us is a thick expanse of seemingly never-ending woods. I watch as she takes the laces of each boot, wrapping them with a slow enjoyment around each coil. The sensuality of simplicity luring her out to play.

A bell jingles: supper's ready.

?

At first, we wait in the sitting room. Other guests are sitting around in silence. We copy. Then Marcello comes in and introduces us to another couple. With the exception of the evening meal, here, guests are encouraged to talk to one another. The tables are shared, not exclusive. Then we go through to the reception and are given our napkins. Two rolled into one brass circle with our bedroom name on it: St. Francis of Assisi.

We walk through to the restaurant. There's no electric light, only candles. We sit at the table at the far end. A woman sits with us and we don't even have to exchange pleasantries: here, dinner is served in silence. The three of us sit facing the wall, in which creamy white, monkish candles sit flickering on black candle sticks in jagged holes. Throughout the meal, only water is served. Each course is brought to you, removing the anxiety involved with ordering. There's nothing to order, only receive. No small talk to be made, only the Gregorian chanting playing to be enjoyed.

The first plate arrives: it looks like cabbage that's been massaged with some kind of sauce. My hand picks up the fork and, scooping up a hearty mouthful, rushes it to my open mouth. Quickly my lips close around the fork, pulling in the cabbage and enjoying discovering heaven in a mouthful. Out goes the empty fork, around goes the cabbage in my mouth, as my teeth rip into it and my taste buds dance in delight: *oh Christ!* The small plate is gone quickly. Next, I eat a small roll. My lips come to its soft warm crust, and something around my diaphragm releases in silent reverence. The bread is gone, my eyes close. I feel tiredness sink into my muscles. I hear what sounds like voices, ghosts of a past rustling by like autumn winds in the breeze. It's an utter relief not to speak. I pour some water from the terracotta jug, listening as it sloshes into my glass in a way that makes me want to convert my whole kitchen into a shrine for all things terracotta.

I wish that Evie was here to experience this deep deep peace. To share the profound joy of sitting in silence with others. I remember how breakfasts would be eaten in Spain at a yoga camp I went to for two summers at the age of eighteen. After five hours of yoga, we'd sit on a bench overlooking the Ibizan hills eating bowls of fresh fruit and porridge in utter silence. No one had to talk; if you were desperate to, you could go and sit at the talking table, which was generally empty. You didn't even have to look at anyone in the eye and smile, you could be gloriously miserable. Steadfastly focused on eating and only eating. No social niceties needed. And how glorious it felt to walk past someone and not even need to smile. Sometimes liberating moments happen in portals most unspectacular. Nevertheless, their legacy is felt for a lifetime.

I turn to look at Tom. He's sitting straight, looking ahead. I kiss his neck softly three, four times, as silently as I can. Then I lean against him, reaching out for his hand, which he holds back. I feel myself coming back to him through the utter peace of silence. The sensuality of the food, of tasting, listening, feeling. By being given space.

Tom and I fight so habitually, which is crazy given that we do love each other and care for one another and given how much we both have wished to be together. Yet despite all this, we war too frequently. And yet when our pride and fears finally release, there is such magic waiting, and how I wish we would remember it more regularly. Thank god then for Italy. For where our minds sluggishly recall memories of heaven, Italy simply exhales them.

Later, when we go to our rooms, we undress quickly and get into our single bed. I turn the light switch off on the walls, and then turn to Tom, our bodies facing one another. We move towards love-

183

making slowly, all the while my attention stays in my body, the chatter of my mind stilled.

For those times when I have allowed my body to respond at her own pace, the result is always that I'm able to show up for love-making. I feel my body pressing against Tom's, skin on skin, and of the depth of our kissing, and I feel aroused in a way that I haven't for too long, as the trembles travelling all over my body bring me closer and closer to the sensuality of that woman who I rediscovered walking in the woods yesterday. I can feel so much I'm almost overwhelmed. And so, the waves crash, the sun and the moon rise and then sink, as the earth spins and two humans hopefully work it out.

silver lining

At some point between arriving in the Rome airport and leaving the airport, I lose my passport. Most likely last destination: the rubbish bin into which I'd dropped the newspaper that I'd swiped from business class on leaving the airplane. Subsequently, instead of returning to England on Sunday evening, Tom and I have to stay the night in Rome, as I have to be at the British Embassy first thing on Monday morning. I don't have an appointment, as we only came to the decision on Sunday morning that my passport was indeed residing in some recycling plant.

At 8 a.m. Rome time on Monday, I call the British Embassy, getting through to a woman. The only potential flaw in this is that this woman is not sitting in an office in Rome, but in London.

"All the appointments are full. Why don't you call at 9 a.m. when they open?" she suggests.
"But wouldn't it make more sense if I was there at the embassy at 9 a.m. in case they can see me immediately?"
"You can try. But they won't let you in without an appointment."

Luckily, I have some pretty good motivation to get me home: the wish to see my daughter, or rather the very powerful longing to *be* with my daughter. Appointment or no appointment, I'm getting my replacement passport, and despite the fact that his birthday weekend has ended with him staying in another hotel, I vow that the both of us will be getting on a plane that afternoon. After a rushed breakfast, I head to the Embassy. I've too much pride to leave behind my rucksack, which is at breaking point it's so stuffed, for Tom to take in the car. Google Maps says that it's only a twenty-five minute walk away, so I strap it over my shoulders and march out of the hotel. Unfortunately, though Monstro is a handsome looking rucksack, it's rather useless at its job, because rather than decreasing the weight of what's inside him, he actually accentuates it. Like one of those baby carriers that leaves you feeling as if it's not limbs and blood of a wee mortal that you're carrying, but planet Jupiter itself.

The walk ends up taking about forty minutes. Losing faith in Google, I start asking passersby for directions. They end up being even more unreliable than Google and I'm sent this way and then another before finally being sent an entirely different way by someone else. As a result, I arrive at the Embassy looking exactly like the kind of person that security is trained to keep out. I call the number to book an appointment, whilst pacing up and down trying to work out where the entrance is. I get through to a woman, location of desk unknown.

"I'm a mother," I pant at her. "I have a four-year-old daughter. I must get home tonight." I'm ready to launch into a monologue, whose dramatic arc I'm hopeful will persuade this woman of the utter necessity of me returning home that day, but it seems there's no need. At times when things appear to be crumbling, once again, I am filled with a determination to reassure both myself and my daughter that our lives will remain normal. Whatever that may mean. My being home for Evie is our normal, hence my determination to be there for her now.

"Can you be here immediately?" the woman asks. "I'm here now."
"Where?"
"Security."
"Okay, they'll let you up in three minutes." I'm shown the room to leave my belongings in. Monstro, my backpack, is too big for the locker, so I leave him sitting on a chair in the waiting room. "Just

leave it there," says the security man.

"Will it be safe? It has my computer in there."

"Yes, yes," he says, waving away my concerns as if I'd told him it contained a couple bags of pasta. When I'm let through the door on the other side, I jog around to the main entrance. A man on a bike is in front of me, and I stop jogging, not wanting to make him feel awkward lest he find it strange that a woman is coming behind him, and then I think screw this, and run ahead instead. At the reception, a woman with iridescent green nails is on the phone. She's wearing heavy make-up, a thick metal Galliano belt and a bored expression.

"Lift around the corner, second floor on the right," she explains, gesturing me away. I race around, get upstairs and go to the counter. There're two men there behind the glass counter. I explain my situation. Say I've paid online.

"Laura Fraser?" One of the men asks.

"Yes, yes, that's me." They give me two more forms, one to check and initial. Then the other man says, "We'll let you know later."

"But I'm a mother, I have a four-year-old daughter, I have a flight returning this evening. I have to be back. My mother, she can't look after my daughter." There's a woman behind me.

"Did I say something? Did I say that I did not know these things?" the man speaks in a tone that makes my skin crawl. "Where's your son?"

"My daughter. She's in England. With my mother."

"Ah, she's in England. I see. We have some other things to do, then we do yours." "Oh, you can do it today?" I say with relief, realising that I'm not being fobbed off. "Yes."

I retreat and sit down. A few moments later, a couple, who I guess to be in their sixties, walk in. Seeing that they're just as confused as I was when coming out of the lift, I point to where the men are. "It's just around there," I gesture.

"Oh, great, thanks," says the woman.

Later, once it's clear that we're all going to be waiting there for a time as yet unknown, I ask the woman if she's lost her passport too. "Yes - in Sicily!" We start chatting, and introduce ourselves. It's a conversation that discovers a few connections between us. They live in a community called Findhorn, in northern Scotland, where Bruce works for the organisation Trees for Change that I've just been reading about in George Monbiot's book, *Feral,* which I'm currently devouring.

We talk about Eileen Caddy, the co-founder of Findhorn, and of her consistent courage in following her inner voice. A woman, who when she found herself complaining that there was no room to meditate in her caravan which she shared with her husband and their five children, heard her inner voice reply, well there's room in the public loos, so go there if you want to practice. So that every morning, around 4 a.m., no matter the miserable Scottish weather, she'd walk to the public loos to meditate. We talk some more. They used to live in an eco-house that they'd built in New Zealand whilst living in a community there. "We built those mud bricks ourselves," Lucy says, pride in her voice.

"God, how was your sleep?" I ask. They look at me oddly, a little surprised.

"Well, actually..." And then she tells me about how they were living off the land, and completely off-grid, but despite all this, the power that was supplied to their house was "dirty electricity." Apparently if electricity comes from the wind turbines, it's okay, but if it goes through these cables into your house, it can be incredibly disturbing.

"We hardly slept for eighteen months." "God, you must've been exhausted." "We were. But we were in denial. It was so ideal. It was Bruce who said we need to go home." Lucy paused and then continued, in a quieter voice. "I had a cancer scare. But Bruce. Bruce has cancer. Those cables caused it." I look at Bruce standing tall in his sandals and grey beard. His dappled blue eyes alive with a quiet strength.

"It was Bruce's inner voice that told us to leave," Lucy added. "May I ask where your cancer is?" I ask Bruce. "I had a tumour on my tongue. That's been sorted out. But it's now in my lungs. I've got lung cancer."

"What's the prognosis?"

"The doctor said I won't be alive by Christmas."

"But Bruce had an insight. His intuition told him he has five years," adds Lucy, hope and something stronger: trust, shining in her eyes.

"How do you feel?" I ask. Bruce smiles, shrugging his shoulders.

"Okay, a bit phlegmy sometimes around the throat."

"If you don't mind me saying, you don't look like someone who only has till Christmas. Your life-force seems so strong. You seem so vital." He smiles good-naturedly.

"I probably shouldn't say this," says Lucy, looking around, "in the British embassy and all," her hands gesturing around her, "but he's been taking CBD oil." Referring to the non-hallucinogenic part of the cannabis plant that's said to have powerful healing qualities to it. "It's incredible."

"Yes!" I say. "Yes, it is! I've been taking it for my asthma. In the vaporiser form."

"Bruce has been taking it for five months now; we went recently for another scan and the doctor said the scan looked exactly the same as before. The cancer hasn't grown at all!" I tell them about Tom's brain tumor. About how he had surgery and then used to go to the healer John of God once a year in Brazil, and how he credits that with his healing.

Then I'm called up, and another woman has come in and I sit down and she chats with them. I pick up a newspaper. I'm then told my emergency passport will be available in an hour. I'll go out to a cafe then, I say. I want to ask their email addresses but feel embarrassed in front of the woman, so smile and say goodbye in case they're not around when I get back.

I find a local market. Buy tasteless black grapes, and giant nectarines that resemble squashed cabbages, along with a punnet of raspberries that I don't realise are mouldy until I've sat down at a nearby table and popped a couple into my mouth. Beside me are five Italian men in their seventies, sitting around a table talking loudly with empty espresso cups in front of them. I sit and write, and after forty minutes return to pick up my temporary passport.

Walking through security, I pass Bruce and Lucy coming in. His arm swung loosely across her shoulders. They look relaxed and at ease with each other. They clearly love and care about one another, and I feel a surge of longing in my heart. We smile at each other, stop and say our goodbyes, and then go our separate ways. I wanted to ask for their emails, so that we might stay in touch. But I don't, feeling shy. And this time I can't even blame the other woman.

alternative means

But our meeting has a legacy. Because a couple of months later, here I am, with the ambulances outside my house again. The local doctor has been here on another home visit, prescribing steroids as "the only thing that'll stop the asthma attacks." I take one, and it makes my womb creak. I remember Bruce and Lucy, and him trusting his intuition, and I think screw this, and so I borrow one of the pots of cannabis oil that my mother's much loved housekeeper Grace has brought, one for herself and one for her sister for her grade four cancer after I had told my mother and her about meeting Bruce and Lucy.

I go with my intuition, and start with the weakest strength. After a couple of hours of taking the oil, and this is after four days, maybe five, of chronic constant wheezing, my asthma stops, my airways relax. I can breathe. And then I start getting better. Slowly and with a dip about three weeks later, as after a few nights of minimal sleep and a couple of late nights out, I get bunged up again, feeling the tightness return in my chest. But I continue with the CBD oil and slowly my health returns. No steroids needed.

coming back

It's Sunday morning, on 11th December in 2016. We're in London, at Tom's apartment which overlooks the park. Tom's still sleeping, jet-lagged from returning from the States yesterday, and there's a pale blue sky stretching outside the windows. I turn on my phone, check my emails, and then go on Facebook. The first thing I see is that the food critic and writer A. A. Gill has died. I read the few articles that there are online so far about his death the previous morning from cancer. It's two weeks before Christmas. He leaves behind his partner and four children.

After reading the articles, I meditate, sitting there in the room, the morning light coming in from the park. I don't so much as watch my mind as let it run. Sparked by the whisper of the thing that in the end probably propels our efforts to transform our lives, more than this wish to simply heal. When faced with the prospect that our lives could be over any day now, what we're most grateful for is our family and our friends. Thinking we have forever, though, we continue with our dramas; healing can be for tomorrow.

Except sometimes, it can't.

After eating breakfast and recording my dream of the previous night, I walk to the bedroom which is at the back of the apartment. The whole apartment is saturated in this warm glow. There's a softness in the atmosphere. The room is deep with sleep. I look at Tom, who's fast asleep, and then sit on the bed, just watching him. He stirs, and I get under the duvet, and into the nook of his arms, and lie there beside this Silver Bear, simply full of this experience of watching him. This man I love and am so often utterly perplexed by.

People often ask, "What do you love about Tom?" A question I struggle with because it feels like there's a right answer and a wrong answer, and I always come away with the sense that I've given the latter. Lying here now, it's clear to me why, or at least how, I love him. I love Tom not because of the best of him, but because I know the worst.

I fell in love with Tom because of his light, and yet I can love him because I know his darkness. Which is to say, the last two years we've weathered too many arguments and disagreements to remember. We've both dreamt of running in the opposite direction, but we haven't: we've stayed. And really the truth is that I love Tom not because I'm invested in being with someone who's so good, so kind, so wise, or even because I can accept his weaknesses, his instabilities and insecurities, but because in spite of all that which I can get so fixated on, "he's all this, or he's all that," the place where his loving and my loving really happens has nothing to do with any of that. Just like those Cambodian nuns showed me.

Tom's not perfect, and nor does he have to be. And my god if anyone knows my ability to be mean, critical, dominating, selfish, haughty, patronizing and maybe a little bit pious, it's Tom. And yet he loves me. And because most of the time when he tells me this, yes I hear it, but I don't really absorb it; my defence is too on. And yet this morning, it hits me: *Lau, what can there be that's more precious?* Because at the end of the day, when our life slips into death, what is left other than the essence of how we loved; how far did our love stretch?

But I regularly flounder from this because sometimes the struggle to remain afloat amidst the dramas and tensions between us means the only way that I can fathom us remaining together is to ask for space apart. And yet slowly, I'm learning to, instead of asking Tom to leave and go to London for a night, or more, instead of saying go, I'm learning to say stay.

I've heard the solution towards arguing is to go towards instead of away from that which hurts. But the tendency to bolt is so engrained in me, as it is in Tom, that to move to the opposite end of the pole and remain where I am is both unsettling and a deep relief for me. Cutting off ties can feel like clarity and closure, but if it's done too brutally, it can leave a hole, that only denial that it doesn't exist or the will to address it, can heal. But nevertheless, our coming together is happening, although fitfully at times, and occasionally with a drama that can be exhausting. And yet something is brewing between Tom and me, as we come to experience what relationship means for us, given who we are, how we are, and why we are as we are.

So here it is, right here in the gap between his shadow and his light; here exists the real essence of him untouched by either what is most wonderful or what is most rejected and most dark; the creation, as it were, of what lies beyond all of his most brilliant and worst capabilities: the essence of what makes us all human. And it is to this that my heart is rehoming and in this journey discovering a person I've known all along.

The rest is just distraction.

golf: minimal appeal

The following day, Evie and I head out to the park to roam, and end up playing miniature golf. Evie soon grows bored of trying to bat the ball into the holes, and so the golf stick is dropped, and instead I watch as she embraces the mounds, rivers and bridges for what they truly are: a landscape to play out a whole world.

And because we're alone, apart from another mother and her daughter who every five minutes or so lies on the floor to scream, it seems okay to abandon the rules of miniature golfing for now. I want to go over to the mother and hug her, but instead sit offering a smile of comradeship that I hope says I totally utterly get it, but her gaze is so fixed on the ground that it goes unnoticed. I turn to my phone and start writing, and then my battery dies, so I meditate as Evie scampers about. After twenty minutes or so, a waitress comes out.

"Your pizzas are ready," she calls and so we head inside, and rip at the hot tomato cheese-drizzled bread. Noticing the music, Evie comes up for air, and puts hers down.
"Can I dance, Mama?"
"Of course," I say, and so she gets off her chair and stands by the table and begins to twirl and lift her arms around her head. Her movements are not big gigantic moves, but small, contented ones. I wish I had the guts to join her. But in the company of other families, namely another table made up of two fathers and several kids, I feel too choked by my own Britishness and so, instead, sit back and watch Evie dance. The fire in her heart kept stoked.

⊠

New York

We're in the Children's Museum in New York, or at least we're trying to be. It's the day before New Years Eve, and it's raining. Subsequently the place is heaving, as we stand in the queue with other families politely snarling at one another as we fight for place under the awning.

Tom, Evie and I have come to stay at Tom's father's apartment in central New York. And now here we are, inside the Museum, in a windowless room that reminds me of that place where Pinocchio's taken along with the other boys, all of whom are running around like lawless attaches on anything's that's vaguely climbable before being turned into donkeys.

If only we were so lucky.

Judging by my fellow parents, there're two options to fill our time. One: flick mindlessly through your phone, or two: failing being able to physically evacuate the building, do the next best thing, which is kind of similar to that father in the playground a couple of years previous: pack your psychological bags, shove a kick into your mindfulness aspirations and head right out there into the cosmos, as your attention atrophies and you drift off into some kind of space-time continuum black hole. Judging from the amount of blank eyes that're staring out into this sea of over-sugared, nature-deprived, lung-hacking slices of the next generation, this is the favoured option.

In the loos, Evie and I pass a mother standing with her bawling child as she dries her hands. "Hmmm, isn't this fun?" the mother asks, in a voice that implies she chose the second option, and has yet to return.
"Meet your future," I say to Tom, as we meet back outside the play area. He grimaces in reply.

easy

Afterwards, we head to Central Park. Immediately Evie sees six squirrels and sprints over to them, chasing them like Bongo to the trees, which she circles. The squirrels even seem to be enjoying it. Don't these little people normally come towards them with outstretched hands and peanuts instead of chasing them like those four-legged animals? One goes to dash up a tree, only to twist a one eighty and bound off in the opposite direction.

My entire system settles.

We walk over to an Alice and Wonderland statue of the Mad Hatters Tea Party, donated by a husband in memory of his wife, "because she loved children." And then we make a deal to one another: we have five days remaining in New York. Let's ditch the tourist stuff and hang out in the park.

It's a deal whose terms don't need negotiating.

🄯

better

The next day, we return to the park, to climb mountains that we'd seen on our way to The Children's Museum. Some large black rocks, close to the knackered-looking horses whose fate it is to pull selfie-taking tourists around a park that they're not even looking at. And whilst Tom and I wobble behind her, Evie leaps across ravines of increasing girth, whilst we call out for water breaks and time outs. Truth is, this is the most fun I've had on the trip so far: chasing my daughter across these black rocks in the middle of Central Park, enjoying the feeling of my body being used.

Evie's a fluid climber. Attempting parts that I wouldn't even have imagined considering at her age, and which require me pulling my almost five-month pregnant and heavily winter-clothed bulk up with the help of a hearty push from Tom engaging his full strength as he heaves his hippo of a woman up a narrow ravine in Central Park.

"Are you sure you want to do this?" he asks, panting, both hands on my ever growing buttocks. "Yes!"

When we're done with the climbing, we head over to the playground, which looks like a miniature metal stone castle. We embark on a game of tag, Tom chasing Evie and me first. We run, climb, jump over and we laugh. My god we roar. Along with water and tissue breaks, Tom and I kiss often and Evie comes and over to wipe a snotty nose over Tom's face. Eventually we collapse into a heap on the asphalt. Evie doesn't want to leave. Two kids in superhero outfits launch themselves nimbly into the ocean nearby.

"What are they playing?" Evie asks with longing in her eyes, as her two more senior playmates lie hyperventilating on the ground beside her. A boy of about eleven runs past with the speed and silence of a deadly assassin, whilst a girl in a t-shirt, with gloves and wiry, stick thin legs, stands atop the slide with a bunny hat on her little head. Her father stands nearby and I wonder if her mother saw her outfit before they left the house.

Then two kids come along and start playing some music. We lie on the floor watching them. Evie and the little girl, dressed for more temperate climates, start dancing together. Jiggling their hands and shaking their waists. One of the guys runs and flips himself into a somersault as he soars over the asphalt bank. The other cartwheels and flips and turns and we watch and clap. When they stop to take a break, I go over to them.

"What's the name of what you're doing?"
"Oh, there're loads of names: free running, gymnastics, tricking. Look, this is more like gymnastics," the young man speaks excitedly and then swivels to the left with about three short strides catapulting himself into the air, as he lands three aerodynamic somersaults and then some kind of spin thing on the floor. "And this," he continues, "is free running." He makes his way over to the railing that runs around the playground and casually leaps over it, before turning back to it again and propelling himself over it gracefully.
"Like that guy in the James Bond film!" I reply, feeling not too dissimilar to a dorky teenager. He ignores my comments and continues chatting, the young man by his side joining in.
"Yeah, so I earn a decent living doing this."
"You do this professionally?" I ask, impressed. "Yeah, well I do it all the time so I might as well get something from it." I can't help but wonder if he's telling the truth, or an inflated version of it. I want to believe him. "My cousin over there, he's a gymnastics coach." He gestures to the young

man who Tom's chatting with, his voice tender with pride.

"How long have you been doing this for?" I ask.
"Me? Oh me, like for six months," replies the younger boy.
"He's thirteen," the older one says, turning to look at me. "And yeah, well I've been doing it probably since I was about eight." He tells me how they do kids parties "and things" and I sense a pitch. I say goodbye, and the three of us head back.

Turning to us after supper, Evie says to Tom, "Today was a long day."
"Yes, it was."
"Yesterday was a long day. But today was a long fun day."

We agree, sweetheart, we agree.

⁂

Never again

We left for our trip to New York full of the excitement of possibilities. We return a single time zone family. Or rather such has been the horror of jet-lag on top of a generally sleep-deprived family that Tom has sworn off all travel involving more than a two-hour time difference EVER AGAIN. It's a way of thinking that's to become a source of much disgruntlement between us, as the yearning to show Evie other parts of our world takes a stronger hold. But for now, at least, we're joined by a common view to not go so far, in such cold weather, to places that don't even want us there. We get off the plane thinking never again, and then Evie turns to us as we stand in passport control.

"That was a wonderful holiday, Mama. When can we go again?"

⏍

a stand

Towards the end of the month, Evie, Tom and I head to London one weekend to protest the day after Donald Trump has been sworn in as President of the United States. My chest virus is refusing to go and Evie's sick as well. We drive up, coughing and snotty with my throat feeling as if it's been razored.

"Are you sure you want to do this?" Tom asks. "Yes! It will be inspiring, it's important, it will lift us, I want to take part." And so we arrive in London and Evie starts screaming because we've piled about twenty-two coats and jumpers onto her, and she can hardly move, and our plan, okay my plan, of walking over the bridge towards the tube is crumbling, so we order an Uber and head to Le Pain instead for hot chocolate, and croissants, to boost morale.

Arriving, we eat a huge breakfast, I down three coffees, all the while fobbing off Tom's looks, "I'm fiiine." And then we Uber it again to as close to Berkley Square as we can get and we get out where the statue of the animals is and Evie's excited to see them and then we follow the others there towards the square: for my and Evie's first march. We've bought her scooter and she falls off and is grumpy and tetchy, so I pick her up and Tom's looking at me in that way that says she should be walking and my asthma is starting to kick off, but I refuse to leave, I want so much to be a part of this moment, to say no to Donald Trump and everything that he represents, there's something bigger and more magnificent than you and it's represented by all the thousands of people who are here.

People's faces show awe and wonder, and maybe a little bit of shyness; the rarity of us all coming together and making a stand for what we believe in. The square's packed and on the way a young woman tells us that there's a family part to the march and shows us where to go. When we arrive we are surrounded by toddlers carrying banners, kids in prams, kids being carried and older kids moving about. Dogs scuttle about too. Evie's grump disappears and there's this sense of magic in the air. We head towards the Ronald Reagan statue; Margaret Thatcher's gift to the American Embassy.

"Can we go there, Mama? Can we go there?" Evie's pointing and we head as close as we can towards the statue atop which people are standing, and cheers are breaking out and people are clapping and everyone's waiting and there are balloons and helicopters in the air and students calling out to each other and shouting to their friends and apart from one woman in a wheelchair with a hand-held tannoy shouting, "Fuck the fascists! Fuck the Fascists!" the whole vibe is one of excitement, togetherness and strength.

Evie wants to be close to the action, there's a sense of almost waiting for someone to speak, for something to happen and then very slowly, without any fanfare, the procession begins: families leading the way. And so we start walking with them, and as the walk turns down to Pall Mall, we stand aside and walk towards Hyde Park. We've only been here for about forty minutes, but both Tom and I acknowledge there's zero chance of Evie making it the two miles on her scooter, and we both lack the juice to carry her, and we've come, turned up and I'm guessing there's going to be plenty more time to come on protests over the years, and so we walk away towards a fountain which is covered in ice and pigeons, which Evie alternates between breaking and chasing, and then we make our way to the roundabout and order another Uber and head back to Battersea, to our cars. If we leave now, we can beat the traffic.

☐

don't tell anyone, but...

I'm growing my armpit hair. It wasn't a deliberate decision, it's just winter, which means that my arms are generally always covered, and as it's country-life living, generally, my armpits remain covered as well, hidden in layers of clothes.

I did try to grow it deliberately last year in the spring, and then got scared by this dark tuft sticking out of my arm and so shaved it all off. But then came December which passed by without any need to shave and so too did January. And now here I am, a week into February, the snowdrops, crocuses and daffodils are appearing in our garden just as the brown tufts of soft hair are lengthening in these grooves at the top of my arms and neither has the world ended nor has anyone pointed at my arms and fainted in traumatized horror.

"Have you noticed I've grown my armpit hair?" I asked Tom the other night as we lay in bed. He lifted one arm above my head and I can't remember exactly what he said other than the feeling that to him it didn't really matter either way.

Which maybe is a good thing, as I have another secret: I've got hairy calves too. Although this one is known by Gabrielle, an acupuncturist who has started to come and see us over the last month since sleep has drizzled away again and this bloody virus which is lurking in everyone's lungs is refusing to evacuate this piece of somatic real estate that it's taken possession of.

I'm also vaguely aware that I need to do something to my bikini line before we go away to Morocco next week. Thing is, courtesy of the baby bump, unless I jut out my pubis bone, and suck in my belly, the reality of my wildly abandoned bikini line is something that I'm blissfully sheltered from. I'm aware, through the sensory organ of touch that I also need to trim my pubic hair, but finding that moment when memory, scissors and nakedness come together is rare. So it continues to grow unabashed.

To be honest, I'm not so partial to the hairy legs but there's something about the armpit hair that I wish I had the guts to be more okay with. I shave for no other reason than that not to do so would repulse the menfolk, and people would think I was a stinky old hippy with a hygiene problem. Thing is, I've spent some time with hippies with long armpit hair and they were neither stinky nor bad to look at. In fact, I thought they looked absolutely beautiful. And yet such is the conditioning that a part of me is wriggling in discomfort, lest anyone discover my guilty secret.

So here I am, with my clandestine armpits, feeling closer to my body as a result. And whilst I don't think I'll have the guts to keep these armpits hairy come our North African trip, and that, even if I do, for sure these long, soft hairs will be razored away by the time our British climate manifests our version of a season called summer, for now at least, my hair follicles are being emancipated. So that, though I probably don't have a whole year to enjoy them, at least I will, for one more week.
⍰

Morocco

After nearly a three-month break from Instagram, I return to it on the last day of a holiday in Morocco over the February half term. It's all so... instant, bringing with it the illusion that every notification is a priority, that every comment needs to be answered immediately, which creates an internal frenzy, like fish-feeding.

Later, waiting in our bedroom, the fire crackles as the mist descends outside amidst the darkening sky, as Evie lets out a yawn before falling asleep in her room off this sitting room where I sit on a cushion on the floor.

The following morning is as cold as Switzerland in February, bringing with it a freshness and the necessity for Evie to cover her bare arms. At 10 a.m., after a breakfast that refuses to end, and in which my pregnant belly gives me the perfect frame to indulge: no one thinks I'm bloated from over-eating, merely blooming in pregnancy. An illusion I gluttonously take advantage of.

Then we head out with Pepito the donkey and his owner, a man of about four feet eight with a hunched back and wiide smile that reveals a large front tooth, and a gentle demeanour that never changes. Evie, preferring to walk, goes in between Tom and me as we follow Pepito upwards over the red Moroccan earth. Though it's fresh when we leave, it's hot on our return. So hot in fact that my limbs grow heavy, and I curl up on my left side in foetal position whilst lying by the pool. Tom takes Evie to play chess in the room. The sun warms me, I don't want to get up, but know I have to. I get up, lumbering to the restaurant like a buffalo who's just been drugged, resisting the urge to lie on the floor and fall back into a deep rest. We've spent eight nights here so far, two of which have seen me get about five hours sleep, the others six, averaging around three to four hours: I am blitzed by tiredness. After lunch, we go inside, the clouds have come, and Evie's watching Babe on my computer, and I retreat to a hot bath with two books. After a while, I think Babe has been going on a long time, but the books are good, the water's still warm and so I stay, marooned in my aquatic nest a little longer. When I do leave, *Babe* seems to be taking a really long time to get past the middle part of the film.

"Bubba, have you rewound it?"
"No, Mama."
"Are you sure, bubba, because it's taking a really long time to come to the end." A pause.
"It did it itself, Mama, it took itself back to there," Evie says, leaning forward and pointing at the halfway point on the bar at the bottom that tells you how long's left of the film.
"Okay bubs, enough now," and I close the computer and there's some stomps and grumps. "I'm going to be strict with you now, Mama." And then she starts writing on a postcard, or rather angry drawing in circles, followed by a request for me to write the letter 'c.' I do, and then she asks me to write the word "pillow" but I've gotten over-zealous, and am busy writing the letters 'u' and 'n' too, to show how they're the same shape as the lower case 'c' just positioned differently. This upsets Evie, greatly. She takes the postcard and pen and hides them in a book. Then returnd, bringing them back. "Mama, I didn't ask you to do that, please be responsive," she says, looking at me with an expression of disappointed seriousness. "I'm sorry, bubba, I got over-excited." And then I'm given a second chance, and she brings out the postcard again, and I write the word 'pillow' under her name.

Then she goes to meet Tom up at the top of the hotel. "I'll go ahead, Mama, I'll see you up there." And she runs off and I make my way up five or so minutes later. Before I leave, though, the luxury of of simply sitting here on my knees, doing absolutely nothing; an unexpected moment of utter peace and stillness, too delicious to resist.

man on a bridge

"Laura?"

I'm walking over Albert Bridge in London with Evie, and turn to look back, and there he is: a man I became so very quickly besotted with who wasn't so besotted with me but who played with my heart in a way that the last time we were together, he literally left me standing on my bed in Ladbroke Grove, my mouth open in a silent plea for him not to walk away as he not so much walked out my front door but leapt out of it. And now here he is, standing at the arch of Albert Bridge. We walk towards each other, with Evie in my arms, and kiss each other's cheek hello.

"Help!" I say, laughing. The wind's blowing, and Evie's scrambling all over me, her scooter's dangling over my arm, and my six months pregnant belly is, well, pregnant. I mean, help me walk my daughter to the end of the bridge, but he looks at me confused.
"This is your daughter?"
"Yes!"
"She's beautiful," he says. Evie squirms over me like a monkey. I look at his face and notice, not unhappily, that he's podged out a bit, causing a reduction of his sex appeal that kind of delights me.

I have actually seen him a couple of other times; the last time I was about the same stage pregnant with Evie. He didn't notice then and I don't think he's noticed my pregnant belly yet today. We chat a little more, and then say goodbye because what else is there to say, and by the time I've got to the end of the bridge, I've forgotten about him and it's not till the next day I remember again and think *shit, I've barely thought about him.* And then spend my time thinking about that. I think too of how, despite his ability to cause a good bruising to my heart, his arms were arms that as soon as my head touched at night, my mind would mellow, my body would relax, and I'd drift off fast asleep.

"Just like that!" he commented once. "Asleep!" To which I had no reply; the answer was too weird. Because I had known a place where I felt that safe before and slept so deeply, but not since I was a child: the arms of my father.

🯄

grief

I don't remember the last time I saw my father, but I do remember every single moment when my mother walked towards me as I played with friends and my brother, who'd just turned five the previous day, on the stretch of green outside my grandmother's house in West Wittering in the South of England. I remember looking up and seeing my mother walk towards me. I remember her solemnness, and I remember the way her boyfriend stood silently by her side. I stood up, and went towards them, doom booming in my stomach. And as we walked over the stones and pebbles down to the beach, before she said anything, I knew.

"Something's happened."
"It's Daddy."
"Yes, darling. Yes it is." After she'd told us, I sat watching my brother building a sand castle.
"It's for Daddy. We can show him when he comes back."

After the initial shock of my father's death had retreated into numbness, my imagination began to try and soothe the pain with suggestions I was all too willing to accept: *Daddy isn't really dead, he's just simply gone away.* What I couldn't work out was why no one could tell me where he'd really gone. And so I watch the film *The Railway Children,* which explains the whole situation: clearly something similar had happened to my father and all I had to do was keep a lookout for the day that "my daddy" was going to come home. And so I listened endlessly for potential loops in the conversations around me that might provide clues for where my father had gone, and why he had yet to return.

Over the years, occasionally I dream about my father. No matter the content, there's always that extraordinary moment of seeing him alive again. And although often I discover that the reason that he left was that he has a new family, I don't care; at least I get to see him again.

Daddy! I call.
Sometimes my father will look at me blankly but with an expression that says clearly: *who are you?*
She's your daughter, Malcolm, a friend will remind him.
Oh, he says. He's forgotten who I am. And yet I've not forgotten him.

Although of course I've tried, in that way where you push down or away those memories of ones we've loved who are no longer around, because you don't have the space to reflect on what it meant to have them alive, nor the courage to reflect on what it means to have them dead. Maybe because of this, the grief has hung around.

⏻

easier to project

When it became clear that the width of my feelings for the French man were slightly at odds with his somewhat horizontal feelings for me, I emailed Lydia, a family friend who lived to her late nineties in Sydney, Australia and with whom, though I never got to meet her in person, I corresponded via email for around a decade asking for her help with my dreams.

"This man has a quality you need to embody yourself," she replied to me one day, after I'd sent her a dream which included the French man, and after I mentioned that although my head could see that he and I were not meant to be, my heart was struggling to let go.

"The question is, what is that quality?" The only thing I could think of was the peace I felt in his arms just before I fell asleep. Which was bizarre, as I hardly knew this man, and I'm not sure peaceful is necessarily the quality that I would use to describe him, but then I'm not sure I would use this word to describe my father, either.

A couple of days after bumping into each other on Albert Bridge, I received a Facebook message from him saying it would be nice to go for coffee sometime.

"I think my coffee drinking days are behind me," I reply back, "but if you and your family are ever in Battersea Park, let's all hang out."

The answer to Lydia's question was finally clear: the quality was peace of mind. The solution to finding it: not falling in love with unavailable men, but learning to trust my heart. Because mirages of water appear when a bodie's capability is so stretched that our subconscious tries to create a convincing image of what's really needed, in the hope that it may give us a second wind, and spur us on a little longer. The danger is when we're so convinced by this mirage that, instead of redirecting our search towards what is really going to quench our thirst, we end our search. It's then that instead of growing lighter with the expansion and rejuvenation that true refreshment brings, we become heavier and stagnant with atrophy as the mirage chips away at the most essential part of ourselves that we need as vital luggage if we are to continue on our way to searching for that place where we know that all we long for exists.

⏎

cloud drifter

Which is to say that this heart has had enough of the battles that can take over each day. The loud vociferous battles, and the subtler, harder to detect ones that only those who play them often know.

So that it's a funny one, because there're these ropes pulling me back to earth, and I can see this ship and I can feel the clouds falling further away as I'm tugged back down. And I feel mildly resentful about the whole pallava: cloud surfing being a particularly wonderful pastime that can be hard to let go of. But as I get closer, I see all these people who make my heart crumble, expand and dissolve: in particular, my daughter Evie.

Whenever I get the chance, I will tell others, "I have a daughter!" Often, it's the first thing I want to share. "Hello! I have a daughter!" This little person who I'm watching grow up, always so her own person. And this is a relation that I'm slowly, slowly getting. So that everyday life gifts me the chance to get to know Evie all over again.

She who is a lover of all things sequins and adores her cousins Freddie and Lottie with a heart of a lion and loves shows like... well actually no point in me saying which show, because they do seem to change quite frequently, and who likes to watch the T.V. with her nose pressed against the screen, lest it disappear.

Who's teaching me the importance of consistency, and boundaries, and softness, and perhaps most of all kindness. And who is my greatest inspiration that the shit in your head don't matter nearly half as much as just showing up. And I sense she's trying to teach me something else, or not so much teach but show, but I keep missing it, I'm so earnest in my seriousness to my devotion to parenting in the right way, dear daughter, I'm continually missing what you want to show me.

Or maybe it's because our children will ask of us what is hardest for us to give, and it has nothing to do with princesses. I've written about it being to do with presence, but now I'm not so sure.

?

finding a rhythm

It's 5.10 a.m. on a Monday morning and I've been lying here for about an hour, willing myself to get out of bed. But finally, I'm out, I turn the lights on, brush teeth, put on bra, then t-shirt and jumper whilst keeping my pajama bottoms on; few things beating their comfort. Then I tip-toe out of my room, past Evie's bedroom, towards the stairs; the first of which is a creaker. The second, too. I misjudge where the creaking starts and place my foot squarely on what sounds like the creakiest part of the whole staircase. Shit. My second step is just as creaky, as are the others.

Bugger. Bugger. Bugger.

I head to the kitchen. Maybe I didn't wake her. I creep about, lighting candles and pouring water and stirring in these repulsive probiotics and various morning concoctions. I open my computer, and feel the blankness in my mind. Nothing. I'd like coffee, but I'm pregnant, so avoiding caffeine. Then I hear creaks from upstairs. Little creaks. A moment later Evie's face appears around the banister. I go to her.

"Why are you up, Mama?"
"Bubba, I'm writing. Come on, come to bed, it's still the middle of the night." I thank the lord for the darker mornings now it's mid-September. As we get to the top of the stairs I see from the open doors that she'd gone into each of the spare rooms to see if I was there. I wrap Evie up in her blankets and bring the duvet up to her. Leaving her door a little open as I walk away. I go back to the blankness as I try to negotiate this book. I write some crumbs and then again I hear little movement, and sense my daughter watching. I look up and see the mound of her head behind the banister. I go to her again.

"Mama, why are you up?"
"Because sometimes adults get up early to write. Come on Bubs, go back to bed."
"Well sometimes kids are hungry in the middle of the night." I crumble. Of course I do. Then I retract; the sleep trainer wouldn't approve. Aren't I sending confusing messages? But then if I give her something to eat, there's more chance that she'll go back to sleep and I'll get a chance to write. It's now 5.53 a.m. She didn't have much supper last night and Tom's keen that I stick to the *well if you don't eat your supper, fine, but then no snack till the next meal* deal; something I've been able to uphold at least once.

"What would you like?" Silence. I realise my error: presenting a question with too many options. I leap to make amends: "A cracker with butter or an oat biscuit?"
"Cracker with butter please, Mama."
"You stay here, bubba, as it's light downstairs." Please, stay where it's dark, stay sleepy. Don't wake up...
"I'll wait here, Mama," Evie says as she sits at the top of the stairs, her little feet side by side. So I head back downstairs, butter two crackers, pour some water in a glass and place one of her straws in it. Then I walk back upstairs, a mixture of anxiety and annoyance beginning to boil in my system: why did I wake her up? Now she'll be tired at school. She gets up and we walk towards her bedroom.
"Will you move the toys there, Mama, and I can put the other cracker there," she says, gesturing towards the steps of her bunk bed, where some wooden camels hang out. She's eating one and I give her some water, which she gulps down.

Then, again the ritual of her getting into bed, me wrapping her up. Blanket then duvet then kiss then words: "Stay in bed, bubba." I half-believe them myself; this time I sound almost begging. Downstairs again, the writing is flowing this time, and Evie remains in her bedroom, for a while at least.

?

sensuality of a house plant

A couple of weeks later, Evie and I are heading to Devon. It's a Friday and we're heading off three hours later than I'd planned after an impromptu swimming session administered in the hope that my four-and-a-half-year-old daughter will have an outlet for her energy to compensate for the long drive. But that's to underestimate Evie's energy levels... The journey takes three and a half hours and it's only in the final hour and twenty minutes that her eyes finally close and she sleeps.

When we arrive, Evie carries in her white basket, the one that was mine as a child, and which she's filled with a collection of her toys, including the big soft elephant, her wooden lions and various other animals and creatures she plays with.

My friend Erika, who's hosting the weekend, is at the entrance and shows us our room. I haven't seen her for maybe two years and I'm being all cool and low key, when really what I want to do is hug and grab her shoulders and say thank you thank you! Because when she sent out the email asking if anyone was interested in coming together for a weekend in Devon and yes, our kids are welcome, after kissing my phone I responded in the only way my intense longing to share with Evie this culture of retreat amongst friends and strangers who no doubt become friends knew how: by replying **YES.**

Whilst I unpack, Evie heads downstairs to meet the others, in particular Saiorse, Erika's twenty-year-old daughter who's studying mathematics at university and doing some work at the kitchen table. Or at least attempting to, but there's Evie, all questions and "Hello, I'm Evie, what's your name?" So that for now, at least, her work is put aside. Which is not too dissimilar to the state I find myself in: given the fact that there're six other kids there, ranging from Henry, who's nearly five, and Aryan who's twelve, I barely see my daughter for the rest of the weekend so that it's *hi mum, bye mum* and at the same time, there she is, Evie: growing, blooming, phasing into a new stage of her childhood, and here are we at this precipice of welcoming her baby brother so that this period we've spent so much together, these last four and a half years, is coming to an end. And here we are, with the both of us in heaven. Evie because she has these awesome willing and friendly playmates around her, including Alice in Wonderland, who's been doing Vipassana retreats since apparently she was first born, and is also a mother. But there's one major difference between us: Alice has never lost her temper.

"What, never?" I ask her.
"No, I just never went there," she replies. I ask the other two mothers present, the four of us all single mothers, "Well, what about you guys?" and both nod their heads and look at me with grimacing expressions and guilty eyes.
"Um, no, definitely lost my temper," says one.
"Christ, me too," says the other.

So here is Alice in Wonderland with whom Evie hangs out with for two days, which means I get to join in the yoga; the longest practice I've had in years. Afterwards four of us dance around the room. Erika comes around and runs a mist through our hair, an aroma that is pungent and opens up my senses.

"What was that?" I ask afterwards. "I feel like I need it when I give birth. It's extraordinary." "It's a South American thing," she tells me and I sniff the bottle and it smells nothing like it did when I was dancing. Because when I was dancing, afterwards I turned to my right and there's this huge plant to the right of me on a ledge and I'm dancing and the light of the South Devon hills is pouring in

207

and I'm staring at this big, long-leafed plant thinking *Christ, that's really beautiful*. As I bob about the room, it strikes me how rare I'm touched these days by the sensuality of life. Yes, I appreciate nature, it revitalises and restores me when I head to the woods, but I'm not soaking in its sensuality, simply benefiting from it at its most simple level: its ability to restore.

What a loss.

Because right now that big, bountiful plant and I are, if not communing, definitely vibing and, well, it feels better than alright because the more I can appreciate the beauty of this house plant, then the more I can feel into the sensuality in my own skin, so that there she is again: that woman who emerged in Italy amidst the lack of electricity and the candles and the little monk room, and here again in a little loft in a very simple retreat centre in Devon dancing with three others, on a Saturday morning before lunch.

Simple ingredients: maximum impact.

⏃

insomnia makes a friend

1.30 a.m. has drifted into 4 a.m. and I'm still awake and so I get up, surprised that I feel, well, awake and I put on my contacts and head downstairs to the kitchen and make a cup of tea and then get out my computer. After about ten minutes, another woman, Judy, walks through. A fellow insomniac, she can't go back to sleep either, and she's also a writer and a mother and this is kind of awesome: insomnia has a friend...

So whilst Judy sits on the sofa near the table, we move between writing, interrupting each other to pass comment about something and making cups of tea. Insomnia doesn't feel half as lonely when you have company to enjoy.

Around 6.15 a.m. there's a sound: Evie's woken and I head upstairs and curl up next to my daughter in her bed and we lie there chatting till Bunny's woken up, because these days I'm exploring just accepting that's she awake rather than trying to get her to go back to bed till the bloody bunny's light has gone on.

"Is Henry awake yet?" "No love, Henry and his mum are asleep." "What about Aryan?" "He's asleep too." "Are you sure? Maybe I'll just go and check." "No love, it's Sunday, let everyone sleep and besides we need to have a shower and wash your hair. You had a pajama day all day yesterday." And now it's my daughter's turn to resist, so that all her energy goes into resisting the inevitableness of this shower. A shower with wonderful eco credentials, but sadly not so accommodating for two bodies, especially one wriggly one who doesn't even want to be there, and whose temperature seems to change every thirty seconds, so that I'm either shielding Evie from being splashed with ice cold or incineratingly hot water. But eventually we find the right temperature and the resistance's replaced by something that feels a lot like enjoyment and so we take our time, washing hair and then getting out, and I give Evie a towel and then reach for the other, realizing my mistake, as this one is the size of a fairy's hand towel. But the coldness invigorates and after we get dressed, I head downstairs and Judy's there curled up on the sofa, her eyes closed, perhaps not asleep, but in rest.

I feel it too, lady, I feel it too.
⏃

stop

Or at least I do until later that morning during the yoga session, when my heavily pregnant body feels torpedoed with exhaustion. I stay there in forward squat, slowing down, sluggish and then feel a pair of hands on my back, slowly stroking and massaging and pressing in deeply around my pelvis. And there I stay, sinking deeper into a squat that despite not being particularly comfortable, my Britishness coupled with my worry that if I temporarily stop her, Gabriella will stop all together, means I feel too awkward to say: this is amazing, but can I just change positions?

But the bliss eventually outweighs the discomfort, and for the next ten minutes Gabriella massages me, so much so that the muscles in my face sag as my nervous system calms down. And later when we head into *savasana* I fall into a deep relaxation; I'm only woken by the sound of my snores.

In other words: I've found my doula.

⏹

I walk on this land, returning.

It's drizzling and I'm walking slowly up the steep incline that takes me to the top of Bepton Downs. I'm seven months pregnant now and this with the combination of not being at my fittest means that I walk at a plod, step by heavy booted step. I pass by where I got to the other day – a halfway point of sorts - a fallen tree trunk that stretches across to the right of the wood and atop which I sat and listened to the birdsong and call of a soaring buzzard.

Today I pass it, I walk for five minutes or so more and then see the clearing of light at the top of the path, marking the end of the path. Here what is already a steep walk arches steeper yet and so slower I go. About twenty or thirty metres from the gate at the top I stop and crouch down. I'm distracted researching aboriginal boy's names for the baby – maybe if I can give him a wild and meaningful enough name, it will compensate for whatever lacks I perceive in my life, the lack of others, the lack of village and the lack of a life lived more nakedly - but more than anything I sense and am responding to that tightness that says my body's tired, the asthma's not far away, I watch that mind that says *Push on! Challenge yourself! If you don't, you'll never make that gate again*!

The part of me, of us, that is forever tyrannically pushing ourselves to do more, be more, to go further and then I stand, turn and walk back down the path as I walk on this land, returning. No event in our life is a separate thing. No sentence alone, bereft of friends, or forefathers. That even though we may live lonely lives, actually we're surrounded all the time: by the spirits in our garden, by our ancestors whose stories still play out in the themes of our lives and by the very aliveness with which every moment breathes. We move, walk, think, talk and take ourselves to be solid blocks. Then we sit, breathe, watch and feel, and realize ourselves to be trillions amounts of cells vibrating and pulsating together to make up this apparition called human.

"It's amazing," said a therapist to me once, "that we don't get down on our knees more often and simply say my god, I breathe, and I have a heart that thumps and eyes that see."
"Yes," I said, "Yes." And I'm still saying yes to this, because like someone, so special to me that I regularly reject him as anything but, said to me, *One day, the sunset will be enough*. In response to which I frowned with a furious look, what a simple thing to say! I thought. What an empty thing to

say and I didn't mean in the *shunyata* Buddhist sense of the word, I meant superficial and hollow with disappointment. And yet, increasingly, I think of this, thoughts returning to this point, to turn it over once more, its truth opening my heart. Because if the beauty of the setting sun cannot return us to our hearts, what can?

always

Well, the woods is a good place to start.

Three quarters up the steep incline that makes up the walk to the top of the Sussex downs, I sit and lean against a tree on the path and read. After a while I sense movement on my right and looked up to see a pheasant; whose only right to life is its ability to provide others with the entertainment to kill. Luckily, in the case of pheasant at least, ignorance is bliss and so this one walked like an emperor, one elegantly placed food after the other. His plume glossy, apparently well-looked after. He carrys on, unbothered by me. About five metres from me. The brown sheen from his feathers matching the brown of our woody surroundings.

After half an hour or so, when the light is fading, I get up and carry on. Willing myself to the top, because I have a theory that if I skip the whole walk one day, I'll grow lazy and begin making excuses about why I can't get to the top. When I reach the top, my heart's pounding. I climb the metal fence and then lie almost immediately amongst the clovers, dandelions and wild grasses in the meadow on the other side. The meadow is littered with pheasants; female and male, and as I make my entrance, they make their exit.

When I get up, I head over to the other side of the meadow. It's not far, but whether because I'm pregnant or have just grown unfit this last month, the walk involves another mental willing to get there. I don't want to go back through the woods; something in me craves the freshness and light of the open meadows. As I walk I spot two deer, about fifty metres ahead. A mother and her baby. I stand there, my mouth open, aware of my breath, my body, belly and heart and make a spontaneous prayer: something my Buddhist teacher urged us all to do: *apply the grandest theories to the most mundane of events.*

I watch them eating, the little one moves away, a moment later scratching her ear with her leg. A moment later they've spotted me. Another young one, who I hadn't noticed and who had been lying by the fence running along the bottom of the meadow to my left, leaps to his/her mother and sibling. The two siblings are lighter-coloured. The two young watch their mother and the mother watches this form of bright blue and grey watching her. Her ears twitch and flutter. She steps closer. I wonder how close she'll come, we're about twenty metres from each other. In your own time, I want to be able to say to her, but at the same time I have to be home in thirty minutes, so how long will this take? I notice one of the young ones has gone back to eating and after a few minutes so does the other.

⬚

the enjoyment of sleep

And then one night I sleep. I go to bed and then I wake and I'm feeling full of energy and I want to get out of bed, but oh shit it must be like 3 a.m. or worse, 12 p.m. and I look at my clock and then I look again and it's 6.38 a.m. Jesus, I've slept. I've slept!

I get out of bed, I have energy! Evie comes through at 7.08 a.m. and we celebrate with miniature chocolate things because right now who cares about sugar: I've slept and my daughter's slept twelve hours through!

"Mummy, can I have these every morning?" "Yes!"
"Mummy, can I wear only dresses that twirl?"
"Yes!"
"Mummy can I watch TV whenever I want?"
"Of course!"
"Mummy, can I have chips with ketchup at every meal?"
"Yes yes yes!"

The day that follows has a radiance and I know it's not a permanent thing and that it's inevitable that I'll have bad nights ahead of me, but at least now I can experience this, this state that arises when I've slept. Knowing that this is normal, not the haggard, low energy, depressed, sensitive, worried, hyper-alert creature that I normally prowl through my days as, and that if I can just find the formula in my head that means I don't behave so anxiously to the things that worry me, then maybe there's still sleep in this woman.

And *my god,* does she enjoy it.

space

It's a Friday, Evie has no nursery today and so we've come to our favourite pub with the chickens in the garden and the tree you can climb and all the little chairs and beds you can sit in and climb. I'm reading a newspaper and Evie's wandering around, arms out wide, singing. There're two other tables occupied; I go up to them.

"Is this okay?" I ask. "Do you mind?"
The first table: "Please, don't stop her. Not on our account."
The second table: "She's charming!"

I go back to our table and sit, watch and enjoy watching this effervescent child exclaim her joy to the world as my own inner child, who so longs to sing with this kind of public abandon and giving over to the joy of the moment even though others are present, watches on, clapping and applauding.
⏾

melting required

It's 6.40 a.m. I've just heard Evie's bedroom door open and she's by my bed, shaking me awake.

I make room for her and morning snuggles, and then she's off, going to play. It's a Friday, no nursery today. I was awake for a couple of hours, maybe more in the night, the promise of the previous night short-lived, and then had shallow sleep afterwards, as is always the way. It's always around 5.30 a.m. that my body relaxes and attempts to sink back into sleep, but still my mind resists.

But this morning, maybe I can sleep another hour more, before she's hungry and needs breakfast. I curl up on my side and snuggle down under the duvet.

And then she's back.

"Mummy, I can't find the pink horse Dodo gave me."
"Look for it, bubba."
"Muuuum, I can't find it."
"Look in the bathroom."
"I've looked."
"Oh the kitchen table, try the kitchen table."
"I've looked, Mum," she says, crawling over me and nudging me like a puppy. "Bubs, I am not getting out of bed to look for it, go and look. Go!"
"Muuuummmmy, I can't find it, I really want it, please come and help me look for it." I stumble out of bed and head to her bedroom. I look for it but it's not to be found. Giving up, I crawl into her bed. She scrambles over me again.
"Bubs, please, I just need to sleep. Your horse is missing. You look for things when they go missing. Or just focus on something else. That helps. Find something else."
Tears. Shit, aren't I meant to try acknowledging her emotions or something?
"I can see it's really important to you," The tears increase. "You look like you're really sad." Tears, great mournful wails. Oh god, I just want to sleep.
"Bubs, it's not going to happen." Her face trembles. I get out of bed and go downstairs to look for it.
"Buuuubba." I call out in that warning voice, seeing a pink pony on the table. Ah, shit, I'm wrong.
"Sorry, bubba it's not the one you want." Evie's down the stairs. I walk past and get back into bed. She follows and crawls over me.
"That's your sister," I say, speaking to the bump. "She's very loud." Evie smiles. The desperation in the mood shifts slightly. And then we chat as I accept that I'm not going to be allowed to sleep. Evie wants me up. I could shut her out of the bedroom, but she'd only cry.

And yet even though my sleep isn't happening, there's happiness, not irritation, in my heart. What if I were able to introduce this lightness into my relationship with Tom? The conundrum of life oscillating through the trials and tribulations of family life, so that whereas our children often melt our hearts; our lovers can too often freeze them.

so close

"We balls wobble but we don't fall down..."

"Mama, will you help me out of the bath?" I've just got cosy underneath the duvet, with my seventh month pregnancy bulk relaxing heavily over and under and wrapped around my pregnancy pillow. I've got a large sandbag over my eyes and it's been about three seconds and already my body, so deprived of the nourishment that deep sleep provides, is sinking into somewhere deep.

"I can't move," I reply to my daughter.

"But muuuuummmmy, I need you to help me out of the bath!"

"You got out fine yesterday when Susanna was here, you can do it." Referring to a friend who came to visit. I am not getting out of the bed, I tell myself. "I need to rest, bubba, please just get out of the bath."

"But Mama, please, please I need your help." Images of my daughter slipping flick through my mind and so I haul my pot-bellied bulk out of my cocoon and go get Evie out of the bath, wrapping her in a towel.

"Carry me, Mama?" she asks.

"I can't ,bubs, my back just went a bit painful. Do you ever get that?" Why am I asking a four-year-old if her back ever hurts her?

"No."

"Oh."

I take her through to her room, attempt to dry her before she scrambles away and then put some pajamas on her before heading back to bed. It's 3.55 p.m. on a Saturday afternoon.

I get back into bed, reorganize myself. I'm meant to be doing this resting and snoozing – not just because I'm having a baby in two months, but because my nights are generally spent wide awake. We've been doing sleep training again, and the last two nights – though Evie has been fantastic and responded so well – have been brutal. And yet despite the fact that my daughter is sleeping, I still can't.

Again I feel myself sinking into *yoga nidra* fast. Then I sense a little being to my left; I've got company. Little fingers wrap around the sand bag covering my eyes.

"No bubba, please. I'm resting. I'm old, I need to rest."

"You're not old, Mama. You're young."

"Okay, thank you, bubba leave the sandbag." It's lifted away. Then she clambers onto the bed beside me. "Bubba, I'm going to be here ten minutes and then we can play."

"But Mama, I want to play with you noooow."

I try and ignore my daughter. Focusing on the sensations in my toes. My eyes are closed. Oh no... I feel my daughter's fingers pulling on my eye lids as she peels open one eye. Then getting comfy she does the same to the other. I will not be distracted, and keep focusing on the sensations in my foot, oh crap no, too subtle, okay thigh? Belly? Head? Hand? Anything. Anything. No matter how remote and unrelaxing it may be having my eyes peeled open, I am going to relax, so help me Tara.

effortless effort contrived

In 2010, during a three-month trip to India, where I was attempting my own version of enlightenment (I gave up early, Himalayan caves look very very cold), a group of us travelled to the place where Siddartha became Buddha: Bodhgaya.

One morning my friend Alex and I woke around 4 a.m. to go meditate under the Bodhi tree; an ancestor of the tree where Siddartha realised his Buddhaness. Along with a merry band of Vietnamese Buddhists, who sat as a group honouring the Buddha in their own unique way. Which immediately served to reveal to me just how precariously limited my own understanding of what Buddha honouring entailed. An understanding that got exploded open, courtesy of the hand-held tannoy that the group leader held aloft in his hands, and through which he projected his voice to the Southern Hemisphere of my brain.

Quite quickly, steam gushed from my ears and poured through my nose. Unable to contain my frustration, I turned to look at my friend, expecting to see a comrade in distress at least. But there he sat, amidst the chaos, and Bodhi tree leaf collectors who would fling themselves at falling leaves to take home and keep as precious reminders of the one who most inspires. Whilst I was red-cheeked and lost in a haze of furious indignation, Alex sat, with undistracted gaze, utterly at ease.

Seeing this, I nearly passed out from the combustion of the whole thing, so that eventually the appeal of taking a loo break was too irresistible to refuse, and so I left, only to return and begin again. And though that time I may have been a little less distracted, given the dismal quality of my previous stint that is a rather frugal claim.

And as I lie here on my bed, thousands of miles from that Bodi tree, with Evie doing headstands right beside my head, I invoke that moment and any other that I hope will help guide me through this moment when my exhaustion and my child's enthusiasm for the joy of being alive are coming face to face. I remember the call of Mark Rashid to use the least amount of energy possible, and how this chimes with my yoga training. So that rather than exert maximum effort in a pose, we come to a place of stillness and steadiness by using the least amount of energy required.

And as Evie leaps from a squat to a headstand, once, twice, three times and more, rather than try and direct her elsewhere, which would only be futile, I lie here, as if in a deep slumberous sleep. Now she's got the sandbag again and another, "Throw them to me, Mama!" and somehow, I'm throwing these sandbags with my right hand and right eye, the only parts of my body that're moving. I focus on my breath, the sensations, anything *anything* so that some kind of rest and rejuvenation can happen, because otherwise I'm going to be comatose in half an hour and I won't make it through the calls I have this evening with au pairs and hell knows what I'm going to create for supper.

And so for about ten minutes we play this catch game, with me exploring using the least amount of energy I can exert whilst simultaneously keeping my daughter engaged and my body rested. Evie wants me to throw them "higher, higher!" but that's taking up too much juice so I go lower, lower and she's laughing and then she's right there beside me again. "Tickle me, Mama! Tickle me!" and her little face is right there in my face and I can't not look at it and beam in response, so even though I'm still trying to do this hybrid *savasana yoga nidra* equanimous snooze thing, I'm tickling my daughter and she's laughing, which in turn makes me laugh. Until the tiredness wins over and I

218

try a new tactic.

"Okay look, take my alarm clock. When this changes to that number, I'll stop." Evie lies beside me utterly still, her eyes watching the clock intently.

After two minutes, "Mama, this is taking a really long time."

Then she gets bored and restless and so I add on another five minutes, and then another, and somehow this gives me fifteen minutes and then I feel it – that shift that says rest has happened and your internal system is rejuvenated enough so that you'll have about another four or five hours of energy.

I turn to tickle Evie and then around 4.35 p.m. I get out of bed: "No Mama! No Mama!"
"But you wanted me out of bed before and now you want me to stay in bed?"
"Yes, Mama!"
"I need to cook supper, bubs."
"No Mama!" and so I haul my belly and butt and boobs out of the bed with Evie hauling on me pulling me back and she's strong and I'm unfit and I fall back once; my centre of gravity is shifting, but on the second time, I'm up.

⏷

slipped standards

part i

There were hints that it was going to happen: leggings worn inside out with the large white label flapping above the rim of the trousers above my bottom; another night when sleep happened in broken pockets accumulating to around three or four hours. And that time I got into the car to go and pick Evie up from nursery and looked down at my feet, seeing the flash of blue to see I was still wearing my old lady blue slippers.

But now it's actually happened: I've arrived at Evie's nursery and here I am, wearing not only inside out leggings, but my blue old lady slippers at the same time: so that whereas the top half of me says I've got my shit together, my bottom half tells another more sleep-staggered story.

There's no other option other than to either get half-naked in my car in the car park and at least revert the leggings, or go forth and boldly claim this sartorial move as one that I've chosen deliberately.

Being lazy, this is the option I choose. And, though inwardly I'm cussing myself, parenthood being parenthood, I'm not even sure anyone notices.

⬚

rules needed

A Monday morning, Evie, Tom and I are snuggling in bed. Or rather Evie's pushing Tom away and moments later they're in full haggle mode about when's the best time to start a session of rough and tumble. "Brush your teeth, and get dressed and then we can rough and tumble," Tom puts down the law.

"You're a rule breaker!" Evie calls out to him. "Mama, Tom's a rule breaker," her little finger points across my increasing girth and palatial breasts at Tom, who's lying dormant beside me.
"We're a family of rule breakers!" she calls out. And as is my way with my child, I can't help but laugh. "A family of rule breakers!" And then Evie runs off to her bedroom to not get dressed, but to play instead, although this morning she allows me to dress her quickly and without battle. Teeth brushing is easy, too. And then Tom's sitting on the chair in our room that he had made for my thirty-fourth birthday, the fabric of which he tried to replicate with the wallpaper in my favourite film, *Tootsie*, which I used to watch as a kid with my grandmother Dean, in that scene where Dustin Hoffman is dressed as Dorothy and lying in bed with Julie at her father's home in the country and she's explaining to him about why she loves this wallpaper because she chose it with her mother, and which has rosebuds on it.

The chair has become the clothes chair and the meditating chair and even though it's 7.50 a.m. and he's taking Evie to nursery in twenty minutes, he's sitting there in his towel, meditating. Neither the green smoothie he sometimes makes on a Monday morning or Evie's rough and tumble game are looking likely. Instead, he comes down and starts tidying out the fridge. This is where Tom goes when he's stressed: into cleaning mode. He's only softened when Evie comes down and runs up to envelop us in a bear hug.

"We're a family of rule breakers!" she says, nestling into the nook, and we hug and laugh.

Meaning happens, sure it can, but only if we allow it to unfold. The meaning's in there, stop trying so hard, stop trying to find it, it's there, it's part of life's DNA; it can't help but exist. As soon as we start saying I'm going to know this thing, it's going to evaporate, dissolve... Meaning, true meaning, can't be defined. No matter what anyone says, no matter what anyone declares. True meaning, it's all a guess. It's all a stick your wet finger to the wind and feel which way it's blowing. Anything more specific than that feeling, that sense, that intuit... it's a game. Not so much a puzzle, but a riddle, of which I'm still trying to work out.

⏻

tea woman

It's a Tuesday. The baby's due date is in eleven days. I'm averaging about four hours of sleep a night. Two on a bad night, four or five of broken sleep on a good night.

The only good thing about chronic insomnia is that at least it can't get any worse; we might actually be the first parents in history who see an improvement in their sleep once the baby arrives. Or at least that's what we're hoping.

Tuesdays are the day Evie usually spends the afternoon at her grandmother Dodo's. A time I use to write. Or at least in theory. Sometimes I write. Most of the time I'm engaged with some online procrastinatory activity (Ellen, Jimmy Fallon and Oscar speeches being three things I can't say no to) but today I pause.

I'm sitting on my throne. Really. It's covered in a cream fur and has a gold elaborate design around the chair. It's kitsch definitely. Pretentious definitely not. A friend of my mother's is a fashion designer. Roberto makes dresses that shift the way you feel about yourself. And I'm a woman who lives in leggings. Roberto's clothes make you feel both provocative and devilish. Like an emboldened goddess that's come to explore planet earth for a day, or night. And our throne, just a little bit celebrated.

It used to live in my bedroom, but apart from clothes being thrown on it, it never really got any use. So it came downstairs to the kitchen to live out its full potential. I sit, legs curled underneath, my favourite £5 mug in my hand that I picked up from Portobello Road. A tea that I normally gulp down whilst tapping away. But today, instead of heading over to my computer, where I'll sit hunched for four hours, tapping away at the screen (watching Ellen interview The Rock), I'm sitting here on our sheepskin throne, drinking my cup of tea very, very slowly.

Broth woman not wine woman; tired not invincible.

[?]

pausing

I write this with my hands resting on my bump.

It's 10.18 a.m. on a Monday and I'm sitting on a newly placed wooden bench at the top of a hill that overlooks the South Downs way. It's the type of place that if you pass someone on the way up, they'll stop for a conversation. Not about the dogs, although they're probably the entry point, but the forest itself. "Enjoy the view at the top," they say, as you continue on your way. In case you might forget.

At the summit of the hill, all of fifty metres up, there's a wooden bench. Just out with the dogs, says the inscription, In honour of David and Sam. It took me a few trips to realise one of these was a human, and one of these was a dog. I sit on the bench, Bongo lying underneath, appreciating the view. The sound of cars hums in the background whilst the forest is alive with the sounds of birds singing. Sussex's version of the Amazon. The babe is due Saturday. We thought he was coming on the weekend. The Braxton Hicks contractions have been putting on such a convincing show, and my nipples are leaking milk, that I sensed the baby's head could appear any moment.

As it turns out, I was just overtired. A false alarm. And we were alarmed.

"You must be so excited," people say.
"Yes," I reply nodding my head, when inside I'm thinking, *but we're just not ready.*

Truth is, I'm appreciating these last few weeks of the pregnancy, and I'm not so sure I want to let go of them, at least not yet. These last nine months have been hard. Tom and I have drifted and come back towards one another and there have been other external stressors about which I have worried so much that my sleep all but disappeared. It's only now that I feel able to really enjoy the experience of being pregnant. Hence why, instead of sitting at the kitchen table editing my manuscript, I'm here, typing a new chapter on a Monday morning overlooking the downs. Not only this, but there's something else stirring, the acknowledgment that this nearly five-year period that Evie and I have had together is about to change. A new person is coming into our lives, and though I'm so curious to meet him and discover what he will be like, there is an ache in my heart at the loss that is coming too.

"Is that Bertie?" A woman in a pink camisole asks, interrupting my thoughts, pointing at Bongo. "No, he's Bongo."
"Oh."
"You have a friend with a dog like him?"
"Kind of." We exchange smiles, then she walks on, turning around the corner down the hill.
"Peaceful up here, isn't it?"
"Very," I reply. But she's gone.

⬜

regression

Bongo's regressing.

It's 12 a.m. and Tom and Evie are currently experiencing a change in the usual routine of me getting up to put Evie to bed if she wakes. It's not going well and I'm downing bottle after bottle of rescue remedies and whatever else I can find in the drawer by my bed to stop the impulse to run in and save the day. Meanwhile Bongo's jumping onto the bed.

"No dog, this doesn't mean you can get in. Off!" he ignores me completely. I haul myself off the bed, and walk around to the end of the bed and place him on the floor. I make this trip four more times. Meanwhile the cries have stopped next door. Peace has descended. I get back into bed and fall asleep. It's now 3 a.m. and Evie's come through again. Tom gets up and carries her back to her room. Silence. And then Bongo, who's been lapping at his water bowl like a dog who's just returned from the desert, needs to go outside and pee, so I take him down and instead of going to his usual spot he disappears.

Completely. *Shit.* Dancing with foxes or something. I can't call out because Evie's room is directly above me, so I sort of whisper,
"Boooongoo?"
Nothing.

And then I hear him yelping, oh god, not so much dancing as fighting. And then he's back, as if nothing's happened, *no drama lady, just sniffing the smells of night.* He strolls past me and we go back upstairs to bed. Dog on the floor, human on the bed, although I'm so tired I'll take wherever, as long as it means I can sleep.
⬚

peaceful place

The next day I tell Evie about the hill and about it being a peaceful place. "Can I come with you, Mum?"

We head off with Bongo that afternoon, as it's a Wednesday and she doesn't have nursery. On Friday we take Tom. It's a day destined for 27 degree temperatures and the long-sleeved dress that Evie's wearing is making her hot and grumpy. She strips it off, scampering away, a partially naked wood nymph, with her Paw Patrol pants, a My Little Pony in each hand, and her blond hair shining in the rays of the sun.

Bongo ambles behind at Bongo's pace, Tom's walking quickly, places to go, things to do: everything about his body language wondering why on earth he's come on a walk on a Friday morning at 9.30 a.m. with a pregnant lady due to give birth tomorrow, a dog who goes at his own pace, and a four-year-old who won't abandon her canine brother every time he stops to sniff a plant or pee.

But slowly we make our way to the wooden bench at the top of the hill. Evie goes to pee by a tree and then play with her ponies on the other bench, which is placed higher up in the shade, whilst Tom and I look out over the view, with him standing a little further away.

His whole body relaxes. "This place is so..."
"Peaceful?"

He looks at me and walks over and smiles, sitting down as we look out at the view together. Evie comes over and we take photos and share the bottle of water and then fifteen minutes or so later Evie asks if we can go home and we get up and she sprints down the steep path as relaxed and agile as a cliff jumper, as Tom and I make our way down more sedately. I watch as my daughter runs the half mile or so the whole way down the hill to the head of the forest, every now and again pausing to wave her arms above her head, and for the both of us to call out a Crocodile Dundee *Ahhhhhuuuuuuuuu!* to each other before the blond half-naked fairy is off again, speeding through the woods, or sitting down occasionally to play with some sticks she's picked up. As we near the final part, Bongo wades into a Guinness-coloured pool of ditch water, his beloved tennis ball floating beside his head, half-submerged. I walk past praying that Tom won't see him.

When Tom walks over the bridge, he's distracted by the note on the post and I hold my breath. Maybe he won't notice him. He turns and walks on, and then, damn, turns again.

"I thought that was a big fish."

And then he's walking quickly and the heat's causing Evie and me to slow down, or maybe just the memory of how our walk went last time: we're nearing the spot where we sat in a sun spot, Evie on what little area of lap my large belly allows, whilst I gave a rendition of *Red Riding Hood*.

"Love, why don't you head off? We're going to go slowly."
"Okay, guys, love you," Tom calls, fleeing at a pace that looks remarkably like relief in motion. Evie and I sit down in a sun spot and Bongo wades off into the undergrowth to munch grass.

We stay for a while.

slipped standards

part ii

I blame the slippers.

It's hot, very hot, 26 degrees. I'm due to give birth any day; in fact my belly's so huge that everyone keeps asking with eyes agog, "Still going?" I've tried wearing this top and that dress, but very little fits me. And then I see it, hanging there prettily in my wardrobe: my favourite nightie. Translucent as the glass on my kitchen windows, yes, but it fits and it's light, and my daughter goes to a liberal kind of school, and so I'm thinking if not now, when?

And yes, you can clearly see my underwear, but like I say, it fits and so be it. This is what I need to wear to collect my daughter from nursery: a see-through rose-coloured nightie, with my pregnancy pants hauled up to the rim of my bra and my giant nipple pads clearly visible, and that're currently soaking up cupfuls of the milk that's guzzling out. I want to tell my breasts they don't need to do dress rehearsals, we've done this before; I want to say to them, it's okay, you can do this.

But I don't think they'd listen.

As I walk across the playground towards the nursery, I feel embarrassed, but just as with the slippers, or maybe because everyone's a little pregnant too, no one says anything. Maybe because people don't particularly think anything funny about turning up in see-through nighties to pick up your child. Really, it's kind of understandable. The true anomaly is if someone turns up looking presentable.

Wow, we say, you look... amazing. Ooooh, we coo in awe, you've got make-up on. *Oh my,* we whistle appreciatively, *you've even brushed your hair.*

Bedraggled, not presentable. Broth woman, not wine. Woman unremarkable, your place or mine.
?

not yet

It's the baby's due date but I don't sense him coming. Physically everything's ready: he's been engaged for a couple of weeks and according to my midwife, "he can't get any lower." But emotionally, well, that's another story.

Ready, and yet not.

Unable to sleep, I've gotten up to walk to the top of the South Downs, but a thunderstorm has broken out, so I'm here sitting at the kitchen table instead, my eyes fogged with tiredness, listening to the birds and the rumble of thunder with the kitchen door open, and the sound of the storm and the rain falling. The light's darkened. I sense lightening. My body's beat, exhausted, longing to return to bed, but I can't quite let it.

I've been awake since midnight, fell back into a light sleep around 3 a.m. and then awake again from 4 a.m. Three hours sleep. But instead of lying there, processing an endless army of thoughts, I got out of bed at 4.30 a.m., had a bowl of cereal and then got into the car with a reluctant Bongo to go for a walk. I don't regret it.

On parking where I normally park, to walk where I normally walk, an internal whisper urged me to continue driving to a nearby shepherd's church. I drive up to it, park outside and haul Bongo out of the car. Super models in the eighties may have refused to get out of bed for less than $100,000; dear Bongo refuses to get out of bed before 11 a.m.

Period.

But the smells wafting in through the open car door are convincing him otherwise, so out he comes, walking by my side as we make our way through the church's graveyard, following our noses, crossing over a field to where a path leads up to the South Downs Way. With me every now and again stopping to take photos of the mist-covered fields and the sun, already high in the sky. We make our way up to the top of the Downs, to an intersection of pathways, and walk over to a steel gate, which I open to walk into the meadow on the other side. Crouching down, looking out over the valley towards the sea, it's a very beautiful place to be surrounded as I am by the inky blues and greens that this little island does so well.

We stumble in our lives, lost in an unconscious search for the paradise that we'd hoped we'd been born into. All the while unknowingly inviting into our lives the very people who, on closer inspection, appear replicas of those we grew up with and who share an uncanny ability to reopen old wounds, wounds we'd hoped we'd grown out of. It's only when we can pause and see these characters in our lives for who they are, and what they are here to teach us: to turn towards the light. Not only in others, but in ourselves first, foremost and always.

story telling place

The baby's due date has been and gone.

Meanwhile, Tom's becoming increasingly silent; his way of shutting down whilst temporarily adrift. The thing is, Tom's in a relationship with a woman whose anxiety is exacerbated by his occasional tendency to disappear. Like an oak in winter, he's still physically around, but in the depth of winter, spring feels a long time coming.

Which is fine, relationships are unfolding dynamics in which we're constantly re-meeting one another, but I'm meant to be a supply house of oxytocin right now, and instead I'm that shop beneath the first-time apartment, with a rich trade in worry and tension. So here we are, in Kingley Vale – a nature reserve that's home to the oldest yew tree forest in Europe – and that's about twenty minutes from where we live. We visit it hardly ever. We plan to, at least once a month. Evie needs persuading at the beginning of the path. Her arms folded across her in mutiny, holding out to be carried. Tom's tense.

"We don't have long, our tables booked for 12 p.m. Let's just walk, she'll follow us." "No love, it'll just get into a power struggle. She'll stand here and scream, and we'll only have to walk back." He looks at me, a collapsed expression on his face.
"It's like the Buddhists," I try, "you know… in order to reach the student they say something that's so unexpected that it shifts the student out of their mindset. That's what we need to do." He looks at me, full of doubt. "Like in New York, remember? When she wouldn't walk and we pretended the fire trucks we heard were putting out fires, and we all ran looking for them. We need to make it fun." His shoulders sag.
"Look, can't you carry her for a minute then tickle her and make her laugh? Then she'll forget all about it and walk."
"Okay, Evie munch," he says, turning, "if you run to me here, I'll carry you for a bit." Evie is already sprinting towards him before he finishes his sentence. Tom bends down and lifts her up on his shoulders. But less than a minute later, she's back on the ground and we're racing. Or rather Tom and Evie are racing, I'm waddling, and Bongo's taking his time sniffing and meandering behind. And this is the way we make our way along the three quarter of a mile walk to the forest. Meandering, waddling, sprinting and running.

"Mama! Mama! I've found a climbing tree!" Evie calls as we enter the forest. I walk over to the tree where she's standing. "Mum, this is the Imagination Tree. We have to press our foreheads against it and see what stories it tells us." I feel the wetness from the rain soaked in the tree.
"Look!" Evie points to a low-lying branch, which has been squirreled away to reveal pink bark beneath. We press our heads against the branch, asking the tree for stories. There's a circle of tree stumps nearby, and when we feel that the trees have imparted their wish for what stories are to be told, we head over to sit and wait for Tom. And whilst Evie sits on a tree stump, her hands on her knees, her expression soft with anticipation, Tom walks off into the undergrowth to pee.

"Mama, I'm just going to whisper my story, so I don't forget it," she says. "Okay, bubs," I say, sitting on the next-door tree stump, and then Tom comes back and we begin.
Evie: *Cinderella,* Me: *A Secret Garden* (a story that will come to have an extraordinary meaning for me in the future of our lives not yet lived), and Tom's: I actually can't remember Tom's, it's an Australian one that has Evie spellbound. As he tells the story, Evie turns to face him, her whole being absorbed by his story-telling. The two of them have a connection I'm not sure they wholly

appreciate. Evie adores Tom in an unquestioning way, and though his eternal bachelor is perennially challenged by family life, he adores her. In fact, when they're in a good place with each other, Evie will always choose to hang out with Tom.

"Mummeee, your stories are boring, let's listen to Tom," she'll say, sitting on his lap with his arms loosely around her. Now, nestled in the nook of the woods, I watch the two of them, the storyteller and the listener, figuring out this thing of step-fatherhood and step-daughterhood; both experiences about to change.

Then we go back a second time to the tree, press our foreheads once more against the trunk and then return and go for round two. Evie: *Beauty And The Beast*, me: *Puff The Magic Dragon* and Tom: a freestyle one about snakes which Evie then copies, and we go back a third time and then head off back to the car. Bongo and I moving slowly, Tom and Evie running ahead. Her hand reaches for his and he holds it gently as they scamper away.

Turning around the corner, I see them wading through some long grass in the nearby meadow and think they must be going for a pee. When we come near, my boyfriend and daughter have disappeared, but Bongo and I discover a tall tree and a little tree standing side by silent side, and we walk towards the trees and hug and sniff them; they come alive, giggle, and then scamper away once more.

About fifty metres further along a tree with blue blossoms and a larger one stand side by side. I walk over and this time press my forehead lightly against the forehead of the smaller tree, and then the larger tree. Again, the trees come to life and off they skip again, two pixies, having not too bad a time after all. Two or three more times this happens, until the path that leads to the car park, all of three quarters of a mile, comes to an end.

The last bit, Evie, Tom and I walk as a three, our hands lightly holding one another's. I look at Tom's face and, although I know his arthritic hip is in agony, his face is relaxed and his eyes are smiling. Evie climbs over the gate but needs help getting over. So we help, and then she hooks her yellow-booted toes over the bar so that as Tom holds her shoulders she forms a plank from his hands to the top of the bar.

He tugs, she giggles with glee.

Then we get in the car and head to a nearby pub for lunch. Everything's softened, the woods have worked their magic; we're ready, imperfectly, excitedly ready.

▣

again

Two hours later, labour begins. Tom's taken Evie swimming, and I sit on the kitchen bench feeling the squeezes in my belly, wondering: are these them? Then Tom and Evie return, and it's the usual rush of supper, bath and bed, so the question gets pushed aside, not to be affirmed until around 10.30 p.m., when unable to lie down anymore, I find myself on all fours breathing through the contractions. But although my body's in the full swing of labour, my mind is resisting.

Umm, dear body, I want to say, I've kind of planned on going into labour *in the day*. In other words, this nighttime labour which is currently unfolding doesn't fit in with the plan. Because when I go into labour – *in the day* – Evie will be picked up by my mother, and then the baby will be born – *in the day* – and then Tom and I and the baby can go to sleep and have a good night's rest.

And so labour gets put on standby.

At 11 p.m. Evie wakes and comes through to our bedroom. I walk her back to hers to begin the vigil of waiting by her bed till she falls back asleep because I've yet to learn that the magic ingredient to a child sleeping through the night is not so much consistency in my methods, or even the methods in others who put Evie to bed (that's the third), nor even having the confidence in her ability to fall asleep (that's second), it's having utter conviction in my sense as her parent to know what's going to benefit the whole family (sleep), and then act in as simple and direct a way as possible to support that process happening, without giving way to guilt. Guilt is a separated parents' nemesis because it leaves us vulnerable to unrooting any seedlings that have begun to take root at the slightest sign that we may be causing our children distress. Rather than learning to hold a space within ourselves for our children, from which they will in perfect symbiosis feel the safety we crave for them, we rush to change the very structures and routine that they so badly need. Which is to say, overcompensation is a sure way to grow grey hairs.

So here I am, kneeling on all fours, having increasingly enthusiastic contractions, whilst whispering sophoric words to my daughter, lulling her back to sleep. Not yet understanding that rather than helping my daughter sleep, my presence actually inhibits her ability to do it herself. Less is not only more, it's trust made real. When Evie does drift off, I go back to bed and try and sleep. Around 3 a.m. I can't lie down anymore, so Tom and I get up and head down to the kitchen. I go to the loo and find blood on my underwear.

"It's fine," says Tom nonchalantly, as he sends a text to our doula, "it's called a bloody show. It means you're in labour." I look at him bewildered. How does he know this?
"My book told me," he says, seeing the expression on my face. "I've texted everyone, they're on their way." Then Evie wakes at 5 a.m. and comes down to the sitting room to lie with Bongo and me, curled up together on the sofa in the sitting room. Tom calls my mother. We wait; labour waits. At 5.30 a.m., Mum arrives.
"Good luck, darling," she calls, making a sort of awkward fist pump in the air as she retreats, Evie and Bongo by her side. Bongo looks mildly relieved; I'm not sure labour is his thing. Then the front door closes, I exhale, relax... Sharon, who's been sitting on the sofa timing the contractions, sits up. The contractions instantaneously shift from coming every nine minutes to every four minutes. I move from the sofa to stand. Everyone's here. Evie's with Dodo. I'm ready. The baby's on his way.

or, almost

"This'll be quick," someone says. Everyone's sitting down, waiting. Tom, Gabriella, our doula, and our two midwives, Sharon and Eleanor.

Then someone starts filling the birthing pool, whilst with every contraction I move; from sitting, to all fours, to the floor, to hugging Tom, to kissing Tom, to leaning over the Tibetan chest of drawers given to me by a family friend and now serving as a perfect aide over which to drape myself and wait out the next contraction. The expectation that this is going to be a swift second labour is palpable, and though I have a strong sense that this won't be the case, I'm keen to reassure. So my head nods like a Labrador's tail wags; everything in its structure wishing to please.

"This'll be quick," someone says.
"Second labours always are," another affirms.

The problem is that, although the contractions are coming every four minutes, the labour isn't progressing. An hour passes, then some more. People start moving, confused. The labour's taking longer than expected, what's happening? Watches are looked at, eyes are closed. Tea is made, a green smoothie as well.

"Would you like one?" asks Tom to Sharon.
"Um, no thank you." Then on hearing the ingredients, which sound less like a green smoothie, more like a chocolate smoothie, she changes her mind, "Actually, I'll have one of those, thanks."

I can feel Manuella moving around in the house. I'm shifting into mammal mode, and my inner hippo wants to be as utterly alone as I can be. My labouring antennae is up, and anxious housekeepers with whom I don't have the best of relationships with are making me feel tense instead of calm.

"Can't you ask if she's alright to go out?" I ask Tom.
"You can't ask her that," he replies. So, we don't.

Instead I take my hearing aids out and head out into the garden, then wander back into the kitchen where everyone's milling about, eating, chatting, waiting... Someone gives me some toast to eat, I nibble on a bit, someone cracks a joke, I smile, but don't laugh. I feel myself pulling back from the world, slipping deeper into that internal space we sink to when giving birth. I see the others and hear them, but words no longer cause the same effect. Like rain sliding down a window, I'm on the other side, turning away, and looking for somewhere to hunker down and rest.
⬚

trust

But I'm not meant to be resting, I'm meant to be birthing. With the lack of progress I can feel anticipation shift to disappointment, confidence to concern.

I go out into the garden, walk around, eat something, drink lots of water, play music, pull a card from a deck of inspiring cards that a friend gave me, ask Tom to read to me from a book I keep in the loo, staying close to him, like a cat who wants to stay close to her human. I listen vaguely to things the others are saying, enjoying my right as a labouring woman to not even have to smile back if I don't want to. And though I'm retreating, externally at least, for now, I'm behaving as expected: being polite and sympathetic. But this phase is not to last for long.

When the contractions come, Tom and I hug. For a while, I slip into a space that's a little bit equanimous, maybe even a little bit erotic. We hug and kiss and the midwives look away, but Gabriella, our Brazilian goddess, is not bothered at all, and comes close to massage my neck. Then around 12 p.m. it's nap time. My body clock knows this is when it gets horizontal time to, if not sleep, at least revive. The fact that I'm in full labour makes no difference at all.

"I need to rest," I say.
"You can't do that," someone says.

But otherwise I can't do this, I think. I'm flagging. The contractions have moved from every five minutes to nine minutes. As well as this, tension is beginning to percolate between our Brazilian goddess and our two midwives. Three women, two different approaches. I don't need to wear my hearing aids to be aware of any of it, I can feel it. But my hippo's growing grumpy at being kept away from lying down in her mud-cocooned wallow, so I make a request instead.

"Can everyone leave us alone?" I ask. They nod, and walk out.

When everyone's left, I take Tom upstairs to our room. We tiptoe past the kitchen so that no one can see us, and then lie on our bed upstairs, curled in a ball. One of the midwives comes up, "I need to examine you," she says. Moments later her hand is inside my vagina, and pulling at some part of me that makes me scream. I think she's trying to turn my womb. It seems that our son has decided to rotate not the 90 degrees he needs to drop down into the birthing canal, but the full 360 degrees around and that this is why labour's taking so long. Gabriella, hearing me scream, is there, looking at me concerned. The midwife says she needs to do that again.

"No," I say, "not again."
"Laura, we need to get this labour moving along," says Sharon. "Do you want some gas and air?" I look at Gabriella.
"What will it do?"
"It will make you shaky," she replies. I want it, I want to be a woman who's so relaxed and afterwards who says things like *the drugs they give you! They're wonderful!* But I'm me, anxious and worried about how they affect bonding, so I say no.

Then I start crying.

Quietly at first. Then louder, deeper, more persistent. My hippo has wandered off, disgruntled, put off, and in her absence I'm left with a woman child who just wants her mother. Which is a bit of a surprise, but it's now in this moment of unrelenting pain and exhaustion that this is the person I want: *mum, mama, mummeeeee.* Everyone's watching me, worrying, thinking, wondering. They draw back and come close, exhaling and inhaling around me, waiting. I'm on my knees on the floor, weeping in exhaustion and pain. I just want to sleep, to rest, and then it finally dawns.

Ohhhh... she really *is* tired. We all go back downstairs, and that's when it's agreed that yes, let her rest. "Rest, Laura," someone says. "You're so tired, Laura, rest."

And so I do. Walking over to the sofa, where I curl up in the corner, head resting on the cushions, and fall into a deep faraway sleep.

a hippo decides

For the next hour, maybe two, the contractions retreat back to appearing every ten minutes. When they appear, the pain is blindingly furious. I try to go with them, to breathe, but I end up fighting them, resisting them, before sinking into a deep sleep, welcoming the oblivion that follows. Ten minutes later, I'm woken by feelings of being stretched and pushed apart. I move from the sofa to the water. From the water to the sofa. My movement is my disquiet made kinaesthetic. Tom and Gabriella move with me, with Gabriella massaging me whilst I cling to Tom.

I start to sing, words from somewhere deep inside me that have no nationality or tongue, just sounds, feelings. I'm normally too shy to sing in front of others, but I'm sitting naked in a tub in my sitting room, navigating my fear around the final stages of birth: worrying about what people think of my vocals is one worry I need not entertain. Tom's in the water with me and I'm leaning into him, on the edge of the tub. It feels wonderful, exquisite and intimate, and I drift off into sleep.

I wake to discover Tom getting a neck massage from Gabriella. My hippo is not pleased. Silently outraged, she flames her nostrils in protest, wades over and nudges him with the full weight of her indignation. In other words, *honey, maybe those shoulders of yours want to find another time to get a massage.* The silence of the message is heard, or rather we're distracted by another round with me and my contractions. Gabriella comes close.

"Don't fight them Laura, go with them. Breathe, slowly, breathe. You can do this, you can do this." I look into her eyes. They're the only eyes now who still believe I can. So, I breathe into them. Tuning into Gabriella's confidence, her sense of herself as a woman, her strength and presence. But I need an outlet for all this pain, and unfortunately, it's the caramel-skinned earth mother whose birthing video I watched in preparation for labour who gets the full frontal of my labouring rage. A string of expletives hurtles from my mouth. Then some more just to emphasise my point. And because hippos have been known to be temperamental, everyone's doing their best to look busy, writing notes, moving things, making tea, going to the loo, hoping that the bellowing hippo doesn't beckon them over. Following my vocal venting session, clarity dawns: I need courage. Dutch courage, mammoth courage, because I'm about to suggest something drastic.

"I need to go to hospital. I can't do this. The pain's too much, please someone take me to hospital." Everyone's silent. The midwives clearly agree. Tom's not sure, concerned how things will unfold once there.
"Laura, we can take you to the hospital if you want," says Sharon.

Gabriella comes close. "Laura, this is your labour, if you want to go to hospital we can." And I want to please, how I want to please. I feel confused, overwhelmed. I want to feel okay about taking the pain relief and for it not to be such a big deal. Women do it all the time, why can't I? I'm standing on the edge of the sofa, people are walking in and out of the kitchen to talk to one another, private meetings carried away from deaf ears that probably wouldn't be able to hear them anyway. Yet they're amiss; it's not the hearing that matters in labour, it's the *feeling*. Gabriella continues looking at me, standing close, I'm holding onto her, breathing together. "Laura, you can do this. This is your labour."

I look at the 60cm pink candles that Tom gave me for Mother's Day and which are almost burnt to the wick. Outside, the sun is sinking, it's late afternoon. I look back at Gabriella, contemplate the move to the hospital, the further delay, the possible loss of control over how things happen.

Damn this, I think. I need this to finish.

I walk over to the sofa and push. I push in a way that I've been told not to. I push down with every iota of power and resilience I have left in me, and right there, with Sharon diligently hovering behind me with her plastic sheet to protect the carpet, in one mammoth explosion all over the floor, my waters break.

I drop to my knees. It's 3.50 p.m. Nothing can be stopped now, no final part of labour resisted (by which I mean that despite best attempts, oh *ring of fire, how soon we are to meet again*). Immediately the atmosphere changes from one of disconnection and doubt to connection, cohesion and focus. *She can do this, she can do this, she can do this.* All my resistance to trying to control the situation has been floored, my ego has surrendered, my fears have changed to one pointed focus. I have exactly thirty-nine minutes left of labour. I'm finally ready to begin.

⏂

new beginning

Remaining on the floor, I ask if someone can get the birthing pool ready. Gabriella's by my side; I won't let go of her. I grip her hands, her wrists, as if trying to extract her strength. I grow bad-tempered. The pain relief that the birthing pool provides is significant, and although Tom and the two midwives are moving at the pace of Formula One champions to reheat it, I'm desperate to get back in.

"But the water's not hot enough!" one of the midwives calls out to me, as I go to get in. "I don't care!" I say. But I hold back, pacing, slowly, trying to flow instead of fight.

After seconds, minutes, I get into the water, before the temperature's ready, when the temperature's ready; I don't know and no one stops me. Once in, the ring of fire happens and it's even worse than I remembered. The aftermath leaves me trembling. Then my body contorts as if under an exorcism, or having a seizure; it's the baby coming down. I know now not to push, to leave the pushing bit to my body's own intelligence, but my Christ, I hadn't known it would be like this. I feel as if a blade of lightening has ripped my body apart in some kind of eternal damnation. I'm shaking and gripping onto Gabriella. *This is horrible*, I want to say. *Hideous.* Horrific. Christ, Christ, there's more?

But I can't actually talk at this point, because the pain is so overwhelming and the fear that more are imminent means I'm all rolling eyes and deranged wild mare who's all hoof and mangled legs. I'm also temporarily mute.

Another contraction, another contortion. One of the midwives is begging me to "Stay still, Laura! Stay still!" I have no idea why this is so important to her. And my bottom continues going in and out of the water depending on what stage of pain I'm in with the contractions.

"Please, someone pull him out," I beg. "We can't sweetheart, we can't."

And then he's there, my son's head and a head full of dark black hair. My fingers reach down through the water to touch him, they dance lightly around the edge of my vagina, sending back the information to the rest of me: *He's here! He's here!* My fingers prod and feel; they're looking, searching: is there any way he can just come, be pulled, anything? But the muscles of my vagina are so tight around him. Nothing's loose. I expected the opposite. At least some kind of baggy bit that can be encouraged and massaged to let my son loose. Then another contraction, and he's half out.

My hands can feel his face, his head, his chest, and still this dance, can he be pulled? Can he? No... he can't, he can't! *Oh dear lord, why on earth not?*

But the impulse to protect him is greater than the impulse to protect me, so there's no pulling, only caressing, and then another contraction, and he's out and I'm pulling him towards me, out of the water into the world. Although it's only two days later, when lying in bed with Tom that I turn to him and say, "My god, I pulled him out didn't I? I did?" A wish granted, the thing I'd most wanted to do.

For now, it's taking him in. His face, scrunched, disgruntled, not comfy. One of the midwives comes over and roughly rubs his hair. *Go awaaaay* I want to say. *Leave him alone.* He cries out. I bring him close, whispering to him, kissing him, "*I love you! I love you!*" I'm so relieved; I was so frightened that after the hell of the labour I wouldn't. I was so frightened to take a drug in case it affected my bonding and now all I can say is *I love you! I love you! I love you!* I'm in a state of hormonal euphoria.

236

The love grows, expands, softens, reassures. I kiss him all over his face. We get out and go to the sofa. The placenta has to be delivered, and again one of the midwives thrusts her hand into my vagina, and I howl with pain. I feel bludgeoned; there should be nothing going into my body now, only out.

I hold my son and lie with him naked, he's on my chest crying and I show him my breast and he can't quite latch and it's clearly hard for him, different. But there's so much happening that I don't get the chance to say to someone, this is different, why's he not feeding easily? It'll only be in forty-eight hours time, on day three, in the morning, first thing, that Sharon will come around.

"Yes," she'll say, peering into his mouth, "just as I thought, a tongue tie." I'm sent out of the room whilst she cuts his tongue and he's brought to me and latches on straight away and all the tension and pain in his face drops away and he feeds, something relaxes.

But for now, I'm here on the sofa. It's over. Done. Or really, a whole new beginning has begun; one that'll bring to the light parts of ourselves that have been forgotten, or plain ignored.

All of our lives have changed, ended, begun, restarted. Magic is sparkling. Who we are now is different and who we are all to become, not yet embodied.

We're simply finding our way.
🔲

siblings meet

Two day later, Evie's coming home to meet her baby brother.

The doorbell goes, I rush downstairs to open it. Evie's there with her beaming face with friends who've taken her to the beach for the day. She rushes in, wrapping her arms around me. Everyone comes in.

"Look at Mummy's tummy!" says Sophie. Evie whips her head around, lifts up my nightie, looking for my belly.
"Mummy! Mummy! He's out! *Where's* my baby brother? Where is he? *Please, please* can we go to him?"
"He's upstairs. Come on, I'll show you." Sophie and her three kids go to say goodbye.
"No, *please* can they come?" Evie asks, already a quarter of the way up the stairs, then turning to them, arms open, "Please come."
"Of course they can." We turn to troop upstairs. Tom, Evie and I, along with Sophie, Poppy, Jasmine and Rocky. Jack's lying on the bed in one of the spare rooms and Evie leaps onto the bed and her little hand reaches out and caresses her baby brother's head. Evie's face beams radiantly, and then, turning to me with such happiness in her eyes, she squeals: "Mummy, when he's older I can play with him instead of you!" I laugh, because what could be a better thing to wish for.
"Guess what his name is, bubba?" I ask her.
She squeals again. "It is, isn't it? It's Jack!" She's singing with delight, reaching out to caress her baby brother's face tenderly and then clasping her hands in excitement.
Tom and I nod. "I was right, Mama! I knew it was! I knew that's what his name was!"
"You're right, bubs, I was so wrong, wasn't I? I thought it was Dylan, but it's really Jack."

And that really is his name. My son, Jack Dylan Bible, named by his sister, his mother and father. A brother to a sister, a son to a mother and a first time child to a father of fifty one.

[?]

what's really there

The love bubble has truly arrived.

It sinks and spreads, encompassing the whole family within its hold.

At first this shared amazement felt at the wonder of being loved by the one you love whilst being no one other than who they really are makes them laugh like children, an effervescent sparkle blooming in their hearts, spilling out into their eyes, causing their feet to grow skittish, so that their children look up at these two supposed grown-ups, both with their predilection towards earnestness and serious hearts and intense engagement and shrugging shoulders, and look at one another with not a small amount of relief, as if to say: finally, finally they get it.

As the love bubble stretches, disharmony becomes harmony, as fears of abandonment and commitment both transform into something more radical: the acceptance that what's really sacred can be neither abandoned nor dominated by another, because instead, maybe just maybe life's granted them something splendid: the chance to create a family that care deeply about one another and that all the grumps and droops of the tail really don't matter as much as we allow them to matter. They're not only distractions, they're simply misleading. They're also persuasive, because often when life does become magical, hell can whisper from a place not too far away, ready to snatch it all away again if you fail to make a stand for it not to.

A stand that doesn't require you to get ready for battle, at least not an external one, but simply to transition from old beliefs that have caused your life to become stagnant that the magic might otherwise make luminous. It's not so much a case of "I believe in fairies," but I believe in the imperfect nature of life, I believe not in the one, but in the you, and in doing our bit to work out this thing called relationship. Yes, we may need a small army of therapists and experts to support us, but no matter. This is us, working it out.

And I've got to trust we'll get there.

just for a while

I'm walking with Jack through the woods near Little Oaks; our home for a while. I'm carrying him in a baby carrier. He's sleepy. And as we near the entrance to the road near our house, his head, which is normally turning to face the world, lolls and rests against my chest, his forehead pressing into my chest.

My heart bursts, sending ripples out. Being a human, so much of what we understand to be true depends on how much we take our thoughts to be accurate interpreters of the life we live. They're wholly misleading, of course. They appear so regularly that we think them friends. When, in fact, the opposite is true. Not so much foes, as mere hallucinations obstructing the real view. So that we spend our lives dazzled not so much by the exquisite transience of our existence but intoxicated by the stories we tell ourselves, through which we relate to the world.

In moments when the thoughts settle, our ability to face our lives with greater resilience emerges. One that looks at the faces of our children, or the haggard tired face of our partner, knowing that our time together is limited. We try so desperately to imprint a memory of ourselves and "the little lives we lead" so that our work and our family can become but boomerangs that we send out and whose return we hope to see soon.

One day though, one day 'out there' when we hurl our boomerang out into the day or evening of our soul, there won't be a return. Instead, it will become our turn to pass, float and stumble on, soaring to someplace else, not having any say if a memory of us remains or not. *Memento Mori* becomes then not a morbid thing, not even a particularly spiritual thing, simply a practical tool that we can use to better appreciate the people we find ourselves sharing our lives with. And when we can stand more confidently in this place, it matters not what those who appear to have a more perfect existence than ours are doing, because what else is there than appreciating those you love?

Appreciation anchors us, dissolving the neurotic need for things to be more like that and less like this. It quietens our anxious whinny for one more go when our time comes. That hidden wish that okay, so yes, maybe one day we'll die, but *please, please, just let us have another chance at being human*. Which is to say that somehow my thoughts find themselves turning to death more frequently. At first, I don't know what to do with them: what place do they have amongst so fresh a birth? But they persist. Showing up in moments where it's just myself and my children. As a mind allows itself to settle, and a heart is inspired to grow.

⁋

cloud drifter

I'm drifting closer.

Evie and Jack are playing in the garden, with Evie making him laugh in the way that only she can. My view widens a bit, there's someone else beside them, the sight of which fills my body with warmth: Tom.

He's standing there and pointing at me. "Okay, Evie munch, who's this?" And then he mimics me sitting on a loo and tapping away furiously on a phone.
"That one," Evie replies, with a big beam, pointing in my direction. And I'm coming closer, and I can smell him. I can smell his sweat and feel his skin and see those eyes. That cold flash when he's angry, and that will also soften uncontrollably when he's at peace.

Tom, whose first gift to me was a crate of oranges, an array of herbs, healing potions and a bag from Whole Foods to help me get over a virus. Tom, who's sixteen years older than me, and who also if I look a little closer is holding onto this suitcase, emblazoned with the word: BACHELORHOOD: USE IN EMERGENCIES. And yet, my god, has he actually put it down, and maybe even nudged it out of the way. Don't tell anyone, but I think he's actually enjoying family life more than he admits.

And now here's his son, Jack, this babe who smiles and giggles and roars with hunger if it's been longer than two hours, sometimes two minutes, since his last feed. And whilst there're still days when I know Tom may want to get the hell away and normally around the time he'll mention "a particularly important meeting" that he needs to go to in America, that'll last, "at least a week," here we are, two people whose default is to go alone being anchored by our family; the pull of which is pulling me closer as I drift back to earth from these clouds I've gotten to know so well.

⸻

241

hormone heaven

Jack's sleeping. Evie and Tom are swimming. Manuella, our temporary housekeeper who's helping us with this period of our lives, is doing her version of housekeeping: folding plastic bags and rearranging the flowers and filling the water filter, whilst damp clothes lie in heaps and an ever- growing clump of baby clothes builds up in the bedroom. "I'll do them later," she tells me.

I'm writing, and although Jack's upstairs, I can feel him around my neck where he likes to crawl his way up, all amoeba coming out of the ocean to rest, as if he's snoozling there now. It's day eight of Jack's entry into the world; and I'm not so much clinging onto these days that are unfurling from this love-nozzled nucleus as wrapping myself around them and fervently, sometimes piteously, praying for this period to extend itself indefinitely.

In other words: oxytocin, won't you hang around?

Awareness of impermanence is meant to increase our appreciation of the preciousness of a moment, whereas depending on which hormones are coursing through my blood this past week, the knowledge that normal life waits somewhere on the horizon, and this utopia of peace and magic that's currently melting our hearts and bringing Tom and me closer to one another will drift on as the routine of our lives takes over.

So instead, I sit here on the sofa, Jack in my lap, and watch my boyfriend talk about all the emails he needs to reply to, and wish he'd close the damn computer and just come and sit with us and soak this beauty up.

A couple of days later, when his family comes for lunch and conversation becomes static, I want so much to go with Evie, Tom and Jack to Peaceful Place in the woods (Bongo's gone back to my mother's whilst we get used to life as a four), look at the view, and eat sandwiches and let the memories of these moments imprint themselves on us at a celluar level.

I want to stop Tom walking out the front door and instead just hug him and walk through the back door that leads to our garden, to go out into the garden with Tom and Evie and now Jack and with Bongo there looking up at us in that way that he does that simply says: *I love you.* To head towards the spot where the sun shines, where we can lie back on the grass and look up at the sky above. Knowing that yes, normal life may be waiting to return, but we're just not ready to welcome it back yet. Because out here in our garden, rewilding in earnest amongst the mole hills and half-painted climbing huts, amongst the Tibetan prayer flags floating gaudily against the trampoline, in all this imperfection, lies us, getting to know one another, starting again, perhaps, discovering life as a four.

Acknowledgments

There were times during the writing of this book where I swore after finishing it that I'd never go near writing again, and instead would hurl myself back into the world of events and whatever it was that I did before I became a mother.

And yet, writing is writing, and memory is fickle. Hence siblings, second books, thirds books and... the very many thank you's to all those who encouraged, cajoled and inspired me on to completing this book. You are all stars in my eyes, and Travels wouldn't be there were it not for the role you have each played in my life. Thank you x

Miles Morland – At the beginning of 2016 I came to yours for tea. "For god's sake, stop blogging," you said to me, "and write a book." And because I'm generally easily influenceable I trotted off, and six months later handed in the first draft of *Travels* to Victoria Roddam, the woman I'd spend the next two years editing the eight drafts of this book with. Miles, your non-advice means the world to me, thank you for giving me the impetus to start something I had no sense of ever even beginning.

Victoria Roddam – "I have the sense that the writing of this is incredibly important to you, Laura," you said to me once. You were right and I am so very grateful to you for teaching me about narrative arc, saying less and trusting the reader. It also meant a huge amount to have an editor who was also a mother and understood the process of working and crafting and mothering whilst negotiating school holidays and sick days *and and and...*

Roberto Rodriguez – for your kind encouragement of the blog pieces I shared with you, thank you. You said things about my writing that gave me the confidence to carry on.

Thank you, too, to Mary Ellis, who introduced me to Cornerstones. Having you and Andy to speak to about the writing process has always been such a joy for me.

To Helen Bryant for creating Cornerstones. *Travels* wouldn't be here were it not for the service and support you provide for writers.

And to Lisa Messinger, for your final edit and proofread of *Travels* before it went to Amazon, thank you for taking the manuscript to the next level and making it one that I am genuinely proud of.

I also want to thank all those who made comments on social media when I first started my blog on lfraser.com. For anyone starting out in the blogging world or making tentative steps towards publishing their first book, it's a tremendously meaningful thing to have people engaging with your writing. (And for anyone reading this, if you have any friends who are blogging and trying to build their confidence up about their writing, for god's sake: comment and share their blog posts!). And for all those who made the effort to read a post and then comment on it, I want you to know it meant the world to me. In particular, I want to thank Dee Kumar and Alex Power for their always supportive and warm=hearted words of support – you're angels, big time. And to Alex, who refused to give me her address to send a copy of Travels to, until I allowed her to pay for it. That refusal is probably one of the most touching I have ever received in my life. Thank you dear friend, you're a distant friend geographically, but a close one in my heart.

Also to Hassen Bali and Andrea Cassandro, two men who reached out with encouraging and generous words of support with regards to my writing. You may not know the impact of you taking the time to be supportive, but your kindness and thoughtfulness in the words you chose meant an immense amount.

Because when you're writing, you begin to doubt that what you're doing is even real – hour after hour spent alone, focusing on something you're not even sure is ever going to come to fruition. And then you go back into the world and talk with friends about careers that are grounded in events and products that you can touch and talk about, and then there is your world, largely coming from your memories or imagination: a world as of yet unshared!

So, in particular I'd like to thank:

Jose Fonseca: "You must do it, darling!" You're always supportive and encouraging of my work. Thank you for providing the encouragement that I should finish this book. It spurred me on. Thank you for believing and having faith. It mattered.

Gypsy Gold: (Yvonne) you're a golden precious friend, another gift from the universe, as somehow you're this integral part of my world, and yet our meeting or staying in touch could so easily not have happened. Thank you for hearing me read the opening chapters of *Travels* and your feedback, and for helping me gain clarity about how to progress, not only with the beginning of this book, but perhaps with my life too.

Susanna Petitpierre: Thank you for always picking up the phone to me, for traveling to bleak spots with me (literally and figuratively!), and for being up for going for a walk, no matter how hard core the rain. For your awesome laugh and kind heart: *thank you.*

Also, to three friends whose entrepreneurial ingenuity & general all round *okay, lets go for this,* I've often reflected on and been inspired by: Natasha Bateman, Rebecca Glenapp & Ryan Kohn.

To Eugenie Cunningham-Reed for being a friend my daughter adores as much as I do.

To three writers who opened doors for me and in their own way made me believe I could craft a way for myself:

Caroline Morehead, thank you for being open to meeting with me to talk about a possible idea I had for a book (not this one) and humouring me with a "hmmm, that's sounds good..." and then asking me this wonderful question: "Would you like to see where I write?" That was such an awesome moment for me. To see a real life author's writing space was so deeply inspiring. Thank you.

Rachel Kelly, thank you for meeting me for coffee to talk about writing. You're brilliant and brave, supportive and inclusive and I deeply appreciated your time.

Bryony Gordon, for reading one of my blog pieces and encouraging me to get it published, and then sharing with me the details of an editor who might do just that. For being a woman who's supportive of other women, no matter how busy you are: you're awesome, generous and kind.

To the online women's circle I was a part of: Elspeth Duncan, Nimmi Johal, Rose Long, Susanna Petitpierre, Thalbir Shokar and Vanessa Soodeen. Thank you for being a lifeline for me when I was immersed in the act of writing this book. I loved our time so very much, and carry our laughter and our wildness in my heart.

Simone de Hoogh: your presence and guidance in my life has been a gift I shall be eternally grateful for. Thank you for every piece of wisdom you have passed my way; I cannot imagine having navigated motherhood, or my relationships without you, and I am so grateful that I have been able to refer to you at some of the most intense moments in my life, and be guided by your wisdom, generosity and consistently kind perspective.

To Geoffrey Bible: for your incredible generosity, and your kind-hearted inclusivity: thank you.

Paul Davis-Openshaw: You're an incredible reflexologist and compassionate conversationalist. Thank you for also being there for me in times when I've needed someone. You've been an integral part of helping me off-shoot some of the impacts of insomnia.

To the team at CBD brothers: I'm so grateful to you for putting your incredible product out in the world and to the difference it has made in my life and my ability to heal. Thank you.

Charlotte Cline for creating my beautiful lfraser.com website and giving me a logo that still makes me beam. Thank you.

Matt Hobbs from azoprint.com, thank you for all your patient edits of *Travels* as we prepared it for printing.

Sophie Neish: When my mother very kindly gave me the gift of you coming to help fill our fridge twice a week whilst I finished the first draft of Travels, I was at first nervous: the kitchen was my office, after all. And yet for two hours, twice a week, I experienced a harmony and a deep sense of support from you that I was so deeply grateful for, and that Evie adores you as much as I do has always touched my heart. Thank you, thank you, thank you – for your grace, respect and kind, gentle nature.

Sheila David, for passing the manuscript on to Pippa in your team. I really appreciated this, thank you.

To Beatrice Bartlett for being a wonderful therapist in a turbulent time. I think of you often. Thank you for your kind gentle guidance in my life, on which I still ponder and am touched by.

To Camelitta, for being there for my family and helping me when I need help. I love you. You are a great gift to me and my family, thank you.

To my mother: for the last 3 months of when I was finishing the first draft of *Travels* when you noticed that Eve and I were eating a lot of pasta and pesto, and for bringing Sophie into our lives... Thank you for being a grandmother who makes a difference - helping with school drop offs and school picks ups. And for opening your home to us when we've needed one and for tidying my home every time you come to visit. These acts of kindness I am profoundly grateful for.

Burkhard von Schenk: The gift that you gave me in 2009 is one of the greatest gifts anyone has ever given me because it allowed me to focus completely on motherhood, and then writing; two of the greatest joys I've ever known. So, thank you Burkhard, I will always hold your generosity with profound gratitude in my heart; without it, this book wouldn't be here.

To Dzongsar Khentsye Rinpoche: Thank you for making me remember that remembering is innate, and forgetting is simply habit. And may any lifetime I re-emerge on this planet always include you as my guide. But may it be in this lifetime that I finally absorb and apply the gift of your teachings.

I am so grateful too for the writings of your father, Thinley Norbu. His writing carries with it a magic that deeply inspires me. I know that what enabled him to write the way he wrote was his view, and that I only have a sense of that because of everything that you teach about the view. If you had not accepted me as a student, I would never have come across your father's writings, and had I never come across his writings, I would never have you as a teacher.

To Charles Eisenstein: Thank you for holding this vision of the *more beautiful world our hearts know is possible*. Your way of being gives me the confidence to better trust my own.

To my grandmother 'Dean', Jean Lyell, and my uncle Nicky Lyell. Both of whom sowed the seed of the love of storymaking in my heart. To Deanie for always encouraging me to "write about it darling, write about it." Encouragement that without I might never have trusted that *my love* of writing was enough to justify the doing it.

And Nicky, my beloved dear uncle who died of asthma when I was a child, and whose lap I would sit on whilst he told me his stories of Mystic Meg. It was Nicky who I learnt the love of creation from and also devotion and joy for the act of creating a story that you can share with others. My dearest uncle: your kind heart and gentle nature provided some of the most nurturing support I knew in my childhood: thank you.

After my grandmother died, a play she'd written was discovered in a drawer. The subject matter is private to her, but the writing was beautiful, elegant and wise; just like she was. And though no one other than our family has seen this play, part of the motivation to complete *Travels* was to do so in the spirit of honouring her and Nicky's love of writing, perhaps entwined with my own. And I am really grateful for this motivation, because I think if I hadn't had it, maybe I would have given up on this book. Without the love, support and encouragement of these two beings in my life, I don't think I would ever have had the sense to trust and enjoy this love of writing as much as I do. For maybe it is not only mine, but all of ours.

And I don't know how to craft this next sentence – but I do want to articulate it. To acknowledge every being, seen and non-seen, who has helped me, and continues to help me to bring this book into being: *thank you thank you thank you*. Life is a far more magical and mystical event than I'd ever realised, and quickly slowly, I'm learning to pay attention.

Equally, were there no natural world to go out into, motherhood would have been a very different experience for me. Our home is an alive one, and one to whom I'm learning to relate with greater and greater appreciation. Dear Mother Earth: your absolute fecundity is a source of great nourishment, healing and joy for me and my family. Thank you in every single language that exists, and every single expression of gratitude that has ever been expressed. May I develop the courage to truly honour you in everything that I do.

Also, dear life, I imagine you have ears to hear this, and perhaps even fingers to turn the pages of this book to this very section to read this part - because I want so much to say thank you, dear life, for giving me a life where I have this thing I love so much to do. To sit here at the kitchen table, where time disappears and there is me, or rather no me, just typing. Sometimes what returns me is the sheer joy of my fingers tapping across the keyboard, in such a way that in rare moments I feel I'm a pianist at her piano. Not so much a woman writing, but revelling in a rhythm through which something travels that I cannot force, but only appreciate.

Thank you for giving me something that, for a person who's been stuck in this incredibly convincingly thicket of emotions that come and go but seems so real that I can give them names and invite them in for tea... only to discover there's no one coming, there's no one giving and there's only something I haven't even got a true sense of yet, other than to say: *my god, thank you,* because sometimes it's the writing that brings me closer to it.

Tom: I can't imagine how one must feel to have a part of their life shared through a perspective not their own. Thank you for trusting me to share some moments of ours, I truly value this gift.

Eve and Jack: being your mother is the greatest joy I've ever known. If it's true that our children choose their parents: *thank you thank you thank you!* I love to be with you both, watching your joyful expressions and enjoyment of being alive. Thank you for being the inspiration to learn about tough but transformative things like boundaries, consistency and presence. I love being your mother with all my heart and my hope is that this book will be a resource for you to dip into, and remember all that was magical. Thank you for being my motivation to complete this book. And Evie, it was you who encouraged me to sell this book, "but where can we sell it, Mummy?" you asked me, when 100 copies arrived for me to give to friends.
"Oh no, I'm not selling it. Just giving it as a gift."
"But why?" you asked, a look of confusion on your face. And because I realised this was not the example I wanted to set you, well, here it is, on Amazon. Because this was you, waking me up. Too easily we women doubt our value. And it has taken this woman, to move closer to her dreams as an author, after a pep talk from her 7-year-old daughter.
And dearest Jack, for the ways you shake me from my slumber too. But well, that's another story...

So dear life, thank you for these many gifts you have given me: from the friends and allies and support. And there, too, with its own heartbeat: this writing. Writing so very much entwined with motherhood, because it was only when I became a mother that a woman called Turiya asked me, "So Laura, if you knew you couldn't fail, what would you do?"

"Damn," I replied. As I sat crouched on the floor, looking into Ben's computer, where we were having our Skype conversation.
"Why do you say that?" she asked.
"Because I know the answer, and now I know the answer, I'll have to do it."

The answer was something I'd never allowed to even be a question. Having pursued so many different careers (law school, events, social impact & charitable work, yoga teacher), it was through becoming a mother that the reality that one day my daughter would come to me and say *Mama: did you chase your dream?* That maybe I needed to stop making excuses and start moving towards this dream I'd kept most private.

So thank you to the TED talk (though I can't remember who gave it!) where a beautiful point was

247

made that there's a time when your children have grown and they come to you and say: "I know what I want to do! I know my calling!"

To which we reply (probably a bit eagerly): "That's wonderful! Darling, what is it?"

And this is when they look at us (probably a bit solemnly, for dream-sharing comes from a place most tender): "To make ice cream." And now there's a pause, because the only way we have the right to say *go for it* is if we went for ours. Because it's only when you go for your dream that you know all the sacrifice, hardship and smashing of ideals that it involves, and so only because of having walked through that, and come out the other side do we have the right - right here in this moment where our children are sharing the trajectory that they wish their lives to take, and the gift they most want to give - to turn to them and say: *go for it*.

So really, this is me, saying to you, Evie & Jack.

My darlings.

Go for it.

Thank you so much for reading Travels.
If you enjoyed it, would you consider leaving a review on *Amazon?*

It's super easy to do, simply type in *'Travels With My Daughter: An Experience of Motherhood*
Laura Fraser' into the search panel on Amazon, it will then take you to the book's page, and if you
scroll down you'll come to *'Write a Customer Review,'* and there you are...

This small act helps writers like me immensely, because it shows that there are readers who
believe in my writing and would like more of it -all of which agents and publishers want to see! So
that when I finish my second book, (close!) and start looking for an agent, I can show her
(yup, I'm rooting for a woman),
all these amazing 5* reviews
and she's listening...

If you'd like to stay in touch with my latest writings, head over to: www.lfraser.com
where you'll get a kickass free ebook when you subscribe with links ot audio tracks and
short stories all around the theme of remembering. Remembering what you ask? Well
to find that out, head on over to the website, subscribe & your inbox will hold the
answer...
|
If you'd llike to follow me on Instagram, I regularly break my resolve to leave social
media
& write there too.
You can find me here: @laurafraser.

Thank you so much for reading,

Laura x

About Laura

My back-ground is in events, small & large. From ones that have brought people to gather "'around the campfire" to be entertained & inspired, or to go out to their favourite venue in London on a Saturday evening and raise money for young people who's lives have been affected by violence in the capital. I've set up pilot projects in Cambodia, co-founded dinners for Wonderful Women & Marvellous Men all the while immersing myself in the worlds of yoga and meditation whenever I got the chance.

Since becoming a mother in 2012 to Eve, and then to Jack in 2017, I've continued bringing people together. Whether for an online womens group for which we met once a week for a year, or writing circles that gather in my sitting room after morning drop off.

I've completed Yoga Campus's 250 hr Yoga Teacher Training and Godfrey Devereux's 500hr. I've trained with yogi masters Rod Stryker, Danny Paradise and David Swenson. I'm a Buddhist student of an incredible Bhutanse lama. Everything I learn is about unlearning everything I've ever accepted as true. And everything I write about, is about sharing that.

May all beings be happy. May all beings come to feel the freedom inante in their own heart & in the meantime, may we all carry on "walking each other home."

Printed in Great Britain
by Amazon